VERTICAL MARKET
STRUCTURES

Helmy H. Baligh

Leon E. Richartz

Graduate School of Business Administration

University of Illinois

VERTICAL MARKET STRUCTURES

Allyn and Bacon, Inc.
Boston

Preface

An economic system of exchange is characterized by the pattern of relationships that exists between its elements. Four important kinds of relationships make up this pattern: cooperation, competition, control, and coordination. Of these, only competition has received any serious attention in economic theory. The vertical aspects of market structures have been given virtually no place in economic theory, although they are those most closely involved with the other three relationships.

If the subject of vertical market structures is placed uniquely in marketing and excluded from economics, then both disciplines suffer. The advancement of knowledge cannot, and must not, be constrained by arbitrarily set limits on the disciplines. That such limits exist is unfortunately not an idle fear. We have encountered views from people with whom we have discussed this work which indicate that they thought our work was not "economics." By implication it is suggested that it would therefore not interest economists. There are also some who claim and imply exactly the same with respect to the marketing discipline. If economists are willing to expand their analysis of the various aspects of economic phenomena, and if marketing scholars are interested in the development of theoretic foundations in their discipline, then this book may serve such people, in some small measure, to attain their goals. Real world phenomena do not always take on only those character-

v

istics which the scholars find it useful to include in their theories. Abstraction in theory development is indeed useful and necessary but should be coupled, within a discipline, with continued efforts to integrate the partiality it engenders. The understanding of something like an economic system is grossly retarded by the invention of mutually exclusive disciplines.

The theory developed in this book should not be viewed by the economists to be outside of economics because of its subject, but rather as a possible source for more and different theories in economics. To the marketing scholar the methodology of this work and its economic flavor should not stamp it as "not marketing," but as a source for the strengthening of the methodology of the discipline. It is suggested that each scholar approach the work by seeking what it might contribute to his discipline. We hope that it will be judged on this basis and not on the basis of how much or how little it also contributes to some other discipline.

This book belongs in the disciplines of economics and marketing alike. It is in the former because it treats an economic phenomenon by using the basic concepts of economic theory. It is in marketing because the subject of vertical market structures has for many years engaged the attention of marketing scholars, and because it deals with the basic concept of the co-operation that is necessary to permit exchange. We have not felt at all concerned about using in our analysis whatever concepts we thought would help our understanding of vertical market structures. But along with the concepts and theory we have developed, we make use of tools normally associated with Operations Research and other more conventional techniques. We use these techniques in order to derive *theoretic* conclusions in the areas of vertical market structure analysis and price theory. The constraints on the use of concepts are purely those of our knowledge and capacities and not the traditional distinctions made between business and economic disciplines.

It is quite obvious that no analysis of vertical market structures would be of value if the individual firm's problems were not considered. The relevant problems in this case are those which involve the efficiency of exchange transactions. The problems analyzed for the individual firm involve the choice of the characteristics of its membership within the vertical market structure. Combinations of overlapping structures in turn make up the even more complex organization that is the economic system. The particular decision problems treated in this work are chosen on the bases of their general relevance to all exchange transactions and the magnitude of their effects on the structure's efficiency.

The book has many blank pages—figuratively speaking. We could not hope within a lifetime to cover the subject of vertical market structures completely. The subject deserves many more minds than our own, and this book is designed largely to foster an awareness of this need. Our work is intended to be a broad framework within which much more analysis by many researchers could be developed, and to present the first stages of the analysis of the subject. To this end we have used mathematics to state clearly the conditions under which our conclusions hold, and to make certain that the conclusions do indeed follow from the premises. Logic and mathematics are our bulwark against inconsistent and loosely formed theory. We have attempted to make the theory as realistic as clarity of exposition and our abilities would dictate without any loss of rigor. We are fully aware of the limitations of this work, but we hope that it contributes its share to the creation of the properly designed theory to help us understand vertical market structures.

We are grateful to Professor Louis D. Volpp of the Graduate School of Business Administration, the University of Illinois, for his help, criticism, and encouragement in the development of the early parts of this work. We also thank Miss Romayne Skartvedt for her help in the proofreading of the manuscript.

Helmy Hamdollah Baligh
Leon E. Richartz
Urbana

Contents

10 Possible Directions of Advanced Analysis

I

Theoretical Analysis

The concept of a vertical market structure

The theoretical analysis of vertical market structures developed in this work consists of a series of models varying in degrees of complexity and differing in the extent of their comprehensive treatment of all variables. A different combination of characteristics of vertical market structures is incorporated in each model. Inherent in any one model is an identification of a particular phenomenon. Once the model's variables are given substance, no further description or characterization of the phenomenon is necessary. However, since the original subject of the study is very complex, no one model mirrors faithfully all the characteristics of the phenomenon of which there are now many descriptions. Only some characteristics of the total concept of the object of study are represented by corresponding variables in any one model, and such correspondence is not perfect since it involves a simplified view of the characteristics. The overall concept of a subject matter for theorizing is often hard to comprehend under such conditions, particularly when the phenomenon is not directly observable. Where one's interest in theory is in part determined by the desire to understand the phenomenon, the need for identification and description in general terms becomes necessary.

A vertical market structure is a marketing channel. Since the term "marketing channel" has been used by different people to refer to economic phenomena with varying characteristics, its use here is avoided. The phenomenon referred to by the term "vertical market structure" has specific characteristics, many of which are common to most concepts of the marketing channel. These common characteristics in fact, are those which are described in the models.

The term "structure" assumes the existence of certain elements—firms and consumers—in the economy. A pattern of relationships between any set of these units is termed a structure. Since, furthermore, these units are engaged in various activities, the term structure also refers to the patterns of relationships between the activities of the units. The entire structure can thus be viewed as a system, the output of which derives from the *activities of its member units* and from the *relationships that these activities have to one another*. Similarly, the inputs into the system depend on these two interrelated characteristics which, in the final outcome, determine the relation between the input and output of the system.

A market structure is a number of firms and consumers, all belonging to a given set. Membership in the set is determined by the application of one or more criteria to the relationships that exist among these firms and/or consumers. A horizontal market structure is thus a set of firms, and membership of all firms in this set is determined by the fact that they are all potential sellers (or buyers) of the same products to the same firms in another set. Thus, firms $\{A_1, \ldots, A_m\}$ make up the set which identifies a particular horizontal market structure if they *compete* with one another for the purchases or the sales of another set of firms identified as $\{X_1, \ldots, X_n\}$. The study of the various characteristics and the behavior of such sets of firms has occupied economists for some time. A monopolistic structure is identified by the fact that the set has only one firm; the number of differentiated products handled by the set of firms forms another important variable in economic analysis.

The set of firms $\{A_1, \ldots, A_m, X_1, \ldots, X_n\}$ could also be viewed as an economic system—a vertical structure, in fact. Here membership for a firm in the set is determined by the existence of a *cooperative relationship* that this firm has with at least one other firm in the set although competitive relationships may or may not exist. A cooperative relationship is that which permits the exchange of goods or services among firms within the set. It does not refer to collusion, and hence is limited to relationships between firms in different levels or sub-sets in the set or vertical market structure. Firm A_i is considered a member of such a set, or a part of the vertical structure, if and only if it engages in such cooperative activities. Its membership is independent of its being in competition with any other A_j for the purchase or sale of any of the relevant products to any of the firms in the sub-set $\{X_1, \ldots, X_n\}$. In effect, a vertical market structure is made up of sub-sets, known as *levels*, each of which identifies a horizontal market structure.

The characteristics, efficiency, and behavior of such vertical structures (levels cooperating with one another to effect exchange transactions) form the subject matter of this work. An example of the problems to be considered is the comparison of the costs of effecting a certain level of exchange of two different vertical structures, one identified by the set of firms $\{A_1, \ldots, A_m, X_1, \ldots, X_n\}$, and the other by the set $\{A_1, \ldots, A_m, R_1, \ldots, R_w, X_1, \ldots, X_n\}$. In the first set, members of the sub-set of competing seller firms $\{A_1, \ldots, A_m\}$ cooperate directly with the members of the sub-set of competitive buyer firms $\{X_1, \ldots, X_n\}$ in order that exchange of products may be effected. In the second case, these two sub-sets cooperate directly with a third sub-set $\{R_1, \ldots, R_w\}$, made up of w competing intermediary firms. When the ultimate result of this second arrangement is still the same level of exchange between the sub-sets $\{A_1, \ldots, A_m\}$ and $\{X_1, \ldots, X_n\}$ as in the first arrangement, then a comparison of the costs of the two structures permits a direct comparison of their efficiency.

This brief exposition of the concept of a vertical market structure is extremely simple. For one thing, the exact nature of the structure, and hence its costs and outputs, will depend upon the exact degree and nature of the cooperative relationship existing within it. If cooperation between the sub-set $\{A_1, \ldots, A_m\}$ and the sub-set $\{R_1, \ldots, R_w\}$ existed in those aspects of exchange dealing with information transmittal but not in those dealing with inventory carrying, the equilibrium structure and its costs would be different from the case where cooperation in both areas would be found. If all vertical market structures were distinguished from one another only on the bases of the numbers of sub-sets (levels) and the number of firms in each sub-set making up the total set of firms in the structure, many of the subtle differences between such structures would be ignored. Different patterns of the allocation of the activities related to exchange among the sub-sets, or levels, are associated with various cooperative relationships. The essence, therefore, of any vertical market structure is the *cooperation* that must of necesssity exist for exchange to occur. The allocation of activities among the levels and the number of such levels and firms within them are the characteristics which affect the efficiency of vertical market structures. It is this last contention that the models prove and determine rigorously.

Cooperation, competition, and coordination

The outputs of a vertical market structure are exchange transactions. It is such exchange which increases in some fashion the profits (utilities) of the parties to it and is the reason for the existence of the structure. Exchange, however, involves the use of economic resources by the members of the structure—its output is not forthcoming without incurring costs. The entire structure is an economic input-output system, the design of which determines the relation between the levels and forms of inputs and outputs.

The characteristics of the system's design are described by the patterns of decisions made by individual members on the use of economic resources. The activities involving the use of economic resources which relate members to one another determine the nature of the relation between the system's total inputs and total outputs. Such activities are those which "bind" the members into a system through the effects they have on the well being of more than one member. If one assumes that every system member optimizes his behavior, then all activities by all firms which affect the conditions of the optimality of any member's decisions are bonds which determine the structure of the system. Any activity by firm Y which has an effect on the nature of the optimal decision of firm X must be considered an element in the design of the system to which X and Y belong. If no such cross effects are present, then it cannot be said that X and Y form a system. System efficiency is dependent upon the nature of such effects, and hence upon the patterns of relationships between its members.

The specific patterns of member relationships are discussed in the models. General dimensions of system design, or classes of relationships between members in the system, are identifiable. Economic theory has tended to concentrate upon one set of these, namely, that of competitive relationships. These are the results of activities which lead firms (or consumers) to share actual or potential buyers (or sellers). Competition within the vertical market structure is the basic element which defines any level of the structure. It is employed heavily in the discussion of equilibrium and optimal system states. The existence or possible existence of competitive relationships has a strong effect on the manner in which cooperative relationships between firms affect the system's efficiency. Individual firm strategy is more richly viewed in terms of its dimensions of competition *and* cooperation rather than of one alone.

As competitive relationships form the horizontal bonds of the system, so cooperative relationships form the vertical bonds. One subject of this work is the discussion of the manner in which such cooperative relationships affect the input-output functions of the system. The *simultaneous* treatment of cooperative and competitive relationships may produce new concepts of optimum and equilibrium system states.

The concept of relationships between firms to coordinate their behavior involves as integral elements the nature of the cooperative and the competitive relationships within the system. Cooperative relationships may take on particular forms as a result of the coordinating relationships derived from the state of competitive relations in the system. Firm strategies within the context of vertical market structures involve choices from the available sets of cooperative, competitive, and coordinating relationships.

Empirical aspects

For purposes of theory, the number of firms in each of the sub-sets and the number of such sub-sets, in the total set which identifies a vertical market structure, can be considered as either endogenously or exogenously determined variables. Considered as given are the initial set of sellers, the initial set of buyers, and the number of firms in each of these two sub-sets. These two numbers, referred to as m and n, need only to be assumed to be finite for the solutions to the models with respect to costs and equilibrium to be meaningful as a basis for the comparison of structures. However, in order to apply the models, even in the most general of forms, the limits on the two numbers of firms in these sub-sets and the characteristics of the two sub-sets require some identification.

Assuming that it is possible to identify an economy, then the sub-set of initial sellers $\{A_1, \ldots, A_m\}$ could be viewed as the set of all the producers of some given product or some given number of products. In other words, it could be viewed as an industry in which membership for a firm is determined on the basis of a set of criteria. These criteria would include the cross elasticities of demand for the products of the firms, the production characteristics used by the firms, and the physical characteristics of the product. The exact weighting of these criteria is determinable in terms of the requirements of the analysis, namely, the degree of generality of its conclusions, and the accuracy with which any such generalization can be applied to the individual member of the set. In the economic theory of the firm the criterion most often relied upon in the identification of the set of firms making up an industry has been that of cross elasticity. In the analysis of marketing channels the marketing literature has tended to concentrate on the physical characteristics of the product which, of course, are not totally independent of cross elasticities of demand. For purposes of this work the sub-set of initial sellers $\{A_1, \ldots, A_m\}$ could be determined on any of the above criteria. The more restrictive the criteria, the smaller the number of initial sellers.

The same analysis applies to the sub-set of initial buyers $\{X_1, \ldots, X_n\}$. The member units in this sub-set may be retailing firms or consumers. It is clear, however, that the criteria used to determine membership in the sub-set $\{A_1, \ldots, A_m\}$ must also be used to determine membership in the sub-set $\{X_1, \ldots, X_n\}$. If the first includes all producers of all products, then the second should also include all buyers in any given sub-set or level as this has been previously defined. Finally, it is quite meaningful to limit, for purposes of empirical analysis, the membership of both sets on the basis of some other economically justifiable criteria. That is, if for some reason a geographic distinction between markets permits reasonable treatment of each separately, then any of the models could be applied to a vertical market structure. Here the initial sub-set of producers or sellers $\{A_1, \ldots, A_m\}$ and the initial sub-set of retailers of users $\{X_1, \ldots, X_n\}$ are limited to those firms located in a geographically distinct market.

In each of the models the criteria determining the numbers of initial producers or sellers and retailers or users are apparent in the assumptions made. As a rule, the bases for defining the limits of these two sub-sets are the characteristics that serve to distinguish the product exchanged from all other products. The analysis is one of partial equilibrium because it ignores possible effects of one vertical market structure on another. The vertical market structures that exist for each product form a complex, interdependent, and overlapping structure in any multi-product economy. Membership of firms in one vertical market structure in which one product is handled does not preclude their membership in other structures in which other products are exchanged.

The analysis does not distinguish between products on the basis of the same set of characteristics throughout. Whatever the set of characteristics employed, the effects of the multi-structure memberships of firms on the equilibrium conditions, costs, and efficiencies of the vertical market structure for the one product identified, are generally ignored. This point is elaborated in the following section and for the moment it is sufficient to point out that the usefulness of any model in explaining empirically identifiable economic phenomena depends, in part, upon the degree to which it is capable of developing a characterization at total equilibrium. Use of the models is, therefore, to be made only with the understanding that they treat only sub-sections of an economy and ignore the relationships that exist between these sub-sections.

Characteristics of the theoretical analysis

The entire content of this work is theoretical, with no description of existing vertical market structures and no empirical testing of the models. Though the analysis is prompted in part by a desire to explain a particular kind of economic phenomenon through the development of a rigorous theoretical framework, it does not relate these frameworks to any specific empirically observed case except where such a relationship is rather obvious. This stress on theory should not obscure the fact that the ultimate goal is the understanding of the process of exchange in an economy and the increase in the efficiency of exchange.

The basic hypothesis underlying the development of models of vertical market structures is that exchange transactions are not costless and that in consequence there exists the possibility that these costs of exchange can be reduced. If one were to dwell for a moment on the historical developments of various types and kinds of wholesale and retail middlemen, and if one were to make the reasonable assumption that such firms could exist only if they served some economic purpose by performing some activity more efficiently than would be the case in their absence, the hypothesis would seem to be reasonable indeed. It is with the aim of developing a theoretical framework to test this hypothesis that the models are built. It is possible, of course, for one to explain various empirically identifiable vertical market structures for specific commodities. The marketing literature is replete with such works.[1] This work, however, stresses the generality of the theoretical framework by dealing with those factors or variables that are common to large numbers of vertical market structures.

The development of models that would permit the discovery of those vertical market structure configurations that improve the efficiency of exchange means that the sources of costs of exchange must be investigated. This is merely another way of stating that there is a need to understand those activities that could or must be performed by the members of the system in producing a transaction between the two initial sets of buyers and sellers. Such activities can be viewed as decisions by firms on the inputs into the process of exchange. The decisions affect the total system's output. Given the cost associated with these activities, such as inventory carrying, it then becomes possible to investigate the way in which such an activity can be allocated to various sub-sets of firms in all possible vertical market structures. This permits the determination of both the equilibrium structure and the most efficient structure for the performance of this one activity.

Most of the models relate the vertical market structure to the cost of an activity associated with effecting an exchange transaction and to the output of the structure in terms of the returns from exchange associated with such an activity. When individual sources of the costs of exchange are so treated it is possible to develop models which combine several activities and treat the costs and returns to each simultaneously. Some of these sources of cost are unavoidable if exchange is to occur at all, that is, they are necessary conditions of exchange. Other activities are determinants of the efficiency of exchange though not necessary to it. This distinction is clearly pointed out in the models. In the one case the most efficient level of the necessary activity could not logically be zero, while in the case of the activity that is not necessary to the process of exchange, such as inventory carrying, the most efficient level could logically be zero.

The issue of limiting the variables which are endogenously determined within the vertical market system to only some of the sub-sets in such a system already has been briefly mentioned. A question could well be raised regarding the treatment of the number of firms in the sub-sets of initial producers m and initial buyers or users n, as being exogenously determined in the models of specific costs of exchange. Why are the two sub-sets $\{A_1, \ldots, A_m\}$ and $\{X_1, \ldots, X_n\}$ treated as given and determined independently of the behavior of firms in the vertical market structure in all but the discussion on prices in Chapter 9 ? The answer is pragmatic. There is so much involved in the analysis with *m* and *n* treated as given, that to permit them to become endogenously determined variables in all the models would in all probability obscure the results of the analysis, as these pertain only to vertical market structures. Only after some detailed knowledge about both kinds of structures is presented would it be reasonable to link vertical and horizontal market structures and to solve for the equilibrium conditions of both simultaneously.

In short, if the process of exchange involves costs, the equilibrium conditions for all sub-sets of firms in the economy must include these costs. The economists have tended to concentrate on the equilibrium of horizontal structures, and here we concentrate on equilibrium of vertical market structures. Once vertical market structures are understood at a level comparable to horizontal ones, neither set of equilibrium conditions must be determined by assuming that the other does not exist or is irrelevant. Some indication of the interrelationship between the two sets of equilibrium conditions is obtained once the models of specific costs of exchange are developed. These interrelationships are then analyzed in the discussion of price. There the link between current micro-economic analysis of horizontal structures and that of vertical market structures is forged. The concept of simultaneous determination of the equilibrium values of variables of the horizontal and the vertical market structures is developed and the equilibrium determined under certain limited conditions. The basic link is, as would be expected, under the heading of price.

Equilibrium and optimal vertical market structures

A characteristic of the theoretic analysis is its economic orientation. The variables incorporated into the models are almost all economic in the sense that they treat costs and revenues or the economic values of inputs and outputs. In consequence the notions of equilibrium and optimal vertical market structure are purely economic. In this sense and usage, both terms have received much attention in the economic and management science literature. It is not intended, therefore, to discuss more than briefly what is meant by economic equilibrium or optimality.

A vertical market structure is in equilibrium if three conditions hold. *The first is that every firm within the structure be incapable of changing the cooperative relationships which it has with other firms already in the structure to its economic advantage.* This means that no firm within the structure finds it *profitable* to alter the structure. The second condition applies to firms not in the structure but capable and willing to become a part of it. *In equilibrium no firm from without the structure finds it possible and profitable to alter it by entering into cooperative relationships with those firms already a part of the structure.* A structure is in equilibrium if it contains a unique number of firms in levels between the initial level of sellers and the initial level of buyers. This number has an absolute maximum which occurs when the total system costs are equal to the costs of direct exchange between the two initial levels. Under some conditions, and the assumption of constant output, the number will be below this maximum and total system costs plus firm profits will sum to the level of the initial costs of direct exchange. Under no circumstances can there be an equilibrium system which is less efficient than the one of direct exchange. Furthermore no firm will enter into cooperative relationships which exclude it from performing any function in the structure. *This implies the third condition—that every firm in the structure at equilibrium performs a function.*

It will be recalled that the sub-sets of initial sellers $\{A_1, \ldots, A_m\}$ and initial buyers $\{X_1, \ldots, X_n\}$ are considered givens in the analysis of the equilibrium structure viewed in terms of specific cost-incurring variables. This means that the second equilibrium condition of a vertical market structure, that which deals with those firms not in these two sub-sets but capable of becoming member units in them, does not apply to these two sub-sets of firms. That is, in equilibrium a vertical market structure does not entail economic equilibrium in these two sub-sets or levels. The equilibrium determined by most of the models is thus a partial one for the entire structure, and the development of more general equilibrium conditions would rest only upon treating the determinants of the equilibrium number of the m and n firms as endogenous variables. However, it is still true that if a vertical market structure is in partial equilibrium, any firm in either of these sub-sets does not individually find it possible and profitable to alter the cooperative relationship it has with firms in the structure or those willing to enter it. By cooperation it is meant the required conditions of exchange and not collusion. It refers only to the relationships of firms in different levels or sub-sets in the vertical market structure.

In no case is the equilibrium vertical market structure based on the assumption of only one kind of competition between firms in any one level or sub-set in it. Though the exact nature of the structure in equilibrium will vary with different competitive relationships among firms in each level, no one kind of competition needs to be assumed for an equilibrium to exist. In part, the analysis of the equilibrium of a vertical market structure is aimed at uncovering the relationship between an equilibrium structure and the nature of competitive relationships that exist among firms in any one sub-set in the structure.

An optimal vertical market structure may be defined in a number of ways depending upon the group or groups of firms, consumers, societies, and the like, whose goals are applied as criteria. In its most general form an optimal structure is considered to be one which maximizes the degree of attainment of the goals of any firm or group of firms in the structure, or those of groups not in the structure. In this context, therefore, there are three points of discussion: (a) whose goals are to be chosen?; (b) how are goals of any group of individual firms to be aggregated?; and (c) how are structures to be compared for purposes of choosing the optimum when the degree of goal attainment is constant in the aggregate but variable in its distribution among firms?

It is *assumed* throughout that all firms in a vertical market structure and those willing to become a part of it are motivated by the desire for profit. The goal aggregation problem is thus a fairly simple one and involves the summing of all profits of the firms whose goals determine optimality. If one of the levels in the vertical market structure is considered to be that of the consumer, then conceptually the problem of aggregation is still capable of solution. Consumer utilities could conceptually be measured along a monetary scale, and aggregation would remain a question of summing up amounts of the same thing—money. The problem of summation is simple since it is assumed that the things added have a common unit of measure.

Vertical market structures are evaluated in most models below on the basis of social costs and returns, as these are determined by the costs and returns of the firms in the market structure. Greater profits, *in toto*, for all firms in the structure, with no change in the prices at which the consumers purchase the product or in their total utilities as measured in monetary terms, mean a structure closer to the optimum. The greatest aggregate profit level identifies the optimum vertical market structure under the given conditions of the particular model treating a specific set of economic variables. If the consumer is treated as part of the vertical market structure, then the optimum structure is that which maximizes the total profits plus monetary value of consumer utilities. In either case the same output to the vertical market structure is achieved at the lowest cost of the performance of some given activities associated with exchange.

The models thus identitfy optimal structures with respect to the performance of functions such as those of contact and communication and inventory carrying. When the prices at which consumers receive the products are allowed to vary, the analysis of optimal structures is more complex but still possible. In all models it is shown that the characteristics of a vertical market structure affect the efficiency of its operation, and that it is thus possible to identify the optimal pattern of relevant relationships.

In every model, it is a condition of cooperation and for membership in the structure, that each firm not reduce by its cooperation the profits of any other firms which are party to this cooperation. The total increase in profits that might occur with variation in the structure through such cooperation may or may not be conterbalanced by lower profits that stem from increased competition that the new firm brings. If there is any decrease in the profits, or the monetary value equivalent of utilities, of any member in a vertical market structure, then the change in the structure which brings it about leads to a movement of the structure away from the optimum. The structure reaches an optimum by the entry of the last possible firm which can increase firm profits (or consumer utility) in the resulting new structure (including the entering firm), without decreasing the profits of any other firm already in the structure. It is in this sense that the general concept of optimum is applied to the structures developed in each model, and it is one which meets the requirements of a Pareto optimum. In some cases, the optimum is based upon the profits of one sub-set, or an identifiable group of sub-sets not covering all firms in the structure. Where this is done it is pointed out clearly that the optimality of the structure is based on the specific set of goals of these specific sub-sets and is not a general optimum.

Often in the models, the optimality of a vertical market structure is based on the assumption of a constant output to the system and a variable input. The minimum input is then the optimal one for that output. In other cases output is allowed to change with the structure, and the effects on vertical market structure optimality of various forms of competition among firms in any of the sub-sets are incorporated into the analysis. In any case, whether output is held constant or allowed to vary, the analysis of the optimum would ignore the effects of monopoly power over time on the returns to society and to units in the structure. Thus, suppose it is possible to state that the optimum structure for the performance of the contact and communication function is that which is identified by the set $\{A_1, \ldots, A_m, R_1, X_1, \ldots, X_n\}$. The number of initial sellers exceeds two, that of buyers exceeds two, and that of the middlemen (the sub-set R_1) has only one firm. If, after entry, this middleman realized that no firm could possibly compete with him, it may be possible for him to alter the distribution of the profits in the structure in his favor. That is, over time he might move away from the optimum as defined. In the models, vertical market structures are treated as static phenomena, but even if that were not the case, the middleman could not manipulate profit distributions if the assumption is made that the two sub-sets $\{A_1, \ldots, A_m\}$ and $\{X_1, \ldots, X_n\}$ could find some other firm willing to replace him. That is, the threat of non-cooperation by these two groups would persuade the middleman not to take to himself any more than the profits from the structure which his presence in it generated. The threat of cooperation by the two sub-sets with yet another firm would not permit him to take even that much. The exact distribution of the increase in net output of the structure resulting from the presence of the middleman in it will vary as the strength of the threat of entry of new middlemen varies, and will depend upon the bargaining powers of the m, the n, and the middlemen. These powers are in turn determined by a large number of variables——costs of operation in different structures, cost of entry, losses from non-cooperation, and the like.

In general, it is sufficient to say that the concept of optimality refers to the lowest cost structure in terms of the performance of the functions associated with effecting exchange. This assumes a constant output. Where output is allowed to vary, the optimal structure is that which maximizes the algebraic difference between output and input weighted by economic prices.

Structure, behavior, and performance

It is possible to define a structure in terms of characteristics that do not include behavioral relationships of the member units or firms in it. Thus a vertical market structure could be identified in terms of the number of firms which buy or sell any given product regardless of the existence of any behavioral relationships between them. In economics a "duopoly" is a horizontal market structure in which only two firms are engaged in the sale of a given product in the same market. The behavior of the firms, given certain profit-making capability assumptions, is then inferred from the characteristics of the structure. Such behavior is not an element of the structure but might be entailed by it. Because this is the case, a great deal of theorizing must precede the tying together of particular structures to particular behavior patterns. The empirical application, in turn, must depend upon the validity of this theoretical analysis and the inferences it makes.[2]

The definition of structure is not limited to a number of firms, characteristics of a product, and the number of levels. It also includes the fact that the firms cooperate with one another. Firms have a certain minimal behavioral relationship which is predicated upon their profit maximizing behavior. Since our analysis deals with the efficiency of this kind of structure, it is true that the efficiency of such self-interested cooperating behavior, given certain other structural conditions, is also the subject of analysis.

The competitive relationship between firms is also a defining element of the vertical market structure phenomenon. Since the efficiency of such a structure is dependent in part on the competitive, as well as on the co-operative behavior, it is necessary to state clearly in the analysis the assumption regarding the former. For example, if the efficiency of a vertical market structure depends on the presence or absence of perfect competition among the firms in any one level, then the model indicates whether such competition is present or absent when it relates the vertical market structure to a level of efficiency. No attempt is made to repeat the economic analysis which relates competitive structure to efficiency, but whenever such an analysis is relevant it is explicitly assumed. Generally it is the efficiency of behavior of the cooperative kind that forms the main subject of analysis. Since the two kinds of behavior determine efficiency and may be dependent on one another, competitive behavior is considered an integral part of the analysis of the efficiency of vertical market structures, but is treated mostly as an exogenously determined variable.

Variables determining efficiency of exchange

The literature on marketing contains a large number of different lists of the functions or kinds of inputs associated with effecting exchange. Essentially, the work in this area is faced with the problem of (a) identifying *a priori* or *a posteriori* the different needs for the functions performed; (b) developing criteria for ranking these functions in terms of their importance in marketing in general, or for the marketing of specific products in particular; (c) attempting to explain the patterns in which the decisions on the levels of these inputs are allocated among the various levels in vertical market structures; and (d) to explain why the amounts of the inputs are the way they are observed to be.

The models presented accept on a pragmatic basis some of the functions listed in this literature as a starting point. The reason is that our interest is the development of a theoretical framework showing the relation of these inputs to outputs, and hence the arrival at some conclusion as to what kinds of vertical market structures ought to be expected, or ought to be designed, under certain conditions. One application of the results of such research is the development of a theoretically proven group of functions that affect the efficiency of exchange. Another result would be the identification of the economic criteria and the proper ranking of the functions in order of their economic importance to the efficiency of exchange, given the special conditions of any product considered and the parameters of the model.

There is no intention at this point, or at any other point, to enter into the controversy on just what the functions of marketing are.[3] There is also no attempt made to criticize the lists submitted in the literature on the basis of the failure of list-makers to state explicitly whether the list is descriptive or theoretically derived from the analysis of the output of marketing and vertical market structures. A glance at the literature would be sufficient to suggest that this line of analysis may have reached the point of diminishing returns.

The choice of the inputs to be studied is not completely arbitrary. The literature on marketing has served to indicate in many respects just which might have the greatest effects, or those absolutely required for the output associated with the exchange which vertical market structures serve to produce.[4] In this respect such activities as contact and communication, inventory carrying or storage, financing, and physical distribution costs suggest themselves as rather obvious subjects for study. Another criterion used in choosing a dependent variable for study is that of its general applicability to products and vertical market structures of varying characteristics.

The models below, for these reasons, treat contact and communication, inventory carrying, financing—the supplying of non-waiting utilities to buyers, the implementing of exchange transactions, production, buying, and selling. Each is treated separately, and models are also developed to treat combinations simultaneously where relationships between these inputs might exist. Finally, various stages of market imperfections are incorporated into the models, and their costs, outputs, and effects on efficiency and equilibrium are uncovered.

Four basic theoretic treatments of vertical market structures in the literature ought to be mentioned briefly at this point. In varying degrees each forms either a source of hypotheses for theoretic constructs or an obvious parallel treatment to be compared with this work. The first such theoretical analysis is that of Alderson,[5] who is concerned with the explanation of the existence of exchange through intermediaries in terms of a small number of critical variables. He contends that the efficiency of vertical market structures in which levels of intermediaries exist between the initial sellers and the initial buyers or users is improved by the performance of two functions——matching and sorting——by these intermediaries. The arguments given in support of this contribution are theoretical, but they are restricted to specific variables and are not rigorously demonstrated, a great deal being left to intuitive truths. The main differences, therefore, between Alderson's work and ours are in two areas: (a) no attempt is made here to hypothesize an *a priori* ranking of the variables determining efficiency of vertical market structures on the basis of the magnitude of their effects as Alderson does; and (b) the methodology employed here is not that of one broad and general argument based in part on intuitive truths and designed to explain in one great stroke the existence of intermediaries in vertical market structures. Rather, the method involves the concentration of rigorous models on specific variables followed by the integration of these models.

Revzan's[6] theoretical work is similar to Alderson's in that he too relies on arguments involving elements that are expected to be intuitively acceptable. He differs from Alderson in that he does not concentrate on a small number of critical explanatory variables. In fact, his analysis incorporates such a very large number of variables, that it becomes difficult to explore relationships in a detailed manner. Here his work differs from our models, since these portray a simplified view of the economic phenomenon and involve rigidly demonstrable conclusions, rather than a complex view with arguments less rigorously developed.

Ralph Breyer's[7] work on marketing channels is oriented towards the development of cost measures for different configurations of vertical market structures. The number of such structures which he discusses is small, and the stress is not on the comparison of the theoretically or empirically determined efficiencies of each. His aim is to identify different kinds of costs and to use the results of their measurement in the choice of a channel for a particular firm in a particular set of circumstances. The theoretical aspect of the work is mainly in the general discussion of why channels will vary in efficiency, and is limited to generalizations which seem to be intuitively and empirically obvious.

Finally there is the work of Balderston[8]. As is clearly indicated in the next chapter, Balderston's work forms the basic force of the first model, and all subsequent models build in various ways upon his general view of vertical market structures. However, whereas the Balderston model considers only one variable the ones below attempt to cover systematically many more variables and to treat them simultaneously in various combinations. Furthermore, this work relates the concepts developed on vertical market relationships to the concepts on horizontal market relationships of micro-economic theory.

Uses for the models

The models developed below have application only as broad theoretical frameworks and not as perfect tools for the solution of specific problems. One important use to which they may be put in this manner is as a *guide* to empirical research and analysis of marketing channels for specific products. Presently, marketing channel studies describe a channel for some product X and then often attempt to explain it in an *ad hoc* fashion by reference to some group of variables. For each product or group of products the variables discussed may differ, and their real importance may be unassessed. However, by using the models of vertical market structures, all product channels could be analyzed by reference to a specific set of variables. Inter-channel comparison would then be more meaningful, since the relative values and importance of a given set of variables as an explanation for particular forms of vertical market structures would be available. The models on inventory would, for example, permit the empirical research to focus upon a product's inventory requirements and hence to show whether its marketing channel is or is not explicable in terms of its ability to meet these requirements. In general, by using the models as a framework, the relative importance of channel-determining variables in empirical cases would become easier to estimate.

The models have even greater use as a general theoretic framework on which a solution for a firm's decision problems in specific areas could be based. More specific models of these decision problems could then be developed to enable the firm to arrive at still better solutions. Throughout the exposition of the models, discussion of possible strategies for firms in a structure is found. Specific instances are given wherein the model has led to the formulation and optimum solution of a firm's problem. The models are as yet too general and too restricted by the assumptions to permit a great deal of realism in portraying real problems of firms. Nevertheless, they are a start in the right direction and form a foundation for further developments in theories of channel decisions.

The decision problems for a firm referred to are those which involve choices related to some aspects of channels. For a firm seeking to enter business, the choice of the level in any vertical market structure and the determination of the kinds of functions it is to perform are problems to which the models can be applied. For example, a firm may wish to determine whether it ought to become a wholesale middleman in a vertical market structure for some product; it may also wish to determine whether, as a wholesale middleman, it is to carry inventory or else to operate as a drop shipper. By using the models as a theoretical framework for solving such problems, a great advance is made on pure guesswork or simple "follow-the-leader" rules.

Other problems relating to channels include those on integration, or belonging to more than one sub-set in a vertical market structure. The organization of the members in a sub-set to bargain more profitably with other sub-sets in the structure is another area of use. Here again, optimum solutions obtained from realistic models are not possible with the theoretical analyses cited below. Nevertheless, the analyses serve to improve the formulation of these problems by identifying both their critical variables and functional relationships between these variables. They also indicate solutions to a simplified view of these and similar economic problems relating to vertical market structures. It forms the basic requirements for the kind of development in these models that is to be expected in order that they may become more realistic and hence more useful.

The last general idea wherein the theoretical models of vertical market structures could be of use is that of public policy. The issue on the cost of marketing or distribution is one of social and political significance. Farmers, one often reads, want to know why they receive so little of the final consumer price of the products they produce, and wish to increase this amount both by their own action and by requesting government regulation. Other groups are eager to discover if marketing costs "too much." In both issues, arguments are made that the difference in the price of an item at retail and the price at which the producer sells it is an indication of the increase in social output which marketing causes. Others suggest that this amount, or value added, is essentially an indication of cost and then proceed to argue that it is too large or too small. In turn, attempts exist to suggest criteria other than value added on which to measure the efficiency of the marketing system. Finally, government agencies are drawn into this important issue and, willingly or as a result of well-placed pressure, attempt to enact the required legislation. Such legislation may favor one sub-set over another in a vertical market structure, or it may require the use of a particular structure and no other, or it may take some other form.[9]

The models of vertical market structures permit strict evaluation of the comparative efficiency of certain theoretic market structures. They can thus be used as a framework for the discussion of the issue of public policy, once it is ascertained by the interested parties that there are, in the problem at hand, real phenomena that are close counterparts of the modeled structures. The whole issue of whether "value added" is a cost or an output of marketing, and whether it is, in any particular case, too great or too little, should appear to be of little value to the development of socially beneficial public policy. This would be made on the basis of rigorously constructed theories which indicate how specific kinds of costs associated with exchange vary as the vertical market structural form varies. The models developed are such a broad framework, and form the start for the creation of a theoretical framework more fully applicable to the issue of what vertical market structures the economy *ought* to have, given any well stated social objective.

1   See in this respect some of the following examples:
Breyer, Ralph, *Commodity Marketing* (New York: McGraw-Hill Book Company, Inc., 1931).
Clark, Fred E. and L.D.H. Weld, *Marketing Agricultural Products In The United States* (New York: The Macmillan Company, 1938).
Clewett, Richard M., (Ed.), *Marketing Channels For Manufactured Products* (Homewood, Ill.: Richard D. Irwin, Inc., 1954).
Weld, L.D.H., *The Marketing of Farm Products* (New York: The Macmillan Company, 1919).
Oaks, Ralph H., "An Outline for Studying the Marketing of a Particular Commodity," *Journal of Marketing*, XIV (January, 1950) pp. 602–605.
Ganzenmuller, George, "Current Shifts in Electrical Wholesaling," *Journal of Marketing*, XXVI (October, 1962) pp. 60–63.

2   See in this respect the problems that arise and their treatment in:
Bain, Joe S., *Industrial Organization* (New York: John Wiley and Sons, Inc., 1959).

3   For some insight into this controversy on functions see some of the following references which, incidentally, form just a segment of those written on the subject:
Fullbrook, Earl S., "The Functional Concept in Marketing," *Journal of Marketing*, IV (January, 1940) pp. 229–237.
Jones, Fred M., "A New Interpretation of Marketing Functions," *Journal of Marketing*, VII (January, 1943) pp. 256–260.
McGarry, Edmund D., "Some Functions of Marketing Reconsidered," *in* Cox, Reavis, and Wroe Alderson (Eds.), *Theory in Marketing* (Homewood, Ill.: Richard D. Irwin, Inc., 1954) Ch. 16, pp. 263–280.
Bund, Henry, and J. W. Carroll, "The Changing Role of the Marketing Function," *Journal of Marketing*, XXI (January, 1957) pp. 268–325.

THEORETICAL ANALYSIS

4   For example, the concept of contact as a necessary activity, and hence a cost-incurring input for the exchange of each and every possible object of exchange, is presented in McGarry, Edmund D., "The Contactual Function in Marketing," *Journal of Business*, XXIV (April, 1951) pp. 96–113.

5   Alderson, Wroe, *Marketing Behavior and Executive Action*, (Homewood, Ill.: Richard D. Irwin, Inc., 1957). In particular see Ch. 7.

6   Revzan, David A., *Wholesaling in Marketing Organization* (New York: John Wiley and Sons, Inc., 1961).

7   Breyer, Ralph F., *Quantitative Systemic Analysis and Control: Study No. 1—Channel and Channel Group Costing* (Philadelphia: The Author, 1949).

8   Balderston, Frederick E., "Communication Networks in Intermediate Markets," *Management Science*, IV (January, 1958) pp. 154–171.

9   A partial list of the literature on the efficiency of marketing in general and specific vertical market structures in particular is:
Craig, David R. and Warren K. Gabler, "The Competitive Struggle For Market Control," *Annals of the American Academy of Political and Social Science*, CCIX (May, 1940) pp. 84–107.
Barger, Harold, *Distribution's Place in the American Economy Since 1896* (New York: National Bureau of Economic Research, 1955).
Stewart, Paul W., J. P. Dewhurst, and L. Field, *Does Distribution Cost Too Much?* (New York: Twentieth Century Fund, 1939).
Alderson, Wroe, "A Formula For Measuring Productivity in Distribution," *Journal of Marketing*, XII (April, 1948) pp. 447–448.
Cox, Reavis, "The Meaning and Measurement of Productivity in Distribution," *Journal of Marketing*, XII (April, 1948) pp. 433–441.
Manischewitz, D. Beryl and John A. Stuert, "Marketing Under Attack," *Journal of Marketing*, XXVI (July, 1962) pp. 1–6.

2

Contact and
Communication Costs[*]

A requirement of exchange

It is not possible to conceive of an economy of exchange in which neither contact nor communication exists between the parties to the exchange. The process of exchange involves costs to those who participate in it and hence also to society. Such costs stem from many elements in the process, and one such element is the requirement that contact and communication exist if exchange of goods and/or services is to be effected. If these costs vary with the ordering of contact and communication patterns between firms and consumers, then it is possible that an optimum pattern exists for any vertical market structure. The total social cost of this exchange requirement might have a nontrivial minimum point at some nonzero level of exchange. Furthermore, any profit-oriented firm in the exchange process may

* This chapter is based on "An Analysis of Vertical Market Structures," *Management Science* X (July, 1964), by the authors and is included here with the permission of *Management Science*.

be faced with the problem of determining the contact and communication pattern which it is to share with other units in an economic system.

This chapter develops theoretical models of vertical market structures based on the contact and communication costs. As a starting point Balderston's[1] model is used. To this basic model variables are added by the relaxation of some key assumptions. However, before these additional variables are treated, Balderston's model is shown to be somewhat restrictive. The restrictions stem from two aspects of the model—(a) failure to consider market imperfections and (b) failure to consider costs of exchange other than those of contact and communication. The first of these forms the subject for this chapter, and the second is dealt with in the following chapters.

As pointed out in Chapter 1, a structure is a pattern of relationships between firms. Various levels of firms are related to one another and to groups of initial sellers and initial buyers through the existence of lines of contact and communication. Equilibrium structures are identified in terms of the number of levels of middlemen or intermediaries between the initial groups of buyers and sellers and the location of the performance of the functions concerned. Strategies on the vertical market structure relationships that each of the initial buying, selling, and certain intermediary firms should choose in order to maximize its profits, other things being equal, are treated and identified, and the resulting equilibrium structure is determined.

The output of the system is discussed in terms of the availability of information on each other's price offerings to the initial sellers and buyers. Thus, a structure's output is that sum of information each member of each group has on the prices offered by all members of the other group. Most often, structures analyzed are those which permit every initial seller to be in contact with every initial buyer, thereby allowing each to collect information on offered prices prior to sale or purchase. Such an informational output permits the existence of what Balderston[2] calls "an adequate bargaining network," by allowing all buyers to have price information on all sellers and *vice versa*. In most cases a model's output is, in effect, held constant by the requirement that every initial seller be in contact with every initial buyer, and the costs of various structures having such an output are determined and compared. It also is possible to allow the output to vary and to determine costs under the conditions of limited contacts and hence also, limited information gathering. Finally, there is no problem even where some difference exists in the value of information as a result of its source. The output of the structure can still be viewed as a constant amount of information, and the reduction in its value or utility viewed in terms of the rebates received by the initial group of buyers and sellers. In other words, by holding output constant, rebates, equivalent to the reduction in the value of output, are treated as system costs.

Notations and assumptions used

The notations used in this chapter are as follows:

m = number of producing firms in the system.

n = number of initial and final customer units (retailers or users) in the system.

t = number of different goods handled within the system.

i = the index number allocated serially to a level of intermediary operation in the system, i.e., a level lying between m and n or between any other levels in the system.

w_i = the number of intermediaries or wholesale middlemen in level i.

r_{ji} = total rebate given by middleman j in level i to his suppliers and his customers.

S_{ji} = initial cost of setting up a contact or communication channel for middleman j in level i.

q = cost of transmitting a package of information.

The basic model involves a very minor reformulation of Balderston's work and requires a set of assumptions identical to the ones he makes explicitly or implicitly. These assumptions are as follows:

1. All producers and all retailers deal with a single product, i.e., $t = 1$. This assumption should be taken to mean *zero* product differentiation.

2. The total amount of flow of goods through the system is given ". . . in accordance with the basic cost conditions in the supplying industry and conditions of final demand facing the retail level or the ultimate transaction level in the market."[3]

3. A standard order size, and cost and method of shipment are given.

4. Intermediary firms carry no product inventories; their function is to collect and transmit information and to set up and maintain the communication channels.

5. The cost of transmitting a package of information is not dependent on the amount of information in the package. It is normalized to equal 1; i.e., $q = 1$.

6. The cost of setting up a contact or communication channel is zero, i.e., $S_{ji} = 0$.

7. Intermediaries, the initial group of customers, and the initial group of producers are motivated by profit-maximization criteria or goals.

8. All firms in the system including m and n are indifferent to the identity of the firms to which they sell and from which they buy, and to the profits made by such firms, provided their own profit level is no lower than it was when they dealt directly with one another and not through such intermediary firms. No firm in

the system requires a rebate from the intermediaries; $r_{ji} = 0$.
9. The numbers of producer and retailer or user firms are exogenously determined.
10. Every firm among m must be in contact with every firm among n, and any intermediary firm must be in contact with all firms in the level above and all firms in the level below it in the channel. "Level" is intended to include intermediary levels and the initial producer and user levels. It is this assumption which permits ".... adequate protection in bargaining."[4]

Cooperation and competition

The models developed in this chapter are of a marketing system wherein cooperation and competition are the only two relationships that exist between firms in the system. Cooperation is not used to mean collusion, but to refer to the relationship that must exist between two firms involved in a marketing transaction. Thus cooperation is the necessary condition of contact and negotiation of an exchange transaction between two firms. All relationships along the marketing channel involve cooperation, and consequently, every firm in the system is a member of the system by virtue of its cooperation with some other firm. In their simplest form, the models developed permit one to conclude that every intermediary firm that cooperates but does not compete reduces by its presence the total cost of contact and communication in the system, provided that this unit cooperates with at least two suppliers and more than two buyers or the reverse.

Competition, unlike cooperation, defines a relationship that is not necessarily applicable to every unit in the system at equilibrium. Two firms in the system are in competition if they have the same set of suppliers and the same set of customers, or if they are in the same channel level. Thus, whereas every firm in the system must cooperate, only some will find it necessary to compete. Models of this system permit one to conclude that where a firm is in competition with any other firm in the system, the removal of one would always lower the total cost of contact and communication in the system.

It is possible to view the competition among the m sellers and among the n buyers as perfect. Such an assumption does not *necessarily* follow from the requirement that each buyer know the price offered by each seller and *vice versa*. Where such knowledge is the output of the system, as is often assumed below, where the product exchanged is identical in all transactions, and where no imperfections, such as geographic advantages, exist, then the price at which all transactions are completed will be the same in all cases. However, the models developed in this chapter do not rest upon the requirement that the m or the n are in perfect competition among themselves, and it is not suggested that they are.

The models do not suggest that free entry *into the initial level of sellers or buyers* exists; the assumption is, at this stage, just the opposite. Furthermore, it is not necessarily the case that the structures of the initial supply market, or the initial demand market, are in competitive equilibrium. The analysis is one of the comparative costs of different vertical market structures with a given output, and of the equilibrium structures, given only that the initial competitive conditions of the m sellers and n buyers are identical for all structures.

Perfect competition among intermediaries is basic to some of the models. However, the analysis does extend to models where such conditions may be limited or absent. One example of such a model is that where middlemen in conjunction with the m group and the n group are permitted to cooperate and to limit to their advantage the entry of more intermediaries. The imperfections in the competition among the intermediaries created by such behavior leads to equilibrium structures differing from those obtained under conditions of free entry.

The requirement of an undifferentiated product remains, in fact, the only one applicable to all the models. Such a requirement, while necessary, is insufficient as a condition for perfect competition to exist among the m initial sellers or the n initial buyers. Furthermore, the requirement of a constant system output—providing total information for all m and all n on offered prices—does not entail the assumption of no imperfections in the competition of the supply or demand markets. All it involves is the creation of a market wherein price differentials mirror faithfully all the effects of imperfections resulting from preference for some sellers by buyers. Only market imperfections stemming from lack of information are excluded in the models developed in this chapter.

Finally, before developing the model, it is interesting to note that the total cost of the system to the original groups of producers and customers is the sum of contactual and communication costs *plus total profits of the intermediaries*. Total cost so defined does not necessarily behave in the same manner as the cost of contact and communication alone. One reason for developing the models is to investigate the manner in which profits to intermediaries vary or might vary with changes in the structure of the system, i.e., with changes in the combination of firms that compete as well as cooperate. Such changes in profits permit one to obtain from the model a lowest cost equilibrium solution for the system and hence, an optimum solution for all m, n, and intermediaries concerned.

The fundamental nature of the system

Since all buyers contact all sellers, in the absence of intermediaries the total number of contacts made in the system is the product nm. Under assumptions 4 and 6, the cost of a single contact is 1 unit. Thus the total contactual cost of the system is nm or:

(1) $$TC = nm$$

The entry of a single middleman reduces the number of contacts to $(n + m.)$ This results since all buyers need only contact the single middleman for information about the m sellers and, conversely, the m sellers must contact only the single middleman for information about the n buyers. The middleman enters the system on the basis that he will make all the contacts for the m sellers and n buyers. Thus, the total contactual cost incurred in the system—by the first middleman in the first level—is:

(2) $$TC_{11} = m + n$$

Since the m sellers and n buyers are indifferent to the entry of the middleman, the middleman gains a total revenue from m and n equal to the contact costs of the system prior to his entry or:

(3) $$TR_{11} = mn$$

The middleman's profits are expressed as the difference between his revenues and costs:

(4) $$TP_{11} = mn - (m + n)$$

It should be noted that the middleman's profits will be positive for any $n, m > 2$ since $mn > (m + n)$ for all $n, m > 2$.

Because profits are being made in the system, and because no barriers to entry exist, other intermediaries may be drawn into the system. In particular, a second middleman could enter into the system in competition with the first. He would have to duplicate the contactual efforts of the first and thereby incur contactual costs of $(m + n)$. He also would be forced to share the total revenues gained from m and n—a maximum of mn since m and n will cooperate with the second middleman only if the costs of contacts to m and n do not increase. The profits of each middleman under these conditions can be expressed as:

(5) $$TP_{j1} = \frac{mn}{2} - (m + n); \; j = 1, 2$$

The process of revenue sharing by incoming competitive middlemen will continue as long as profits for the middlemen are non-negative and entry is unimpeded. At equilibrium the total profit of the jth middleman would be:

(6) $$TP_{j1} = \frac{mn}{w_1} - (m + n) = 0; \; j = 1, 2, \ldots, w_1$$

where w_1 is the number of middlemen in the first or primary level.

Expression (6), solved for the number of middlemen, yields the result that:

(6a) $$w_1 = \frac{mn}{m + n}$$

This is Balderston's model with its solution.[5] However, w_1 is *not* the equilibrium number of intermediaries under the assumptions made; it is the equilibrium number of intermediaries in the first level. But there is no reason to suppose that no other levels could exist. In fact, as it is shown below, just the opposite is the case if one holds to the concept of the system that led to the development of Balderston's model.

The formation of one intermediate level of middlemen allows for the formation of additional levels of middlemen. The new levels of middlemen are formed for the same reasons that the first level was created. The entrance of the first intermediary into each new level may lower the contact cost of the whole system; cooperation without competition will always lower total costs unless either of the two levels with which such cooperation exists contains two or less members. That is, from expressions **(2)** and **(6)** the total contact cost incurred by the primary level of intermediaries is:

(7)
$$TC_1 = w_1(m + n)$$

and in general:

$$TC_i = \sum_{j=1}^{w_i} TC_{ji}, i = 1, 2, \ldots$$

where w_i is the number of middlemen in the ith level.

A new middleman in the system, cooperating with the n buyers and the w_1 existing middlemen, would have contactual costs of:

(8)
$$TC_{12} = n + w_1$$

or, in the event of his cooperating with the m buyers and w_1 middlemen,

(8a)
$$TC_{13} = m + w_1$$

In turn, the revenues would be equal to the contact cost of the system prior to his entry:

(9)
$$TR_{12} = nw_1$$

or,

(9a)
$$TR_{13} = mw_1$$

The new cooperating middleman will enter into the system, and thereby create a new level of middlemen, as long as his total revenues exceed his total contact costs; i.e., he will enter if and only if:

(10)
$$TP_{12} = nw_1 - (n + w_1) \geq 0$$

or,

(10a)
$$TP_{13} = mw_1 - (m + w_1) \geq 0$$

Using an analysis similar to Balderston's, the maximum number of middlemen at the new level occurs when the last entering middleman in the level makes a profit of zero. Because *fractional* firms are not permitted to enter the system, this condition can be rephrased as the point at which the next firm seeking to enter would make negative profits. For simplicity, however, the issue of fractional firms is ignored, and the zero profit form of the condition is used. In the purely competitive model, the total contactual costs of all the middlemen in the new level equal the total revenues generated by the middlemen in the new level thus:

(11)
$$w_2 = \frac{nw_1}{n + w_1}$$

and

(11a)
$$w_3 = \frac{mw_1}{m + w_1}$$

The formation of the second and third intermediate levels allows for the possible development of four additional levels in the system. These levels would be formed between n and w_2, between w_2 and w_1, between w_1 and w_3, and between w_3 and m. Similarly, the four new levels could lead to the development of eight additional intermediate levels in the system. The progression of these additional levels would continue as long as *the product of the number of middlemen or sellers in the level immediately above the new level in question and the number of middlemen or buyers in the level immediately below the new level was greater than or equal to the sum of the middlemen, sellers, or buyers in the levels immediately above and below the new level.* This condition states:[6]

(12)
$$\frac{ab}{a + b} \geq 1$$

where:

a = number of middlemen or sellers in the level immediately above the one in question, and

b = number of middlemen or buyers in the level immediately below the one in question.

For any given number of buyers and sellers, the number of middlemen and the number of levels of middlemen existing within the system at equilibrium are maximized when the number of sellers equals the number of buyers. This is proved as follows:

(13) $w_1 = \dfrac{nm}{n + m}$, subject to: $K = n + m$ where $K =$ any given number of initial buyers and sellers. To maximize w_1 set $\dfrac{\partial w_1}{\partial n} = \dfrac{\partial w_1}{\partial m} = 0$ in the expression:

(13a) $w_1 = \dfrac{nm}{n + m} - \lambda(K - n - m)$ where: $\lambda =$ the Lagrangian multiplier.

Then

(14)
$$\frac{\partial w_1}{\partial n} = -\frac{nm}{(n + m)^2} + \frac{m}{n + m} - \lambda = 0$$

(15) $$\frac{\partial w_1}{\partial m} = -\frac{nm}{(n+m)^2} + \frac{n}{n+m} - \lambda = 0$$

The second order conditions require that the relevant bordered Hessian determinant be positive in sign,

$$\begin{vmatrix} \dfrac{\partial^2 w_1}{\partial n^2} & \dfrac{\partial^2 w_1}{\partial n \partial m} & \dfrac{\partial^2 w_1}{\partial n \partial \lambda} \\[2mm] \dfrac{\partial^2 w_1}{\partial m \partial n} & \dfrac{\partial^2 w_1}{\partial m^2} & \dfrac{\partial^2 w_1}{\partial m \partial \lambda} \\[2mm] \dfrac{\partial^2 w_1}{\partial \lambda \partial n} & \dfrac{\partial^2 w_1}{\partial \lambda \partial m} & \dfrac{\partial^2 w_1}{\partial \lambda^2} \end{vmatrix} > 0, \quad \text{or} \quad \begin{vmatrix} \dfrac{2nm - 2m(n+m)}{(n+m)^3} & \dfrac{2nm}{(n+m)^3} & -1 \\[2mm] \dfrac{2nm}{(n+m)^3} & \dfrac{2nm - 2n(n+m)}{(n+m)^3} & -1 \\[2mm] -1 & -1 & 0 \end{vmatrix} > 0$$

$$\frac{2nm}{(n+m)^3} + \frac{2nm}{(n+m)^3} - \frac{2nm - (n+m)2n}{(n+m)^3} - \frac{2nm - (n+m)2m}{(n+m)^3} > 0$$

and $2(n+m)^2 > 0$.

Thus we have a maximum w_1 since $n, m > 2$.

Solving expression (14) for λ and substituting this value into expression (15) results in the following expression:

(16) $$\frac{n}{n+m} - \frac{m}{n+m} = 0$$

In turn expression (16) yields the result that:

$$n = m$$

Because only positive values for the numbers of sellers and buyers have meaning, it can be concluded that the maximum number of middlemen in the primary level occurs when the number of sellers equals the number of buyers.

Since the number of intermediaries in any level is some function of the number of sellers, buyers, and middlemen in the system, the greater the number of middlemen in the primary intermediate level, the greater the total number of middlemen and levels of middlemen the system can sustain. Because only middlemen making non-negative profits from the performance of the single function of contact can be expected to remain in the system, the equilibrium and maximum number in the primary level is $n/2$ when $n = m$. In general the number of middlemen in the primary level can be related to the number of buyers and sellers as follows:

$$w_1 = \frac{nm}{n+m}$$

and

$$w_1\left(1 + \frac{m}{n}\right) = m$$

Since $m, n \geqslant 2$, $m/n > 0$, and $\left(1 + \dfrac{m}{n}\right) > 1$, this implies that $w_1 < m$ and $w_1 < n$.

Thus there are less middlemen in the primary level than there are buyers and sellers. Therefore, by a similar argument the number of middlemen which can be obtained in any *additional* level must also be less than the number of sellers or middlemen in the level immediately above it, and less than the number of buyers or middlemen in the level immediately below it. While this conclusion pertains only to the *formation of new intermediate levels*, it proves that under the assumption that no fractional middlemen could exist, the total number of middlemen and the total number of *levels* of middlemen must converge to some finite number for any finite number of buyers and sellers.

One final conclusion can be drawn from this simplified model—co-operation leads to contactual cost reductions for the system while competition increases contactual costs. In cooperation a middleman assumes the burden of making contacts for a number of firms and is able to exist only because he can reduce the cost of the performance of the contactual fraction between the levels he services. Unless the cooperator can reduce the contactual costs between the two levels he services, he faces negative profits and thus cannot enter. Competition, in the model, results in the duplication of effort by middlemen and increased contactual costs.

This principle is illustrated in Chart 2.1, where the initial system includes only ten buyers and ten sellers. Allowing additional levels of cooperation, further competition in the new levels, and the existence of only whole milddlemen, the system at equilibrium contains twenty-one middlemen and eleven separate levels of intermediaries. A system containing twenty buyers and twenty sellers would allow ninety-eight middlemen and forty-three levels of intermediaries. A system containing 350 sellers and 350 buyers would contain approximately 21,000 middlemen and 11,000 levels of intermediaries. In contrast, Balderston's initial systems would have included

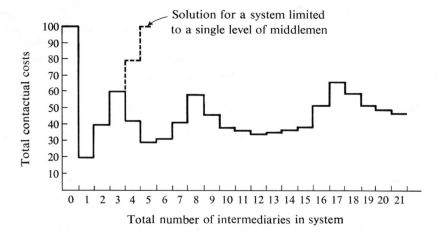

CHART 2.1

only five middlemen in the first, ten in the second, and 175 in the third, since he allows only one level of intermediaries—the *primary* level, or that group of middlemen cooperating directly with the initial groups of sellers and buyers.

Rebates by middlemen

It is possible that firms in the structure would not be indifferent to the entrance of new cooperating firms at their existing levels of profits. One reason for this is the loss of direct contact with the customers which would be incurred by the existing firms as a result of the introduction of new levels of intermediaries—new cooperating firms in the system. Presumably such a loss may have some cost associated with it, and the existing firms will be indifferent only if the new cooperating firms cover this cost by reducing the costs or increasing the revenues of the existing firms by an equal amount. Another reason may be the realization that through bargaining with intermediaries, profits could be increased. In effect, then, new cooperating firms must grant *rebates* to the existing firms in order to gain entrance and cooperation from the firms already in the structure. Such rebates may be viewed as direct money payments or as price differentials. Without empirical evidence there is no *a priori* way of determining the size of the rebate required to create an indifference situation among the existing firms regarding the entry of new cooperating firms. The rebates are, however, now viewed as necessarily of an amount greater than zero, and the influence they have on the "size" of the system can be stated in general terms.

Assuming that the *m* sellers and *n* buyers in the system are collectively indifferent to the entrance of any middleman when the middleman grants a rebate of a size r_{j1}, the total rebate granted by all middlemen in the first level of intermediaries is:

(**17**) $$R_1 = \sum_{j=1}^{w_1} r_{j1}$$

The total rebates granted by the first level can be expressed as some proportion of the total cost of the system *mn*, i.e.,

(**18**) $$R_1 = k(mn); \ 0 < k < 1$$

The total revenue within the system, to be allocated among the middlemen in the primary level is:

$$TR_{j1} = (1 - k)mn$$

Each middleman in the primary level has profits of:

(**19**) $$TP_{j1} = \frac{(1 - k)mn}{w_1} - (m + n)$$

Again the equilibrium number of middlemen is defined as the point at which all middlemen in this level make zero profits, or where:

(20) $$TP_{j1} = 0 \Rightarrow w_1 = (1-k)\frac{mn}{m+n}$$

Thus, the number of middlemen in the primary intermediate level is reduced in proportion to the size of the aggregate rebate, relative to the initial total cost of the system, granted by the middlemen in that level. In turn, a reduction in the number of middlemen in the primary intermediate level results in a more than proportionate reduction in the number and levels of additional middlemen who can operate within the system if the existing w_1 middlemen demand equal rebates from the new middlemen. In effect, each middleman in level 3, the level between the m sellers and w_1 middlemen in the primary level, must give a rebate of:

$$\frac{kmw_1}{w_3}$$

At equilibrium the total profit of each middleman is zero:

$$TP_{j3} = (1-k)\frac{mw_1}{w_3} - (m+w_1) = 0$$

Then,

$$w_3 = (1-k)\frac{mw_1}{m+w_1}$$

where:

$$w_1 = (1-k)\frac{mn}{m+n}$$

or,

$$w_3 = (1-k)\frac{m(1-k)\dfrac{mn}{m+n}}{m+(1-k)\dfrac{mn}{m+n}} = (1-k)^2\frac{mn}{m+2n-kn}.$$

For $k=0$ the equilibrium values of w_1 and w_3 are $mn/(m+n)$ and $nm/(m+2n)$, respectively. To show that the reduction in w_3 is proportionately greater than that in w_1 when $k>0$ it is necessary to show that:

$$\frac{\dfrac{mn}{m+n}}{(1-k)\dfrac{mn}{m+n}} < \frac{\dfrac{mn}{m+2n}}{(1-k)^2\dfrac{mn}{m+2n-kn}}$$

or

$$(1-k) < \frac{m+2n-kn}{m+2n}.$$

Then

$$(1 - k) < 1 - k\frac{n}{m + 2n}$$

Thus the reduction w_3 is relatively greater than the reduction in w_1 for any $0 < k < 1$, since $n, m \geqslant 2$.

Profits in the system

The m sellers and n buyers may demand rebates from all new (entering) middlemen with whom they cooperate as a payment to defer the loss of direct contact with the original market elements which results from the entry of middlemen. The average rebate demanded varies with the *average* loss of direct market contact. The total profits of middlemen vary with the average size of the rebate and the number of middlemen. Chart 2.2 shows how the total profits for middlemen vary when the total rebate granted to the m sellers and n buyers increases at a decreasing rate as the number of intermediaries increases.

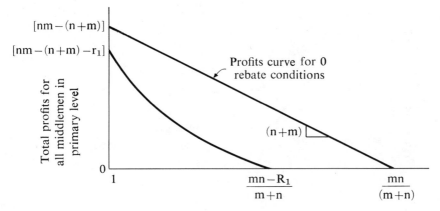

CHART 2.2

If the average rebate demanded by the m sellers and n buyers does not change as the number of middlemen is increased, the total profits curve for the primary level of middlemen is a straight line, as is shown in Chart 2.3.

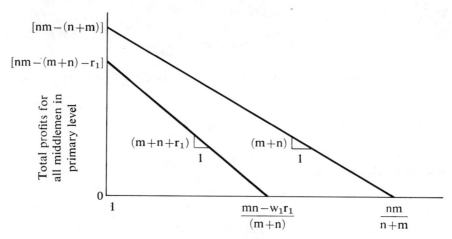

CHART 2.3

If the average rebate demanded by the *m* sellers and *n* buyers increases as the number of middlemen increases, the total profits curve declines at an increasing rate as the number of middlemen is increased. This is illustrated in Chart 2.4.

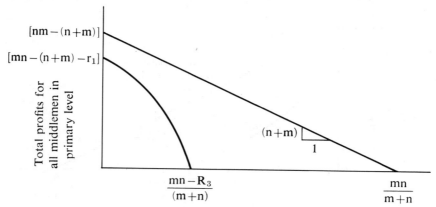

CHART 2.4

Given that no middleman will enter the system unless he can earn zero or greater profits, the contactual costs incurred by middlemen plus the total profits achieved by all middlemen in the system equal the total cost incurred by the *m* sellers and the *n* buyers. This is illustrated in Chart 2.5.

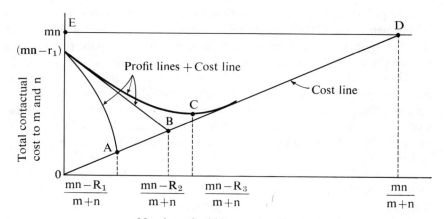

Number of middlemen in primary level

CHART 2.5

Assuming that the m sellers and n buyers wish to minimize their contactual costs, we can state that the number of middlemen in the primary level will be:

$$(21) \qquad w_1 < \frac{mn - R}{m + n}$$

Since the size of R, the total rebates granted by the w_1 middlemen, is dependent on the behavior of the m sellers and n buyers, no explicit number of middlemen can be determined. If the rebate demanded by m and n exceeds $mn - (m + n)$, then $w_1 = 0$ (shown by point E on Chart 2.5) since it is not profitable for any middlemen to enter the system. If m and n demand no rebate then:

$$w_1 = \frac{mn}{m + n}, \text{ which occurs at point D}$$

If m and n demand average rebates which increase as the number of middlemen increases, then the number of middlemen entering the system is shown by point A, where

$$(22) \qquad w_1 = \frac{mn - R_1}{m + n}$$

If m and n demand constant rebates of r_{j1} from each entering middleman, then the number of middlemen in the system at equilibrium is shown by point B:

$$(22a) \qquad w_1 = \frac{mn - w_1 r_{j1}}{m + n}, \text{ since } R_1 = w_1 r_{j1}, \text{ in this case,}$$

or,

$$(22b) \qquad w_1 = \frac{mn}{m + n + r_{j1}}$$

At points A, B, D, and E there are no monopoly profits made by the middlemen. Only if the average rebate demanded by m and n falls as the number of middlemen increases can there be any monopoly profits. This suggests that the bargaining power of the m and n falls as the monopoly power of the middlemen in the primary level *decreases*, and there is more and more competition among such middlemen. Though not impossible, such a state of affairs is highly unlikely, and is probably what is implied by Balderston's conclusion on primary level middlemen profits. It should be noted, however, that Balderston's profit curve is not identical to the one shown in Chart 2.2, since his curve intersects the zero total profit state at $w_1 = nm/(n + m)$. This is impossible under the conditions stated by both Balderston and us, since m and n would never cooperate with entering middlemen if their total rebate were falling as the number of middlemen increased.[7]

It is possible to have profits enter the system under any scheme of rebates providing $[R \leqslant mn - (m + n)]$ if fractional middlemen are not permitted to enter the system. Under such conditions is it possible that the quotient

$$w_1 = \frac{mn - R}{m + n}$$

is not an integer. Thus, the number of "whole" middlemen in the system could be less than the number necessary to drive profits to zero. Chart 2.1 illustrates this condition.[8] Thus, while both the Balderston system and the one developed here are systems in which profits exist, there is little similarity between them. Balderston's system is a special case of the more general system, and in order to generate monopoly profits, a highly restrictive assumption must be made about the behavior of m and n. Profits derived because fractional middlemen are not permitted to exist in the system cannot be defined as monopoly profits, but as the result of the peculiar nature of the model which permits only integers for the equilibrium number of middlemen.

Cost of information transmittal

It is assumed early in the chapter that the cost of transmitting a package of information is constant and equal to one (1). Relaxing this assumption would affect the equilibrium number of middlemen and number of levels of midldemen in any given system of m sellers and n buyers.

Allow the cost of contact and communication to be made up of two parts: a fixed element q and another element which varies with the amount of information transmitted. Let us say, for the sake of simplicity, that the cost of transmitting the price offered by any seller and any buyer is p, i.e., the price of one buyer or seller is defined as a unit of information with cost of transmittal p. The total cost of direct contact between a member of the m group and a member of the n group is now a cost of contact *and* communication, $q + 2p$.

The total contactual and communication costs incurred by m and n, in the absence of intermediaries, is:

$$TC = mn(q + 2p) = qmn + 2pmn$$

Thus, each m sends out his price to all n and each n his price to all m.

The total cost of contact and communication to a single *middleman* entering the primary level that would achieve this same informational output of the system is of two parts. One part is $q(m + n)$, the total number of contacts times the fixed cost of each contact once the middleman acquires the initial price offer of the m and n. To determine the second cost element note that the middleman passes to each of the n buyers a total number of units of information of m prices and asks for one price offer—a total of $(m + 1)$ units of information. The total information passed to all members of the n group is thus $n(m + 1)$. Between the middleman and the m sellers just the reverse holds; he gives each of the m sellers a total of n pieces of information (n prices) and collects one. The total units of information transmitted between the middleman and the m sellers is thus $m(n + 1)$.

The total cost to the middleman of attaining this given output of information for the system is the sum of the costs of contacts and the costs of information transmitted,

(23) $$TC_{j1} = q(m + n) + pn(m + 1) + pm(n + 1)$$

The total profit of the first middleman in the primary level is:

(24) $$TP_{11} = qmn + 2pmn - q(m + n) - p(m + n + 2mn)$$

The profits of each w_1 middleman in level 1 are:

(25) $$TP_{j1} = \frac{qmn + 2pmn}{w_1} - q(m + n) - p(m + n + 2mn)$$

At equilibrium the profits of each middleman are zero, thus:

$$TP_{j1} = \frac{qmn + 2pmn}{w_1} - q(m + n) - p(m + n + 2mn) = 0$$

or,

(26) $$w_1 = \frac{qmn + 2pmn}{q(m + n) + p(m + n + 2mn)}$$

The equilibrium number of middlemen in the primary level in the absence of information transmittal costs, when $p = 0$, is shown in expression (6) as:

(6) $$w_1 = \frac{qmn}{q(m + n)} = \frac{mn}{m + n}$$

From a comparison of expressions (6) and (26) it is clear that the introduction of information transmittal costs leads to a *reduction* in the equilibrium number of middlemen in the primary level in the system. This can be proved by examining the differences in the numerators and denominators of expressions (6) and (26). In the case where $p > 0$ the numerator increases by $2pmn$ while the denominator increases by $2pmn + p(m + n)$. Since $2pmn < 2pmn + p(m + n)$ and $mn > (m + n)$, the equilibrium number of middlemen shown in expression (26) must be less than that shown in expression (6). This reduction, of course, leads to a reduction in the total number of middlemen and levels of middlemen in the system as a whole.

Fixed costs and a minimum acceptable rate of return

In reality, fixed costs would be associated with the entry of middlemen into the structure. The fixed costs might take the form of formal layouts of capital prior to making any contacts, or of below-cost operations for a period of time needed to establish a cooperative relationship among all the buyers and sellers. In either case an investment is made by the middleman in contemplation of a return in the form of operating profits from making contacts for the buyers and sellers. Thus it may be worthwhile to relax assumption (6), i.e., that there are no fixed costs.

In order to induce potential middlemen to invest funds into the marketing structure, the investor must be assured that he will realize a rate of return on his funds comparable with other investment alternatives. Assuming a setup cost of S_{ji} and a minimum acceptable annual rate of return of I, a firm will not enter the structure, at the ith level, unless annual profits are at least equal to IS_{ji}, i.e.,

(27) $$\text{Min}(TP_{ji}) = IS_{ji}$$

From expression (5) and ignoring depreciation costs we can say:

(28) $$TP_{ji} - IS_{ji} = \frac{mn}{w_1} - (m + n), \text{ for all } w_{j1}.$$

Solving for the number of middlemen in the first (primary) level we find:

(29) $$w_1 = \frac{mn}{(m + n) + IS_{j1}}$$

Thus fixed costs tend to reduce the number of middlemen in the primary level, and therefore to reduce also the number of middlemen and the number of levels of middlemen in the whole system.

Segmented markets

Up to this stage in the analysis it has been assumed that the structure is comprised of sellers who sell only one type of product and buyers who are interested in only the single product. Thus, all buyers had to contact all sellers and, conversely, all sellers had to communicate with all buyers. In reality, despite this same condition, we might expect to find market structures in which preference for some sellers by buyers, and *vice versa*, is shown. Such a situation could arise as a result of differing transportation costs, some institutional factors, or differing assortment requirements among the buyers and sellers. As a result there might be a number of segmented markets composed of buyers who desire information about only a fraction of the sellers in the market. One characterizes such a system as an overlapping structure of the kind treated to this point.

As an extreme case we might assume that there are Z geographic areas in which buyers are located so that within each area only some of the suppliers are considered as possible sources, but any buyer in any area can be serviced by all middlemen dealing directly with the initial buyers. Assume also that each of the buyers in each of the Z areas is interested in cooperating with only $\left(\frac{1}{d}\right)$th of the sellers and that $d < Z$, i.e., that sellers may serve more than one area, and an overlap exists. Finally, assume that each of the Z areas contains an equal number of buyers. Thus a single buyer incurs only $\left(\frac{1}{d}\right)$th of the previous contactual costs since he is interested in only $\left(\frac{1}{d}\right)$th of the sellers. The total contactual costs of the system, in the absence of middlemen, is now less than it was considered to this point. The informational output of the system is also reduced. The total contactual cost of this reduced output is $\frac{mn}{d}$.

A middleman entering the primary level would incur contactual costs of $(m + n)$ since he must contact all of the m sellers and n buyers as assumed. Thus the total profit for a single middleman at the primary level in the structure is:

$$(30) \qquad TP_{11} = \frac{mn}{d} - (m + n)$$

Additional middlemen at the primary level would also encounter contactual costs of $(m + n)$ but they would have to share the total revenue, $\frac{mn}{d}$, among themselves. Thus the total profit of the jth middleman in the primary level is:

$$(31) \qquad TP_{j1} = \frac{mn}{dw_1} - (m + n)$$

At equilibrium all middlemen in the system would be making zero profits and the total number of middlemen at the primary level would be:

$$(32) \qquad w_1 = \frac{mn}{d(m+n)}$$

The imperfection of segmented markets clearly reduces the number of middlemen in the first level and, hence, in the system as a whole by reducing the total revenue to be shared by all middlemen and leaving their contact requirements unchanged. The reduction in the primary level is also in proportion to the ratio of all sellers who must be contacted by each buyer.

Rebate strategies by middlemen

Thus far in this analysis it is shown that a number of levels of middlemen can exist within a generalized market structure. Further, a number of factors which limit the number of middlemen in the market structure are discussed. To arrive at these solutions it is assumed that the middleman is a passive individual—that is, he does only what is required of him in response to competitive conditions without attempting to influence them, and he operates at the limit of his constraints. It is wise then that we examine the possible competitive strategies that a middleman can employ, in the theoretical structure, to *maximize* his profits.

In the absence of fixed costs, multiple products,[9] and fractional middlemen we can see that a middleman gains entry into a market structure because he can convince the m sellers and n buyers that cooperation with him is profitable to them. As an inducement to create an indifference to his entry among the buyers and sellers, the middleman might offer some rebate to them. The reasonable question then is what size of rebate maximizes the middleman's long-run profits?

Ignoring, for the moment, the total rebate size requirements of the m sellers and n buyers, the rebate given must be within two limits. One limit is set by the need for the middleman to prevent entry of a competitor. The other limit is determined by the middleman's ability to pay. Where, within these two limits, the final rebate will fall is a function of the nature of the bargaining situation which exists between the potential middleman and the m sellers and n buyers.

To prevent the entry of other middlemen, an intermediary must, as a first condition, offer a rebate to m and n of a size sufficient to insure that no other middleman could make positive profits. This minimum rebate depends upon the rebate demands of the m and the n upon the second middleman. In general, if the m sellers and n buyers demand an additional rebate of r_{21} of the second middleman for their cooperation and his entry, the first middleman would have to offer a minimum rebate of some r_{11} to prevent entry of the second middleman. To obtain r_{11} it may be noted that all middlemen must share equally the total rebate given to the m and n, as they must share equally the revenues received from m and n for assuming the contactual function. The total profits of a second entering middleman would be:

$$TP_{21} = \frac{mn}{2} - (m + n) - \frac{r_{11} + r_{21}}{2}$$

To prevent the entry of the second middleman the first intermediary must set r_{11} such that $TP_{21} = 0$, or he must set:

(33) $$r_{11} = mn - 2(m + n) - r_{21}$$

If the rebate demands of the initial buyers and sellers on the second middleman are minimal, i.e., if $r_{21} = 0$, then the minimum rebate that the first middleman must offer m and n is:

(33a) $$r_{11} = mn - 2(m + n)$$

Similarly if m and n demand an equal rebate from the second middleman, making $r_{11} = r_{21}$, then:

(33b) $$r_{11} = \frac{mn}{2} - (m + n)$$

It would seem that the two rebates described in expressions (33a) and (33b) represent the logical extremes to m and n regarding the disutility to them of allowing additional middlemen to enter the vertical market structure. The first rebate represents total indifference on the part of m and n while the second suggests a constant marginal disutility with respect to the entry of additional middlemen—an economic limit in the sense that the loss of direct contact among the m and n is postulated not to increase at an increasing rate with respect to the entry of added middlemen. Thus the lower limit of what the first middleman grants to prevent the entry of a second middleman lies between the rebates given by (33a) and (33b).

Consider the least restrictive of these rebate conditions, the case in which m and n demand an equal-sized rebate from the second middleman for his entry. The equilibrium profits of the first middleman would be maximized[10] at this point since this profits would be:

(34) $$TP_{11} = mn - (m + n) - \left[\frac{mn}{2} - (m + n) \right], \text{ or}$$

(34a) $$TR_{11} = \frac{mn}{2}$$

This position is an optimal one for the single middleman. Given that it is an optimal position, all prospective middlemen will seek to attain it, and each knows that all others seek to attain it. Thus, if all middlemen were to *bid* for the position and if each were to offer a rebate of $\left[\frac{mn}{2} - (m + n) \right]$

to m and n, any single middleman would have to rely on chance alone to achieve the position of intermediary performing the contact and communication function.

If there is a finite number of prospective middlemen bidding for the position—say A of them—the expected profits of any given middleman are:[11]

$$(35) \qquad TP_{j1} = \frac{1}{A}\left(\frac{mn}{2}\right)$$

Given this prospect, each middleman will consider the possibility of offering rebates in excess of $\left[\frac{mn}{2} - (m + n)\right]$ in an attempt to enhance his expected profits. That is, a middleman may feel that he can enhance his *expected profits* by offering a larger rebate to m and n, thereby improving his bidding position relative to other prospective middlemen. For example, a middleman might offer a rebate of $\frac{mn}{k} - (m + n)$ which would result in an expected profit of:

$$(36) \qquad TP_{j1} = \rho\frac{mn(k - 1)}{k}$$

where: ρ = the probability that a rebate of size $\frac{mn}{k} - (m + n)$ will be large
enough to "win."

Then we can say that a middleman will offer a rebate larger than $\frac{mn}{2} - (m + n)$ as long as his expected profits are increased by the offer, or as long as:

$$\rho\frac{mn(k - 1)}{k} > \frac{1}{A}\left(\frac{mn}{2}\right)$$

Since each prospective middleman will entertain the issue of larger rebates, we shall consider the size of the largest rebate offer. To do so it is necessary to discuss the second limit to the size of rebates—the ability of middlemen to pay. The largest rebate any middleman can offer is of size $[mn - (m + n)]$ since his profits with this rebate are equal to zero, i.e., when $k = 1$ since

$$(37) \qquad TP_{j1} = mn - (m + n) - [mn - (m + n)] = 0$$

We can infer that the larger the number of prospective middlemen or the larger the number of bids by middlemen, the closer the final rebates will be to $[mn - (m + n)]$. If there is an infinite number of bids we can expect at least one rebate bid of $[mn - (m + n)]$; if conditions of perfect competition exist in the bidding there will be zero profits in the structure.

Thus far we have concentrated on the role of middlemen in the bargaining procedure. The m sellers and n buyers also set requirements of their own—the conditions that have to be met before they will cooperate or accept bids. This lower limit to acceptable rebates and its relation to the lower limit set by the middleman's maximum profit requirements are now considered.

The bids for rebate that m and n will entertain, or those which are high enough to cause them to entertain the choice of a *single* middleman, are those which are in excess of the total rebate they could have received if the system were allowed to move toward equilibrium with *multiple* middlemen in the structure. The minimum total contactual costs which can exist within the structure equal $(m + n)$, since in every market structure the minimum functional requirement is that each seller and each buyer be contacted at least once. This minimum cost position is achieved only when there is just one middleman in the structure.

The minimum contactual cost market structure with multiple middlemen is one in which four midldemen exist in the pattern shown in Chart 2.6, where the total contactual costs are:

(38) $$TC = (m + n) + 2(w_1) = (m + n) + 4$$

This market structure will be in equilibrium only if:

$$\frac{mn}{m + n} < 3$$

Least Cost Market Structure for Multiple Middlemen

```
0_____0 m SELLERS
                    0                      w_2 = 1
              0         0                  w_1 = 2
                    0                      w_3 = 1
0_____0 n BUYERS
```

CHART 2.6

For any m and $n > 5$ the market structure shown in Chart 2.6 will not be in equilibrium, and the entry of competitors will increase the contactual costs beyond the $(m + n + 4)$ figure shown in expression (38). Given any m and n, however, a least contactual cost structure with multiple middlemen can be found which is in equilibrium. By definition each middleman's profits tend toward zero at equilibrium and, thus the total rebate that m and n can expect is:

(39) $$R = mn - \left\{ m + n + 2\sum_{i=1}^{i_{max}} w_i \right\}, \text{ all } w_i > 1$$

where i_{max} = number of levels of middlemen at equilibrium.

The total rebate that m and n can expect in any given structure with multiple middlemen depends upon the relation between r_{ji} and w_i—one that cannot be determined *a priori*. This expected total rebate is greater, equal to, or less than the minimum rebate a single middleman must give to insure that no other middleman can enter the structure, as in expression (**33**). This effective minimum rebate is thus the larger of:

$$mn - \left(m + n + 2\sum_{i=1}^{i_{max}} w_i\right), \text{ all } w_i > 1$$

or

$$\frac{mn}{2} - (m + n).$$

At the other extreme the effective maximum rebate is $mn - (m + n)$. Since $[mn - (m + n)]$ is always greater than $\left[mn - \left(m + n + 2\sum_{i=1}^{i_{max}} w_i\right), \text{ for } w_i > 1\right]$ and also always greater than $\left[\frac{mn}{2} - (m + n)\right]$, two limits exists for all m and $n > 2$, and the possibility of strategy employment by middlemen in the theoretical structure exists.

We can conclude, in the light of the existence of strategy and negotiation possibilities by m, n, and middlemen, and in the absence of market imperfections, that the theoretical structure carried to its logical conclusion will result in a system of the original n buyers and m sellers, and a single middleman.[12] The single middleman's profits, under conditions of pure competition among *prospective* middlemen, will be bid to zero and no monopoly profits will exist. Under any other set of market conditions both the level of rebates and the profits of the middleman cannot be precisely determined; only the limits to both are algebraically identifiable.

The introduction of strategy possibilities does not allow for the existence of multi-level marketing channels. A single middleman solution may appear wholly unrealistic, but it is more plausible when we consider that it may well be that organized wholesale markets *operate* essentially as does a single middleman in a marketing system.

Model with market imperfections

The analyses of this chapter can be summarized into a single model illustrating the influence of: 1. information transmittal and contactual costs; 2. segmented markets; 3. rebates by middlemen; and 4. minimum acceptable rates of return restrictions for middlemen, on the structure of the market with regard to the location and numbers of middlemen in the system. Under the conditions stated above, and in the absence of middlemen, the total contactual and information transmittal costs incurred by the m sellers and the n buyers can be stated as:

$$TC = \frac{qmn}{d} + \frac{p2mn}{d}$$

The jth middleman entering the system at the primary level would incur costs of:

$$TC_{j1} = q(m + n) + p\left(m + n + \frac{2mn}{d}\right) + \frac{k}{w_1}mn + IS$$

where:

q = fixed cost of a single contact;
p = variable cost of the information transmitted in a contact;
d = number of segmented markets included in the system;
I = minimum acceptable rate of return required for the existence of a middleman in the system;
S = fixed cost of entry into the primary level for any middleman;
k = proportion of the product mn which must be granted as a gross rebate by the middlemen in the primary level of the structure.

The total profits at equilibrium for any middleman in the primary level can be defined as:

$$TP_{j1} = 0 = \frac{\dfrac{qmn}{d} + \dfrac{p2mn}{d}}{w_1} - \left[q(m + n) + p\left(m + n + \frac{2mn}{d}\right) \right. $$
$$\left. + \frac{k}{w_1}mn + IS \right]$$

which reduces to:

(40)
$$w_1 = \frac{mn\left[\dfrac{q + 2p}{d} - k\right]}{(m + n)(q + p) + \dfrac{2pmn}{d} + IS}$$

The existence of w_1 middlemen in the primary level would lead to the existence of additional levels of middlemen. For example, the jth middleman dealing with the m sellers and w_1 middlemen would have revenues of:

$$TR_{j2} = \frac{qmw_1 + pw_1\left(m + \dfrac{mn}{d}\right) + kmn}{w_2}$$

The new middleman, aside from his fixed investment and rebate, would have to contact all of the m sellers and all of the w_1 middlemen. He would have to transmit to each of the m sellers $\frac{n}{d}$ prices and to each middleman m prices. Thus his total contactual and information transmittal costs would be:

$$TC_{j2} = q(m + w_1) + p\left[\frac{mn}{d} + m + w_1(m + n)\right] + IS + \frac{kmw_1}{w_2} + \frac{kmn}{w_2}$$

At equilibrium, the jth middleman's profits would be zero, i.e.,

$$TP_{j2} = TR_{j2} - TC_{j2} = 0$$

and the equilibrium number of middlemen in this new level is:

$$w_2 = \frac{qmw_1 + pw_1\left(m + \frac{mn}{d}\right) - kmw_1}{q(w_1 + m) + p\left[\frac{mn}{d} + m + w_1(m + n)\right] + IS}$$

The total number of middlemen and levels in the system at equilibrium can be obtained in a similar fashion.

In the simplest form of the model the equilibrium number of middlemen in the primary level is:

$$\hat{w}_1 = \frac{mn}{m + n}$$

This can be obtained from the equilibrium number of middlemen in the general form of the model by setting $p = 0$, $k = 0$, $I = 0$, and $d = 1$.

One argument against the simple form of the model is that the equilibrium $\hat{w}_1$ is very large and consequently the total number of middlemen in all levels is also extremely large. The more general form of the model reduces this unrealism by reducing the equilibrium number of middlemen in the primary level and therefore all middlemen in all levels at equilibrium. To support this contention it must be shown that $\hat{w}_1 > w_1$, or

$$\frac{mn}{m + n} > \frac{mn\left(\frac{q+2p}{d} - k\right)}{(m + n)(q + p) + \frac{2pmn}{d} + IS}$$

This is the same as showing that:

$$0 < (m + n)[(p + q)(d - 1) + dk] + ISd + p[2mn - (m + n)]$$

Since all three terms on the right of the inequality are positive, the proof is complete and:

$$\hat{w}_1 > w_1$$

1   Balderston, Frederick E., "Communication Networks in Intermediate Markets," *Management Science*, IV (January 1958) pp. 154–171.

2   Ibid., p. 157.

3   Ibid., p. 155.

4   Ibid., p. 157.

5   Ibid., pp. 154–171.

6   The product ab is equal to the revenue of the new level and the sum $a + b$, the cost of contacts incurred by each firm in the level between a and b. Thus, firms will enter into the new level as long as there is some prospect of profits or $ab \geq a + b$, which implies: $\frac{ab}{a+b} \geq 1$.

7 A falling total and average rebate function is required to fit Balderston's solution. While a falling average rebate function is within the realm of m and n's behavior patterns, a falling total rebate function is not. See Balderston, *op. cit.*, pp. 159–160.

8 With regard to Chart 2.1, it should be noted that if fractional middlemen were allowed to enter the system, the number of levels of middlemen would approach infinity.

9 These assumptions are made only as a matter of simplifying the analysis, the general conclusions of which would be equally valid if there were fixed costs and multiple products.

10 At all equilibrium positions considered thus far, all profits for middlemen in the primary level have been zero or near zero—where $\frac{mn}{(m+n)}$ was not a whole integer. As this profit position was gained by giving the smallest rebate to gain sole entry into the structure, all other profit positions must be inferior.

11 That is, there is one chance in A of getting profits of $\frac{mn}{2}$ and (A-1) chances in A of getting profits of zero.

12 Since a middleman operating in the system with multiple middlemen can expect only zero profits, there can be little doubt that the prospect of profits of as much as

$$2\sum_{i=1}^{i_{max}} w_i, \text{ for all } w_i \geq 1,$$

will lead him to bid higher rebates to m and n with the hope of eliminating his competitors.

3

Inventory Costs

Inventory cost and exchange

If exchange is to occur the function of contact and communication is a necessary one. It is a source of costs that might be reduced by the presence of middlemen, to the advantage of everyone in the system without changing the output. One function that *may* have to be performed by a marketing system is that of inventory carrying. But in this system, the inventory function is not necessary in the same manner as the contact and communication function. However, both functions may be related to the overall efficiency of the system, and hence the comparative costs of their performance by various kinds of firms in vertical marketing systems can be analyzed in similar fashion.

In the model, inventory theory is employed to determine whether the costs of inventory carrying to the entire vertical market structure are dependent on that structure and the location of the inventories in it. In other words, if the middlemen were to take over the inventory function from the producers, would the total exchange efficiency of the system be increased? If so, is this dependent upon the assumption that the carrying of *positive* inventory levels in the system always increases the efficiency of exchange regardless of who performs the function? What are the equilibrium numbers of middlemen and levels of middlemen when they perform this inventory function?

As in the previous discussion of the contact and communication function the equilibrium number of middlemen and of levels of middlemen varies with different configurations of market imperfections. These numbers are also dependent upon the nature of the demand of the n buyers. Considering only inventory costs, the equilibrium market structure which contains middlemen is again a feasible structure if and only if its total inventory costs are less than or equal to the total inventory costs to the system of direct exchange between the m sellers and n buyers.

Analysis of equilibrium

In the previous chapters the analyses compare various points at which the system is in equilibrium, given the nature and degree of market imperfections. The path by which an equilibrium position is reached is ignored, and the changes in variables over time are not considered. Similarly in this and the following chapter the analysis is one of comparative static equilibria for the system. However, the introduction of the concepts of probabilistic demand, the time period of production, and shortage and overage costs over "time," warrants explanation of the exact nature of the equilibrium conditions of the system.

The stochastic process of demand generation by the users in the system (the n firms) is considered to be in a steady state; *the probability distribution of demand* by the n buyers is stationary over time. The entry and exit of middlemen, however, cause this probability distribution of demand for the goods of any *one* of these middlemen to vary. The assumption is made therefore that this movement of firms into and out of the system occurs only at the end or beginning of the inventory decision period, so that every firm can view the probability distribution of demand for its goods as a given for that period. In addition it is assumed that the length of the inventory period is constant over time and equal to the time period of production, and that unit overage and shortage costs of inventory are also unchanged over time. By confining ourselves to the mathematical expectations of shortages and overages over a fixed inventory-production period we characterize a *static* system. By comparing the costs of the expected overages and shortages resulting from various market structures the analysis is one of comparative statics.

Demand characteristics in the system

The demand for the single and undifferentiated product produced and exchanged in the system is viewed as probabilistic. The n buyers[1] generate a total demand during a given period of time with a probability distribution:

$$f(\mu) = AZ$$

where:

A = a k component row vector describing the probability distribution of orders by the n buyers during the period L.

Z = a transition matrix of size $k \times q$ relating the number of all *orders* placed during the period L to the *units* of product demanded.

μ = total units of the product demanded by the n buyers (retailers or users) during a given time period, L. (Therefore, $f(\mu)$ is a q component row vector describing the probability distribution of the total units demanded by all firms.

The demand for the product from the rth inventory-carrying firm during the period L is:

$$f(\mu_r) = ABZ$$

where:

μ_r = units demanded by the n buyers from the rth firm during period L ($r = 1, 2, \ldots, w, \ldots, m$).

B = a transition matrix of size $k \times k$ describing the probability distribution of orders faced by the rth firm for any given number of orders placed by the n buyers. One might view B as the result of a Markov process involving similar firms tending toward a long-run equilibrium state.

For purposes of this analysis the assumption is made that the n buyers are indifferent in their choice of suppliers. This is reasonable, given the assumption that prices are equal as a result of the perfect information requirements and lack of market imperfections. The nature of competition among the selling firms is such that the probability that any firm receives an order generated by a firm in the n buyer group is dependent only on the number of firms competing in the level of the selling firm. Considering the indifference of the n buyers regarding order placement, the probability of receiving an order once it is generated is $p_r = \dfrac{1}{r}$, where r is the number of firms in this selling level of m producers or w middlemen. Let Z be an identity matrix, i.e., $q = k$, which means that each order is of size one unit of product. The assumption that all orders generated by the n group of firms are of equal size, and the standardization of this size to one unit, is made to simplify the initial analysis .The basic nature of the model is dependent, as is seen below, only on the fact that demand is probabilistic and not on the probabilistic nature of the order size. In other words, demand would be probabilistic if both order generation and order size were distributed probabilistically, and also if only one of them were distributed probabilistically. Making order size nonstochastic simplifies the handling of the probability distribution of demand that emerges and facilitates the development of the basic model. Any element in the matrix B can thus be written as:

$$b_{ij} = \binom{j}{i}(p_r)^i(1-p_r)^{j-i} \quad \text{for } j \geqslant i$$

or,

$$b_{ij} = 0 \quad \text{for } j < i$$

$$\begin{cases} i = 0, 1, \ldots, i_{\max} \\ j = 0, 1, \ldots, j_{\max} \end{cases}$$

The term $i_{\max}$ refers to the maximum number of units ordered from the rth firm, and $j_{\max}$ refers to the maximum aggregate number of units demanded by the n buyers. Since some possibility exists that any one firm will receive the total orders of all the n initial buyers in any one period and each order is of size one, then $i_{\max} = j_{\max} = \mu_{\max}$.

The average demand $\bar{\mu}_r$ for each distribution varies with the number of competitors $r(r = 1, 2, \ldots, w, \ldots, m)$. However $r\bar{\mu}_r = \bar{\mu}$, since the sum of the expected demands for the product of each firm in the group of r selling firms must be equal to the total expected demand. The value of $\bar{\mu}$ is constant since the initial n buyers do not change their demand when the number of prospective suppliers changes. The introduction of middlemen is assumed not to affect the process of demand generation in the model.

Perfect competition and the inventory problem

To formulate the inventory problem of the individual seller, it is postulated that each seller is faced with a probabilistically distributed demand. However, for this postulate to hold in conjunction with a structure of *perfect competition* among the initial sellers seems contrary to some basic notions of the nature of perfect competition. A seller in a perfectly competitive industry can sell all he has at the market price. Why then should the firm view the amounts it can sell as being probabilistically distributed?

This question would not arise if the structure of the competition among the initial m sellers were not a perfect one. The models considered in this work are largely free of the imperfections which lead to imperfect competition. Hence it is essential that the analysis extend to perfect competition to achieve some degree of generality.

The probability distribution of demand, $f(\mu_r)$, implies a given price. Such prices are set in the market by the conditions of aggregate supply and demand, and for every price a different distribution may well result. Whenever a time lag between the decision on production and the availability of output for sale exists, the firm must make some assumption on the ultimate market price in order to determine its optimum level of output. As a result it is possible that the firm would not wish to sell all of its output at the existing equilibrium price.[2]

For purposes of this analysis we define the firms' output, i.e., that quantity of goods it brings to the market for sale, as its *total inventory*. Given the the firm's marginal cost structure and an existing equilibrium market price, the firm can determine an optimum sales level. The difference between the firm's total inventory and this sales level is termed an *overage* when positive and a *shortage* when negative. Consider the following diagram:

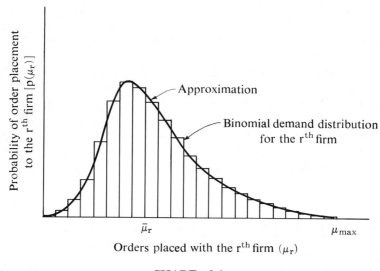

CHART 3.1

D_i is a demand schedule for the entire industry. For each D_i there is some probability that it will be, in fact, that schedule of demand for the industry at the time output is ready for sale. Thus if the total group of m sellers produced a total amount mQ_m (the total inventory) the price per unit received will be p_i with some given probability.

The output problem facing the individual seller is the same as what we term the inventory problem. There is some probability that any amount which the firm produces will be sold at a price below its marginal cost. There is also some probability associated with selling the output at a price above marginal cost by a given finite amount.

Thus the firm's total revenue is probabilistically distributed, and its costs, which are determined by the amount Q_m, are known. Whether it is the price or the amount sold that is probabilistically distributed does not affect the probabilistic nature of the firm's problem. In both cases the problem is to produce an amount, or to determine a level of inventory at the beginning of the production period, that maximizes the expected *difference* between a probabilistically distributed revenue function and a deterministic cost function. One last variation is also possible—the transfer of the probabilistic elements from the revenue function into the cost function by stating all changes in revenues as changes in cost of a different sign, and then to optimize by *minimizing* expected costs.

The formulation of the inventory problem is not contradictory to the conditions of perfect competition among the initial group of sellers m or the middlemen w. Rather than formulate the problem as one of output (sale) determination under conditions of probable prices it is formulated as one of probable sale levels under conditions of given prices. Instead of maximizing the difference between revenue and cost, the problem is stated as one of minimizing costs for a constant revenue. It is the ease of manipulation, and the ease with which the model can be made to incorporate added variables, that has led to its formulation in the manner chosen.

Although it is unnecessary, the model's application could have been limited to a condition of undifferentiated oligopoly in the seller level. Since under such conditions a market price is given to the firm, and since the firm is assumed to have no differentiating characteristics, the total amount of product demanded from it could be viewed as probabilistic and dependent on the total number of competitors in its market level. When total demand is assumed known, there exists for the industry a series of demand curves, each with some probability of being the one applicable at any given time. Under this latter condition the model of inventory choice developed would be applicable, assuming that there is one price at which all firms will sell regardless of which demand curve applies. This would mean that all demand curves faced by the firm are "kinked" at the same price.

Summary of assumptions for inventory analysis

Before developing the model of total inventory costs in differing vertical market structures, we shall recapitulate and summarize the basic assumptions made regarding the environment within which firms make inventory decisions.

1. It takes no to time transfer the product from one firm in one level to another in the next level. This does not mean that there is no elapsed time between ordering and receipt of goods. It means that if a transaction is agreed upon, and if the product is available in the seller's inventory, or when it becomes available, then the *transfer* of the product involves no elapsed time.
2. Production lead time for the product is L days. It takes a producer L days to ready a unit of the product for sale. Production lead time is constant and independent of the level of output as in batch processing.
3. The product is produced at only one level of firms in the system, the initial group of m sellers.

4. There are no setup costs of production and no ordering costs for all firms in the system.
5. Demand for the product by all n firms in the initial buyer group is probabilistic but is evenly distributed throughout the lead period L.
6. There is a positive disutility incurred by any of the n buyers for not being able to find the product in stock when it is ordered from any seller. This disutility is given a money value π_n and is considered an element of the shortage costs to the producers who supply the n buyers. In other words, the seller caught short incurs the cost of the disutility to the unsatisfied buyer by paying him π_n per unit of product short. In addition the unit short is backordered and is sent to the buyer at the beginning of the next period.
7. Each inventory-carrying firm incurs a cost of α_m for every unit of inventory it has on hand at the end of the production-inventory period.

Inventory decisions of individual sellers

Total inventory costs of various vertial market structures necessarily depend upon the manner in which individual firms arrive at their inventory decisions. It is assumed that every firm in the system is capable of employing inventory models to solve its inventory problem, and that every firm does carry the optimum level of inventory as determined by these models. Non-optimum inventory policies ascribed to firms in the system may or may not nullify any inventory cost savings that are associated with certain vertical market structures when it is assumed that all other firms optimize their inventory levels.

In the structure that has no middlemen and involves only direct transactions between the m sellers and the n buyers, each seller faces a demand distribution given by AB. This distribution derives from the analysis of demand and the assumption that all orders, distributed in a fashion given by vector A, are of equal size of one unit. The matrix B gives the probability that any one firm will obtain any given number of units of demand provided any given number of orders is generated. All firms are considered to be equally efficient and have the same costs of capital. The firms also have a shortage cost π_n, the amount paid the buyer for his disappointment, and E, the amount of lost profit resulting from not being able to sell a demanded product. Thus: $\pi_m = \pi_n + E$.

Since there are no set up costs of production, there are no economies to the individual seller of carrying inventories for more than a single period. In addition, any inventory carryovers from one period to the next are never planned as such but result from the positive differences between the quantity stocked and the quantity actually demanded. Any such surplus has some probability of occurring. Finally, the production process is such that output on a continuous scale is not possible. This means that a batch process production in which all units of the product become available for sale simultaneously at some instant in time is assumed.

The demand distribution facing the individual firm is a discrete one. In consequence, the expected total inventory cost equation cannot be differentiated but can be treated by the technique of finite differencing. The total expected inventory costs per period (of *fixed* length L) for any one of the m producers can be expressed as:

$$TEC_m = \alpha_m \sum_{g=0}^{\mu_{max}} \sum_{k=0}^{Q_m} a_g b_{kg}(Q_m - k) + \pi_m \sum_{g=Q_m+1}^{\mu_{max}} \sum_{k=Q_m+1}^{g} a_g b_{kg}(k - Q_m)$$

where:

a_g = probability that exactly g total orders will be placed by the n buyers ($g = 0, 1, 2, \ldots, \mu_{max}$).

b_{kg} = probability that *any* single m will receive exactly k orders *given* that a total of g orders will be placed by the n buyers.

Q_m = total number of initial inventory units stocked by any single seller.

TEC_m = total expected costs of carrying inventories for any single producer per period.

Note; $$b_{kg} = \binom{g}{k}\left(\frac{1}{r}\right)^k \left(\frac{r-1}{r}\right)^{g-k} \qquad \text{for } g > k,$$

where: r = the number of firms, in a single level, carrying inventories. (In this case $r = m$).

The first term in the total expected cost equation describes the expected overage cost. It is the product of the unit cost of overage (α_m) and the expected number of units by which the firm's inventories (Q_m) will exceed units demanded from this firm considering only those cases in which overages can occur. The second term in the total cost expression describes the expected shortage costs. It is the product of the unit cost of shortage (π_m) and the expected number of units by which demand will exceed the number of units stocked by the individual producer when only those cases in which shortages can occur are considered.

Increasing inventories by one unit to $Q_m + 1$ would result in the following total expected costs:

$$TEC'_m = \alpha_m \sum_{g=0}^{\mu_{max}} \sum_{k=0}^{Q_m+1} a_g b_{kg}(Q_m + 1 - k) + \pi_m \sum_{g=Q_m+2}^{\mu_{max}} \sum_{k=Q_m+2}^{g} a_g b_{kg}(k - Q_m - 1)$$

which can be reduced to:

$$TEC'_m = \alpha_m \sum_{g=0}^{\mu_{max}} \sum_{k=0}^{Q_m} a_g b_{kg}(Q_m - k) + \pi_m \sum_{g=Q_m+1}^{\mu_{max}} \sum_{k=Q_m+1}^{g} a_g b_{kg}(k - Q_m)$$

$$+ \alpha_m \sum_{g=0}^{\mu_{max}} \sum_{k=0}^{Q_m} a_g b_{kg} - \pi_m \sum_{g=Q_m+1}^{\mu_{max}} \sum_{k=Q_m+1}^{g} a_g b_{kg}$$

Then the net increase in total expected costs from the one unit increase in the producer's inventories is:

$$\Delta TEC_m = TEC'_m - TEC_m = \alpha_m \sum_{g=0}^{\mu_{max}} \sum_{k=0}^{Q_m} a_g b_{kg} - \pi_m \sum_{g=Q_m+1}^{\mu_{max}} \sum_{k=Q_m+1}^{g} a_g b_{kg}$$

This result states that the increase in expected costs by the addition of one unit of the product to inventory should be the expected increase in overage costs for stocking one more unit of inventory (the unit cost of overage multiplied by the probability that the cost will be incurred) *minus* the expected reduction in shortage payments (the unit cost of shortage multiplied by the probability that the added unit of inventory will be demanded.) When the total expected demand is large, the increase in total expected costs associated with a one unit change in the inventory level Q_m will approach zero when Q_m represents the optimum level of inventories, i.e., when TEC_m is a minimum. Then:

$$\alpha_m \sum_{g=0}^{\mu_{max}} \sum_{k=0}^{Q_m} a_g b_{kg} = \pi_m \sum_{g=Q_m+1}^{\mu_{max}} \sum_{k=Q_m+1}^{g} a_g b_{kg}$$

where:

$$\sum_{g=0}^{\mu_{max}} \sum_{k=0}^{Q_m} a_g b_{kg} = 1 - \sum_{g=Q_m+1}^{\mu_{max}} \sum_{k=Q_m+1}^{g} a_g b_{kg}$$

Using this identity and rearranging terms results in the following decision rule for each of the m producers:

(1)
$$\sum_{g=Q_m+1}^{\mu_{max}} \sum_{k=Q_m+1}^{g} a_g b_{kg} = \frac{\alpha_m}{\alpha_m + \pi_m}$$

This rule states that the individual producer should set his initial inventory Q_m at a level such that the probability that the individual firms demand μ_m will exceed the initial inventory Q_m is equal to the ratio of unit overage costs α_m to the sum of unit overage and shortage costs $(\alpha_m + \pi_m)$.

It can be easily shown that in cases where the expected demand is small the decision rule should be:

(2)
$$\sum_{g=Q_m+1}^{\mu_{max}} \sum_{k=Q_m+1}^{g} a_g b_{kg} \leqslant \frac{\alpha_m}{\alpha_m + \pi_m} < \sum_{g=Q_m}^{\mu_{max}} \sum_{k=Q_m}^{g} a_g b_{kg}$$

This states that the ratio of unit overage to the sum of unit overage and shortage costs should be greater than or equal to the probability that demand will exceed Q_m and less than the probability that demand will exceed $Q_m - 1$.

Chart 3.2 illustrates how expected shortage and expected overage costs for a single producer vary with the level of initial inventories.

Since the producer must begin production a full period in advance of potential sale, the issue of the validity of the single period model might be raised. That, is if demand is less than the number of units stocked for the tth period the producer will end the tth period with positive inventories. If he

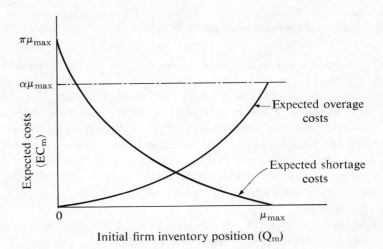

CHART 3.2

has produced an amount equal to Q_m his total beginning inventories for the $(t + 1)$th period would be greater than Q_m, which is clearly nonoptimal for that period. It should be noted, however, that the model does not, by itself, tell the producer what his optimal *production level* should be for *any* period. The inventory decision rule can be translated into a decision rule for production by letting current production (to be sold in the next period) be equal to actual demand in the previous period. Assume that the rth producer began the $(t - 1)$th period with Q_r units. If demand $\mu_r(t - 1) \leqslant Q_r$ then an overage of $Q_r - \mu_r(t - 1)$ units exists at the end of the period. Hence the rth firm must produce $\{Q_r - [Q_r - \mu_r(t - 1)]\} = \mu_r(t - 1)$ during period t to have expected initial inventories of Q_r in period $t + 1$. Similarly, if $\mu_r(t - 1) > Q_r$ then a shortage of $\mu_r(t - 1) - Q_r$ exists at the end of period t. Hence the firm must produce the backordered units plus Q_r or $[Q_r + \mu_r(t - 1) - Q_r] = \mu_r(t - 1)$ to have expected initial inventories of Q_r in period $t + 1$.
Let

$P_r(t) =$ number of units to be produced in the tth period for sale in the $(t + 1)$th period by the rth producer, $r = 1, 2, \ldots, m$.

$Q_r =$ optimal number of units of *initial inventory* to be stocked by the rth producer, $r = 1, 2, \ldots, m$.

$\mu_r(t - 1) =$ actual number of units demanded of the rth producer in the $(t - 1)$th period, $r = 1, 2, \ldots, m$.

The rth firm's decision rule for output during the tth period is

(3) $$P_r(t) = \mu_r(t - 1)$$

Individual middlemen inventory levels

Allow middlemen to enter into the system. The total demand generated by the n buyers is similar to that in the system of direct exchange, and the distribution of orders, A, the same as in the previous system. However, the demand distribution facing the individual middleman may differ from that of the individual producer, since the number of middlemen may differ from the number m. In fact, the individual middleman faces a demand distributed of AB, where again it is assumed that all orders are of one unit size, and where B is a matrix the elements of which depend only on the number of middlemen and the way in which each of the n buyers selects a source of supply (in this case, randomly.)

Each middleman in the primary level has unit stockout (shortage) costs of π_w, and unit overage costs of α_w in each period.

Proceeding in a manner similar to the case of the optimum inventory level for the individual producer, finite differencing is used to obtain the optimum inventories for the individual middleman in the primary level (buying from the m and selling to the n.) This results in the following decision rules for the individual middleman:

For relatively large total expected demand:

$$(4) \qquad \sum_{g=Q_w+1}^{\mu_{max}} \sum_{k=Q_w+1}^{g} a_g b_{kg} = \frac{\alpha_w}{\alpha_w + \pi_w}$$

For relatively small total expected demand:

$$(5) \qquad \sum_{g=Q_w+1}^{\mu_{max}} \sum_{k=Q_w+1}^{g} a_g b_{kg} \leqslant \frac{\alpha_w}{\alpha_w + \pi_w} < \sum_{g=Q_w}^{\mu_{max}} \sum_{k=Q_w}^{g} a_g b_{kg}$$

where: $b_{kg} = \binom{g}{k}\left(\frac{1}{w}\right)^k \left(\frac{w-1}{w}\right)^{g-k}$

Optimal ordering policy:

$$(6) \qquad S_r(t) = \mu_r(t-1)$$

where:

$S_r(t)=$ number of units of product ordered by the rth middleman at the beginning of period t for sale in period $t+1$, $r=1$, $2, \ldots, w$.

$Q_r =$ optimal initial inventory position of the rth middleman.

$\mu_r(t-1) =$ actual number of units demanded of the rth middleman during period $(t-1)$, $r=1, 2, \ldots, w$.

The similarity of these decision rules for individual middlemen to those of the individual producer (see expressions 1, 2, and 3) result, of course, because in performing the inventory functions, the middleman places himself in the identical position of the producer as regards the costs of shortage and overage. The only basic difference between the inventory-carrying characteristics of the m producers and w middlemen lies in the differences in their producing capabilities. Since the middlemen cannot produce products they must order them from the m producers. While the transfer time of products among any two levels in the system is zero, the middlemen must order one period in advance of demand because of the production lead time of L days. If the middlemen demanded a zero lead time the m producers would have to carry inventories, thus increasing costs to the producers and, ultimately, leading to non-cooperation among the producers and middlemen.

Middlemen cost parameters

It is clear that the shortage cost parameter for middlemen is the same as that for initial sellers. To gain the cooperation of the n buyers, every middleman must guarantee them the same disutility payment (π_n) when shortages occur. The middleman must also maintain the same price which the buyers paid in the system of direct exchange. Since E is defined as the difference between the price paid by the initial buyers and the producer's marginal cost of production[1], and since the production costs do not vary with the entry of middlemen, $\pi_w = \pi_n + E$. Since π_m is defined as the sum of π_n and E, $\pi_w = \pi_m$. It may be noted that the unit margin E is passed on to the initial producers, and that middleman profits result only from efficiencies they may introduce in the stocking of inventories.

Efficiencies are assumed *not* to result from any differences between the overage cost parameters for firms. There are no economies in the physical handling of inventories, and it is assumed that $\alpha_w = \alpha_m$. Since the unit shortage and overage cost parameters are equal for *all* firms, all subscripts on these parameters will hereafter be dropped, i.e., $\pi = \pi_m = \pi_w$ and $\alpha = \alpha_m = \alpha_w$.

Inventory levels and system costs

The total costs of performing the inventory-carrying function in a vertical market structure depend upon:

a. the number of firms carrying inventories;
b. the variance of the initial demand distribution for the product by the n buyers and in consequence the variance of the demand facing each individual inventory-carrying firm;
c. the total or aggregate level of inventory in the system; more specifically, the absolute difference between this level and the total expected demand.

Given that the individual firm optimizes its inventory level subject to the parametric nature of overage and shortage costs and the conditions assumed necessary for the various cooperative relations in the system to exist, it will be shown that:

a. the sum of the expected shortage and overage costs associated with the inventory function increases as the *number* of firms holding optimum initial inventory levels increases;
b. the sum also increases as the *variance* of the initial total demand distribution and of the distribution facing the firm increases;
c. the sum of the costs increases as the total level of inventory varies from mean demand.

The last condition is of special interest. The fewer the firms which carry a given level of inventory, the more efficient is the allocation of inventories to points at which demand occurs. If sellers are chosen randomly by the buyers, as is assumed, then the probability that any given number of buyers will find the seller called on without inventory while other sellers are experiencing overages will be higher with larger numbers of sellers. The limiting case is where only one firm carries all the inventory. In this case the probability is zero that the system will incur shortage costs when, in fact, some inventories are to be found in it. In short there is an increasing lack of adjustment of inventories at competing selling points to the placement of orders by buyers, when the number of such selling points increases. Coordination resulting from a reduction in competing inventory carriers brought about by the introduction of middlemen may reduce this lack of adjustment.[5]

Aggregate inventories

The total number of units of inventory carried by any *level* in the vertical market structure for each period is the sum of all inventories held by each firm in that level. Since each firm in the level attempts to optimize its initial inventory position, and since the optimal initial inventory position (Q_r) is common to all, the expected total inventories carried by all firms in the level can be described as:

$$(7) \qquad\qquad E(I_r) = \sum_{i=1}^{r} Q_i; \text{ all } Q_i = Q_r$$

where:

$E(I_r) =$ expected number of units of initial inventory held by the r firms for any period.

Because the demand faced by each firm in a single level is probabilistic, and because production, or ordering, precedes the availability of inventories by a full period, the actual inventory holdings (i.e., the sum of the known order size and probabilistic ending inventories of the previous period) for the beginning of any period are probabilistic in nature. If, in addition, *total demand* is probabilistic, or if the number of firms is greater than one, aggregate inventories cannot be explicitly defined. However, we know that each firm attempts to optimize its initial inventory position at Q_r, and that they employ decision rules (see expressions **3** and **6**) which make all variations between actual initial inventories and Q_r chance or random fluctuations. Then:

$$E(I_r) = rQ_r.$$

In any comparison of aggregate inventory levels over time it is sufficient to compare the sums of the optimal firm inventories for any period, provided that optimal inventory *structures* do not change over the time for which the comparison is valid. Since it is assumed that structural changes in costs do not occur during inventory periods, the comparative analysis of inventories needs to be concerned only with optimal initial inventories. For purposes of analysis let:

(8)
$$I_r = rQ_r.$$

When the values of the overage and shortage cost parameters in the system are such as to make the ratio $\dfrac{\alpha}{\alpha + \pi} = \dfrac{1}{2}$, then each firm in the system will "set" its initial inventories at a level where[6]: $p(\mu_r > Q_r) = \dfrac{\alpha}{\alpha + \pi} = \dfrac{1}{2}$.

The probability that demand exceeds initial inventories is equal to one half, and occurs when $Q_r = \bar{\mu}_r$, since the likelihood that demand exceeds the mean level of demand[7] is $\dfrac{1}{2}$.

Then:
$$I_r = r\bar{\mu}_r$$

and:
$$I_{r+1} = (r + 1)\bar{\mu}_{r+1}$$

where:
$$\bar{\mu}_r = \frac{\bar{\mu}}{r}; \ \bar{\mu}_{r+1} = \frac{\bar{\mu}}{r + 1}$$

or,
$$I_r = I_{r+1} = \bar{\mu}; \ r = 1, 2, \ldots, w, \ldots, m.$$

When the optimal initial inventory for each firm in a level is equal to its expected demand, with unit overage cost equalling unit shortage cost, the total (aggregate) inventory for the system is constant regardless of the number of firms in the system or in any level in the system. When $p(\mu_r > Q_r) \neq \dfrac{1}{2}$, i.e., when $\dfrac{\alpha}{\alpha + \pi}$ is not equal to $\dfrac{1}{2}$, there *is* some question as to which level will have the lowest total inventory costs and hence ought to carry inventories. In the case where the ratio is $\frac{1}{2}$ it is shown that regardless of the number of firms in the inventory-carrying level in the vertical market structure, the total units carried in inventory in the system will be the same. This *does not necessarily mean* that costs will be the same, and that no optimum location of inventories in the vertical market structure, or channel level, exists. In the case where $\frac{\alpha}{\alpha + \pi} \neq \frac{1}{2}$ no *single* precise generalization can be made about the comparative size of inventories that are carried by various channel levels. Nevertheless one can arrive at some general conclusions on the aggregate inventory carried by various structure levels for specific ranges of the parameter $\frac{\alpha}{\alpha + \pi}$. The way in which these aggregate inventories vary as the probability density function of demand facing the individual firm varies, and as the number of firms in the inventory-carrying level varies, can be identified.

Aggregate inventory levels in systems

It is assumed that the total demand generated by the n buyers is probabilistic. The demand facing any given firm (for $r = 1, 2, \ldots, w, \ldots, m$) is assumed given by some distribution with mean $\bar{\mu}_r$ and standard deviation σ_r. The nature of this probability density function of demand facing the individual firm (w or m) is dependent upon the probability density function of total demand and upon the probability density function of the allocation of this demand by the n buyers. Thus, the demand distribution faced by the individual firm may take on a variety of forms.

The aggregate level of inventories depends upon the overage cost, the shortage cost, and the distribution of demand facing the individual firm. It is in terms of these variables that the relationship between two market structures and their aggregate levels of inventory is made. The analysis now turns to the manner in which total inventories in a system vary as the number of firms in the middleman level or in the producing level, each carrying optimum inventory levels, varies. Total initial inventories stocked by all firms is: $r(\bar{\mu}_r + k_r \sigma_r) = rQ_r = I_r$, where, $k_r =$ number of standard deviations from the mean that identifies the optimal initial inventories of any firm in a level containing r firms, i.e., $Q_r = \bar{\mu}_r + k_r \sigma_r$. Where total expected demand is large $k_r = k_h$ for all $1 \leqslant r$, $h \leqslant m$ since each firm stocks inventories such that the probability that firm demand will exceed the optimal initial inventory is equal to the *same* parameter[8] $\frac{\alpha}{\alpha + \pi}$. Hence let all $k_r = k$, and it follows that:

$$Q_r = \bar{\mu}_r + k\sigma_r; \; Q_{r+1} = \bar{\mu}_{r+1} + k\sigma_{r+1}$$

and, $p(\mu_r > Q_r) = p(\mu_{r+1} > Q_{r+1}) = \alpha/(\alpha + \pi)$

We make the following assertions: when $\pi > 0$ then,

(a) when $k > 0$, i.e., when:

$$p(\mu_r > Q_r) = p(\mu_{r+1} > Q_{r+1}) < \frac{1}{2}$$

then, $I_r < I_{r+1}$;

(b) when $k < 0$, i.e., when:

$$p(\mu_r > Q_r) = p(\mu_{r+1} > Q_{r+1}) > \frac{1}{2}$$

then, $I_r > I_{r+1}$

(c) when $k = 0$, i.e., when:

$$p(\mu_r > Q_r) = p(\mu_{r+1} > Q_{r+1}) = \frac{1}{2}$$

then, $I_r = I_{r+1}$

The proofs of assertions (a) and (b) depend upon the validity of the inequality:

(9)
$$\frac{\bar{\mu}_r}{\sigma_r} > \frac{\bar{\mu}_{r+1}}{\sigma_{r+1}}.$$

In the case where total demand is probabilistic, the probability distribution of demand *for the individual firm* is a conditional demand density, and the mean and standard deviation of the probability density for the individual firm are:

$$E(\mu_r) = E[E(AB/B)].$$

Since matrix B is a series of binomial distributions, $E[E(AB|B)] = E[p_r A]$ where $p_r =$ probability that any firm in a level containing r firms receives any *given* order from a buyer. Also let $q_r = 1 - p_r$ and assume expression (9) holds. Then:

(a) when $k > 0$

$$I_r < I_{r+1}$$
$$\text{or} \quad rQ_r < (r + 1) Q_{r+1}$$
$$r(\bar{\mu}_r + k\sigma_r) < (r + 1)(\bar{\mu}_{r+1} + k\sigma_{r+1})$$

which reduces to

$$r\sigma_r < (r + 1)\sigma_{r+1}$$

since $k > 0$ and $r\bar{\mu}_r = (r + 1)\bar{\mu}_{r+1}$

$$\sigma_r < \left(\frac{r + 1}{r}\right)\sigma_{r+1}$$

or

$$\sigma_r < \left(\frac{\bar{\mu}_r}{\bar{\mu}_{r+1}}\right)\sigma_{r+1}$$

since

$$\frac{\bar{\mu}_r}{\bar{\mu}_{r+1}} = \frac{\dfrac{\bar{\mu}}{r}}{\dfrac{\bar{\mu}}{r+1}} = \frac{r+1}{r}$$

or

$$\frac{\bar{\mu}_r}{\sigma_r} > \frac{\bar{\mu}_{r+1}}{\sigma_{r+1}}$$

(b) when $k < 0$

$$I_r > I_{r+1}$$
$$rQ_r > (r+1)Q_{r+1}$$
$$r(\bar{\mu}_r + k\sigma_r) > (r+1)(\bar{\mu}_{r+1} + k\sigma_{r+1})$$

which reduces to:

$$r\sigma_r < (r+1)\sigma_{r+1}$$

since: $k < 0$ and $r\bar{\mu}_r = (r+1)\bar{\mu}_{r+1}$

or

$$\frac{\bar{\mu}_r}{\sigma_r} > \frac{\bar{\mu}_{r+1}}{\sigma_{r+1}}.$$

To prove assertion (9) note that:

$$E(\mu_r) = p_r\bar{\mu} = \frac{\bar{\mu}}{r} = \bar{\mu}_r.$$

Also: $\quad \sigma_r^2 = E[\text{Var}\,(AB|A)] + \text{Var}\,E(AB|A)$

but, $\quad E[\text{Var}\,(AB|A)] = p_r q_r E(A) = p_r q_r \bar{\mu}$

and, $\quad \text{Var}\,E(AB|A) = p_r\,\text{Var}\,A = p_r\sigma_\mu^2.$

Then $\quad \sigma_r^2 = p_r q_r \bar{\mu} + p_r\sigma_\mu^2 = \left(\frac{r-1}{r^2}\right)\bar{\mu} + \frac{1}{r}\sigma_\mu^2.$

Given these definitions[9] of $\bar{\mu}_r$ and σ_r^2, we can say: $\dfrac{\bar{\mu}_r^2}{\sigma_r^2} > \dfrac{\bar{\mu}_{r+1}^2}{\sigma_{r+1}^2}$

since

$$\frac{\dfrac{\bar{\mu}^2}{r^2}}{\dfrac{(r-1)}{r^2}\bar{\mu} + \dfrac{r}{r^2}\sigma_\mu^2} > \frac{\dfrac{\bar{\mu}^2}{(r+1)^2}}{\dfrac{r}{(r+1)^2}\bar{\mu} + \dfrac{(r+1)}{(r+1)^2}\sigma_\mu^2}$$

Then

$$r\bar{\mu} + (r+1)\sigma_\mu^2 > (r-1)\bar{\mu} + r\sigma_\mu^2$$

which is true since $\bar{\mu} + \sigma_\mu^2 > 0$.

Since: $\dfrac{\bar{\mu}_r^2}{\sigma_r^2} > \dfrac{\bar{\mu}_{r+1}^2}{\sigma_{r+1}^2}$ we can say: $\dfrac{\bar{\mu}_r}{\sigma_r} > \dfrac{\bar{\mu}_{r+1}}{\sigma_{r+1}}$ and the proof is complete.

It only remains to be shown that when $k = 0$, $I_r = I_{r+1}$. This follows from the definitions of Q_r and Q_{r+1} when $k = 0$.

$$I_r = rQ_r = r(\bar{\mu}_r)$$

$$\text{and} \quad I_{r+1} = (r + 1) \; Q_{r+1} = (r + 1)(\bar{\mu}_{r+1})$$

$$\text{but} \quad r \, \bar{\mu}_r = (r + 1)\bar{\mu}_{r+1}$$

and, therefore, at $k = 0$, $I_r = I_{r+1}$. These conclusions are illustrated in Chart 3.3.

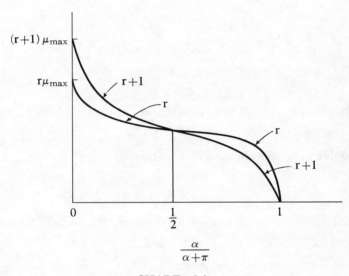

CHART 3.3

In general we can conclude that as the number of firms in a level increases the *absolute difference* between the aggregate level of inventories and expected demand increases, or,

(10) $$|I_r - \bar{\mu}| < |I_{r+1} - \bar{\mu}|$$

$$\text{where} \quad I_r = rQ_r = r(\bar{\mu}_r + k\sigma_r)$$

$$\text{and} \quad I_{r+1} = (r + 1)Q_{r+1} = (r + 1)(\bar{\mu}_{r+1} + k\sigma_{r+1})$$

The single most important conclusion that can be drawn about comparative aggregate inventories at this point is that as the number of firms in a level increases there is a greater tendency for the firms to understock when shortage costs are low relative to overage costs, and to overstock when shortage costs are high relative to overage costs.

Since it is the aim of these few sections to investigate the influence of individual firm inventory policies on aggregate level inventories, we should raise a final question regarding the firm's behavior patterns. What influence does uncertainty have on individual firm inventories? This question can be answered merely by contrasting the inventory holdings of the individual firm when two demand distributions are employed, each having the same mean demand but different variances. In particular, we can say that as the variance is increased (analogous to increasing uncertainty) the firm's inventories vary more from the mean demand.

$$\text{Let } Q_r = \bar{\mu}_r + k\sigma_r \Big\}$$
$$\text{and } Q'_r = \bar{\mu}_r + k\sigma'_r \Big\} \text{ where } \sigma_r < \sigma'_r \text{ since } \sigma_r^2 < (\sigma'_r)^2.$$

Then:

(a)   When $k > 0$, or $\pi > \alpha$
$$Q_r < Q'_r$$

(b)   When $k < 0$, or $\pi < \alpha$
$$Q_r > Q'_r$$

and (c)   When $k = 0$, or $\pi = \alpha$
$$Q_r = Q'_r$$

The proofs can be made in the following manner:

(a)   When $k > 0$
$$Q'_r > Q_r$$
$$\text{or, } \bar{\mu}_r + k\sigma'_r > \bar{\mu}_r + k\sigma_r$$

which reduces to: $\sigma_r < \sigma'_r$ since $k > 0$.

(b)   When $k < 0$
$$Q'_r < Q_r$$
$$\text{or, } \bar{\mu}_r + k\sigma'_r < \bar{\mu}_r + k\sigma_r$$

which reduces to $\sigma_r < \sigma'_r$ since $k < 0$.

Finally, (c) when $k = 0$
$$Q_r = Q'_r$$
$$\text{or } \bar{\mu}_r + k\sigma_r = \bar{\mu}_r + k\sigma'_r$$

which reduces to $\bar{\mu}_r = \bar{\mu}_r$ since $k = 0$.
These results are illustrated in Chart 3.4.

These results can be extended to aggregate inventories since aggregate inventories are merely the sum of individual firm inventories, e.g., if $Q_r > Q'_r$, then it follows that $rQ_r > rQ'_r$. Hence, the *absolute difference* between aggregate inventories and expected demand tends to increase as the standard deviation of the total demand increases, or,

(11) $$|I'_r - \bar{\mu}| > |I_r - \bar{\mu}|$$

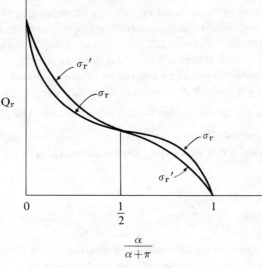

CHART 3.4

where:

$$I_r = rQ_r = r(\bar{\mu}_r + k\sigma_r) \brace \text{and} \quad I'_r = rQ'_r = r(\bar{\mu}_r + k\sigma'_r)} \quad \text{where:} \quad \sigma'_r > \sigma_r$$

·

Alternative order distributions

The generalized conclusions regarding the influence of the number of firms in a selling level and the degree of uncertainty associated with the total demand distribution on the size of aggregate level inventories hinges on the fact that orders are distributed in a binomial fashion among middlemen. In effect this relationship stems from the assumption that the n buyers are totally indifferent regarding their order placements, which results in a random allocation of orders to middlemen. Another result is the pivotal relationship between the mean and variance of the demand distribution facing the firm, proved in the previous section——that as the number of firms in a selling level increases the means of the probability distributions of demand for the individual firms fall faster than the standard deviation, i.e., $\dfrac{\bar{\mu}_r}{\sigma_r} > \dfrac{\bar{\mu}_{r+1}}{\sigma_{r+1}}$.

When the binomial order distribution pattern does not hold it means that some factors that are *not random* enter into the choice of a seller by a buyer. This would alter the particular nature of the demand distribution faced by the individual seller from that generated when the n buyers are totally indifferent regarding order placement. While we will make no attempt[10] at this time to suggest the unique behavioral elements, of firms engaged in a competitive exchange process, which yield nonrandom order distribution patterns, it is certainly worthwhile to investigate the *effects* of such distribution patterns on aggregate level inventories. Only two generalized cases need to be considered here: when the ratio of the mean to the standard deviation of the individual firm's demand distribution does not vary with the entrance or exit of firms in the level—when $\frac{\bar{\mu}_r}{\sigma_r} = \frac{\bar{\mu}_{r+1}}{\sigma_{r+1}}$, and when the mean of the individual firm's demand distribution falls more slowly than the standard deviation with the entrance of new firms into the same selling level—when:

$$\frac{\bar{\mu}_r}{\sigma_r} < \frac{\bar{\mu}_{r+1}}{\sigma_{r+1}}$$

a. *The Case Where* $\frac{\bar{\mu}_r}{\sigma_r} = \frac{\bar{\mu}_{r+1}}{\sigma_{r+1}}$

There exists a family of probability distributions such that the ratio of the mean and the standard deviation of each distribution is a constant. Regardless of the size of this constant, we can assert that as long as the ratio of the mean and the standard deviation of the demand transformation matrix, **B**, is a constant, the aggregate level inventories do not vary with the number of firms in the selling level. They still vary however, with the size of the standard deviation of the demand distribution for the individual firm. Thus it must be shown that

$$I_r = I_{r+1} \quad \text{and} \quad |I_r - \bar{\mu}| \leqslant |I'_r - \bar{\mu}|$$

where by definition:

$$\left.\begin{array}{l} I_r = rQ_r = r[\bar{\mu}_r + k\sigma_r] \\ I'_r = rQ'_r = r[\bar{\mu}_r + k\sigma'_r] \end{array}\right\} \quad \text{and where} \quad \sigma_r < \sigma'_r$$

(a-1) $I_r = I_{r+1}$

or $rQ_r = (r+1)Q_{r+1}$

then $r[\bar{\mu}_r + k\sigma_r] = (r+1)[\bar{\mu}_{r+1} + k\sigma_{r+1}]$

which reduces to: $r\sigma_r = (r+1)\sigma_{r+1}$

Then $\sigma_r = \left(\frac{r+1}{r}\right)\sigma_{r+1}$

or

$$\sigma_r = \left(\frac{\bar{\mu}_r}{\bar{\mu}_{r+1}}\right)\sigma_{r+1}$$

since

$$\frac{\bar{\mu}_r}{\bar{\mu}_{r+1}} = \frac{\dfrac{\bar{\mu}}{r}}{\dfrac{\bar{\mu}}{r+1}} = \frac{r+1}{r}$$

and

$$\frac{\bar{\mu}_r}{\sigma_r} = \frac{\bar{\mu}_{r+1}}{\sigma_{r+1}}$$

which was assumed to be true and, therefore, the proof of part (a-1) is complete.

(a-2) $|I_r - \bar{\mu}| < |I'_r - \bar{\mu}|$

or $|r[\bar{\mu}_r - k\sigma_r] - \bar{\mu}| < |r[\bar{\mu}_r - k\sigma'_r] - \bar{\mu}|$

or $|-kr\sigma_r| < |-kr\sigma'_r|$, since $r\bar{\mu}_r = \bar{\mu}$.

Then we say for all $k \neq 0, |\sigma_r| < |\sigma'_r|$ which follows from the assumed $\sigma_r < \sigma'_r$. For $k = 0$ the equality sign holds and the proof is complete.

b. *The Case Where* $\frac{\bar{\mu}_r}{\sigma_r} < \frac{\bar{\mu}_{r+1}}{\sigma_{r+1}}$

As a point of interest it might be noted that the above inquality requires that the demand distributions be negatively skewed. It means that if system output is unchanged, the standard deviation of the demand density falls faster than the mean as new firms enter the system. Such distributions are considered rare among economic phenomena. For this reason and because this case leads to conclusions on system inventories that are the opposite of those for the case $\frac{\bar{\mu}_r}{\sigma_r} > \frac{\bar{\mu}_{r+1}}{\sigma_{r+1}}$ it is not discussed further.

In summary, we can say that when orders are distributed among selling firms in a binomial fashion, and in all cases where the distribution is such as to lead to the condition that $\frac{\bar{\mu}_r}{\sigma_r} > \frac{\bar{\mu}_{r+1}}{\sigma_{r+1}}$ the absolute difference between aggregate level inventories and expected demand increases as the number of firms in a level increases. When the entry of new firms into a selling level effects no change in the ratio of the mean and the standard deviation of the demand distribution for the individual firm, then aggregate level inventories remain unchanged. Finally, when the entry of new firms results in a more than proportionate decrease in the standard deviation of the firm's demand distribution relative to the mean, and $\frac{\bar{\mu}_r}{\sigma_r} < \frac{\bar{\mu}_{r+1}}{\sigma_{r+1}}$, then as the number of firms in a level increases, the absolute difference between aggregate inventories and expected demand decreases. Regardless of the influence of the entry and exit of firms on the ratio of the mean and the standard deviation of the demand density for the firm, an increase in uncertainty results in an increase in the absolute difference between aggregate level inventories and expected demand.

We now wish to take up the effect of the above patterns of aggregate inventories on the total cost, to the system, of carrying inventories.

Comparative aggregate inventory costs

The total inventory cost to the system is the sum of the stockout and overage costs incurred by the individual firms in the system. Because the demand to all firms is probabilistic, any description of inventory costs for a future period also must be probabilistic.[11] Thus, we will confine our analysis of inventory costs to the comparison of *expected* total inventory costs under various market conditions and formulations.

In the absence of economies or diseconomies of scale in the carrying of inventories (α and π are constant) the minimum expected inventory cost for the system occurs when only a single firm carries inventories. Recall that the individual firms in the selling level devised inventory policies that would minimize their (individual) expected costs. Since the single inventory-carrying firm must bear the total costs of the system, its minimum cost position is by similarity of definition a minimum for the system as a whole. Of course, this does not necessarily mean that the single firm represents a unique optimum. The issues which must be raised then are how do expected inventory costs vary with the levels of inventory, the number of firms carrying inventories, and with the degree of uncertainty for the individual firms in the system?

Employing the notation of the previous section, the expected total cost of inventories for the system when total orders are binomially distributed among the firms and there are r firms in the selling level is:

$$rTEC_r = r\left\{\alpha \sum_{g=0}^{\mu_{max}} \sum_{k=0}^{Q_r} a_g b_{kg}(Q_r - k) + \pi \sum_{g=Q_r+1}^{\mu_{max}} \sum_{k=Q_r+1}^{g} a_g b_{kg}(k - Q_r)\right\}$$

but,

$$\sum_{g=0}^{\mu_{max}} \sum_{k=0}^{Q_r} a_g b_{kg} = 1 - \sum_{g=Q_r+1}^{\mu_{max}} \sum_{k=Q_r+1}^{g} a_g b_{kg}$$

$$\sum_{g=0}^{\mu_{max}} \sum_{k=0}^{Q_r} a_g b_{kg} k = \bar{\mu}_r - \sum_{g=Q_r+1}^{\mu_{max}} \sum_{k=Q_r+1}^{g} a_g b_{kg} k, \text{ and}$$

$$\sum_{g=Q_r+1}^{\mu_{max}} \sum_{k=Q_r+1}^{g} a_g b_{kg} = \frac{\alpha}{\alpha + \pi}, \text{ then}$$

$$rTEC_r = r\left\{(\pi + \alpha) \sum_{g=Q_r+1}^{\mu_{max}} \sum_{k=Q_r+1}^{g} a_g b_{kg} k - \alpha \bar{\mu}_r\right\}$$

Similarly for a level containing $r + 1$ firms:

$$(r + 1)TEC_{r+1} = (r + 1)\left\{(\pi + \alpha) \sum_{g=Q_{r+1}+1}^{\mu_{max}} \sum_{k=Q_{r+1}+1}^{g} a_g b'_{kg} k - \alpha \bar{\mu}_{r+1}\right\}$$

where

$$b'_{kg} = \binom{g}{k}\left(\frac{1}{r+1}\right)^k \left(\frac{r}{r+1}\right)^{g-k}$$

From these cost expressions we can show that when $\pi \neq 0$

(12) $$rTEC_r < (r + 1)TEC_{r+1}$$

or

$$r(\pi + \alpha) \sum_{g=Q_r+1}^{\mu_{max}} \sum_{k=Q_r+1}^{g} a_g b_{kg} k - \alpha \bar{\mu} < (r+1)(\pi + \alpha) \sum_{g=Q_{r+1}+1}^{\mu_{max}} \sum_{k=Q_{r+1}+1}^{g} a_g b'_{kg} k - \alpha \bar{\mu}$$

which reduces to:

$$r \sum_{g=Q_r+1}^{\mu_{max}} \sum_{k=Q_r+1}^{g} a_g b_{kg} k < (r + 1) \sum_{g=Q_{r+1}+1}^{\mu_{max}} \sum_{k=Q_{r+1}+1}^{g} a_g b'_{kg} k$$

A normal approximation to the above discrete probability densities is employed to show this, i.e.,

$$\sum_{g=Q_r+1}^{\mu_{max}} \sum_{k=Q_{r+1}}^{g} a_g b_{kg} k \simeq \int_{Q_r}^{\infty} x f(x)\, dx = (2\Pi)^{-\frac{1}{2}} e^{-\frac{Q_r^2}{2}}$$

Then if $Q_r > Q_{r+1}$

$$e^{-\frac{Q_r^2}{2}} < e^{-\frac{Q_{r+1}^2}{2}}$$

and clearly

$$(r+1)(2\Pi)^{-\frac{1}{2}} e^{-\frac{Q_{r+1}^2}{2}} - r(2\Pi)^{-\frac{1}{2}} e^{-\frac{Q_r^2}{2}} > 0$$

where $\pi \geqslant \alpha$, $rQ_r > (r+1)Q_{r+1}$ and clearly $Q_r > Q_{r+1}$.
When $0 < \pi < \alpha$, $Q_r = \bar{\mu}_r + k\sigma_r$, $Q_{r+1} = \bar{\mu}_{r+1} + k\sigma_{r+1}$, and $k > 0$.

Also,

$$\sigma_r^2 = \frac{\sigma^2}{r} + \frac{r-1}{r^2}\bar{\mu} \quad \text{and} \quad \frac{\bar{\mu}_r}{\sigma_r} > \frac{\bar{\mu}_{r+1}}{\sigma_{r+1}}$$

then,

$$\frac{r+1}{r} = \frac{\bar{\mu}_r}{\bar{\mu}_{r+1}} > \frac{\sigma_r}{\sigma_{r+1}} \implies \frac{(r+1)^2}{r^2} > \frac{(r+1)^2}{r^2}\left(\frac{r\sigma^2 + (r-1)\bar{\mu}}{(r+1)\sigma^2 + r\bar{\mu}}\right) > 1$$

since,

$$r(r+1)\sigma^2 + (r^2 - r - 1)\bar{\mu} > 0$$

which is clearly true for all $r > 1$. Note that when $r = 1$ $rTEC_r$ is a minimum by definition. Consequently $\sigma_r^2 > \sigma_{r+1}^2 > 0$ and since $\bar{\mu}_r > \bar{\mu}_{r+1}$, $k > 0$ it is clear that $Q_r = \bar{\mu}_r + k\sigma_r > Q_{r+1} = \bar{\mu}_{r+1} + k\sigma_{r+1}$.
When $\pi = 0$, each firm carries zero inventories and hence:

$$TEC_r = TEC_{r+1} = 0$$

and, therefore

$$rTEC_r = (r+1)TEC_{r+1} = 0$$

For all $\pi > 0$ expected total inventory costs increase monotonically as the number of firms increases. When $r = 1$ the system is at its unique optimum solution.[12] A second conclusion, drawn from the special case of $\pi = \alpha$ is that even for the same aggregate inventories in a level, expected costs increase as the number of firms in a level increases. This suggests that centralization of inventories tends to decrease the cost of carrying inventories.[13] One reason for this conclusion is that a reduction in the number of firms in a level tends to reduce the degree of uncertainty for each firm relative to its expected demand which in turn tends to reduce its expected inventory costs. To prove this it must be shown that

$$rTEC_r < rTEC_r',$$

where: $TEC_r' = $ expected total costs of carrying inventories for the rth firm when the variance of the total demand is greater than it is in the case of TEC_r

It is known that for $k < 0$, $rQ_r > (r+1)Q_{r+1}$, i.e.,

$$r(\bar{\mu}_r + k\sigma_r) > (r+1)(\bar{\mu}_{r+1} + k\sigma_{r+1})$$

Therefore it is clear that: $\bar{\mu}_r + k\sigma_r > \bar{\mu}_{r+1} + k\sigma_{r+1}$, and $\sigma_r \neq \sigma_{r+1}$.

Thus if firms in a level containing r firms held inventories of $Q_r^0 = Q_{r+1} = \bar{\mu}_{r+1} + k\sigma_{r+1}$ they would incur greater total expected costs than they would if they carried the *optimum* $Q_r = \bar{\mu}_r + k\sigma_r$, i.e., $TEC_r < TEC_r^0$.

Allow the mean of the *total* demand distribution to be held constant and the variance changed so that the optimal decision for all firms in a level containing r firms is to set initial inventories equal to $Q_r^0 = Q_{r+1} = \bar{\mu}_{r+1} + k\sigma_{r+1}$ for the same cost parameters π and α. This implies that:

a. the means of the demand distributions for all firms are unchanged, i.e.,

$$r\bar{\mu}_r' = \bar{\mu}' = \bar{\mu} = r\bar{\mu}_r \quad \text{and, therefore,} \quad \bar{\mu}_r' = \bar{\mu}_r$$

and,

b. the ratio $\dfrac{\alpha}{\alpha + \pi}$ remains unchanged, which further implies that k also remains unchanged.

Hence the optimal decision, under the "new" demand distribution for the firm is:

$$Q_r' = \bar{\mu}_r' + k\sigma_r' = Q_r^0 = \bar{\mu}_{r+1} + k\sigma_{r+1}$$

but, since $Q_r > Q_r^0$ we know that:

$$\bar{\mu}_r' + k\sigma_r' < \bar{\mu}_r + k\sigma_r.$$

Since $\bar{\mu}_r' = \bar{\mu}_r$ and $k < 0$, this reduces to:

$$\sigma_r' > \sigma_r$$

The same result applies for $k > 0$ by a similar argument, and, therefore for any $k \neq 0$ we can conclude that $(\sigma_r')^2 > \sigma_r^2$. By definition:

$$(\sigma_r')^2 = \left(\frac{r-1}{r^2}\right)\bar{\mu}' + \frac{(\sigma')^2}{r}, \quad \text{and}$$

$$\sigma_r^2 = \left(\frac{r-1}{r^2}\right)\bar{\mu} + \frac{\sigma^2}{r}$$

Since $\bar{\mu}' = \bar{\mu}$ it is clear that $(\sigma_r')^2 > \sigma_r^2$ if and only if $(\sigma')^2 > \sigma^2$, i.e., only when the variance of the total demand distribution is increased.

Since $Q_r' \neq Q_r$ when $k \neq 0$ it must be concluded that $TEC_r' > TEC_r$ and, thus, that:

$$rTEC_r' > rTEC_r$$

In summary we can say that the expected total cost to the system of carrying inventories increases as the absolute difference between the aggregate inventory level and expected total demand increases for any given α and π. This difference, in turn, increases as the number of firms in a selling level increases.[14] Also, holding aggregate level inventories constant, total expected inventory costs increase as the number of firms in the selling level increases. Finally, any increase in the degree of uncertainty (variance) of aggregate total demand tends to increase the system's total expected inventory costs.

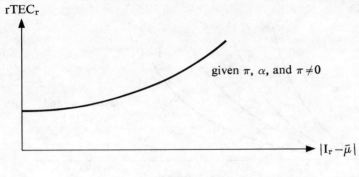

CHART 3.5

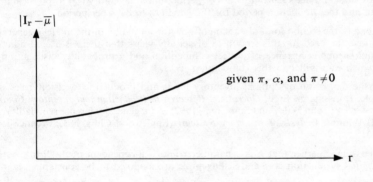

CHART 3.6

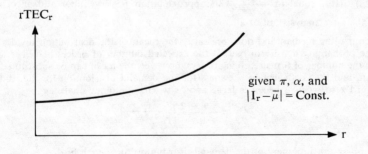

CHART 3.7

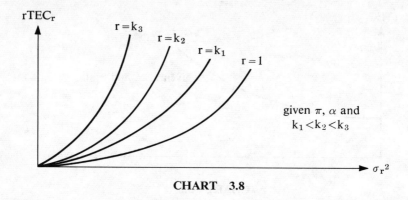

CHART 3.8

1   All notations used in earlier chapters are used in the same context here and below. In addition, new general variables are shortage costs (π) in dollars per unit short per period, overage costs (α) in dollars per unit over per period, initial inventory (Q) in physical units per period, and the production period for the good (L) in days per period.

2   See end of the section for a discussion of how the limitation of the model's generality would remove the need for this section to dispel any views that there is a contradiction in the simultaneous occurrence of perfect competition and a probability distribution of demand which each seller in this competition faces.

3   For the derivation of optimal inventory levels and production decision rules see, for example, Hanssmann, Fred, *Operations Research in Production and Inventory Control*, Ch. 4 (New York: John Wiley and Sons, Inc., 1962). As a general reference see Hadley, G. and T. M. Whitin, *Analysis of Inventory Systems* (Englewood Cliffs, N.J.: Prentice-Hall, Inc., 1963).

4   It is assumed earlier that E is a parameter and is independent of the firm's output level. Marginal production cost and selling price are assumed to be constant.

5   The subject of coordination is discussed at greater length in Chapter 5.

6   For the sake of simplicity, in the body of the text, we will substitute the term $p(\mu_r < Q_r)$ for $\sum_{g=0}^{\mu_{max}} \sum_{k=0}^{Q} a_g b_{kg}$, and the term $p(\mu_r > Q_r)$ for: $\sum_{g=Q_r+1}^{\mu_{max}} \sum_{k=Q_r+1}^{g} a_g b_{kg}$

In addition, to simplify the notation and the analysis resulting from the discreteness of the demand distribution, the inequality relationships will be ignored and changed to equalities. We assume, in effect, that because n is very large it is possible to find a $p(\mu_w > Q_w)$ that is equal to $\dfrac{\alpha}{\alpha + \pi}$ This approximation is very minor and affects the results of the later analysis not at all.

7   Of course the median and not necessarily the mean of the distribution divides the area of the probability density in half. If the expected number of orders placed is large relative to the number of firms receiving orders, however, the mean can be substituted for the median, and the coefficient of skewness for the demand distribution for the rth firm tends toward zero when $\bar{\mu}$ becomes large and/or when r becomes small, i.e.,

$$\delta_3 = \frac{\mu_3}{\sigma_r^3} \simeq \frac{r-2}{\sqrt{\bar{\mu}(r-1)}} \xrightarrow[\bar{\mu}\to\infty]{} 0$$

where:

μ_3 = third moment of the demand distribution for the rth firm.
σ_r = standard deviation of the demand distribution of the rth firm.
$\bar{\mu}$ = expected number of orders placed in the system.

8   We use a normal approximation to the actual firm distribution to produce this conclusion. Since the average *firm* and industry demand is expected to be quite large, this approximation results in negligible distortion.

9   For a derivation see, for example, Feller, William, *An Introduction to Probability Theory and Its Applications*, Vol. 1., 2nd Edition (New York: John Wiley and Sons, Inc., 1957.)

10   Some of the more obvious reasons for nonrandom order distributions are trade customs, differential pricing policies, personal preferences, spatial location problems, public policy restrictions, product differentiation, and imperfect knowledge on the parts of buyers and sellers regarding the existence of other buyers and sellers.

11   The single exception would be where total demand is known and only a single firm carries inventories. Under such conditions total system costs, overage and shortage, will always be zero when the single firm employs an inventory policy of setting initial inventories equal to the known demand.

12   Note that the case of $\pi = 0$ is most uninteresting for it says that no one will carry inventories and, therefore, the inventory function is not performed.

13   This should not be construed to mean that a centralized distribution system is optimal since we have not considered many kinds of distribution costs. It merely means that the internal cost of stocking inventories is minimized when they are centrally located.

14   This is subject, of course, to the inequality that $\frac{\bar{\mu}_r}{\sigma_r} > \frac{\bar{\mu}_{r+1}}{\sigma_{r+1}}$.

4

Inventory Cost
and Equilibrium

Inventory holding cost: the financing function

The identification of the suppliers of the physical storage facilities has been a major concern of the marketing literature. The interest here lies with the issues of who undertakes the *responsibility* of incurring these costs of storage prior to the returns obtained from carrying inventories, and who *makes the decision* on the amounts to be stored or carried in inventories. It is quite possible for the person who actually supplies the physical facilities necessary for carrying inventories *not* to be the performer of the inventory-carrying function. He is, in this case, the seller of services to the performer of this function. The person who pays the cost of carrying inventories in anticipation of returns and who determines the amounts to be carried is the performer of the function. The supplier of physical storage facilities, if he is someone other than the inventory carrier, in turn performs an inventory-carrying function in terms of the product he sells——storage space and services——and not for the product handled by the system being exclusively studied.

The discussion of the costs of holding inventories brings up the issue of the financing function, especially regarding the aspect of undertaking the responsibility for the costs of financing the carrying of inventory. The main interest is not the actual supplying of the funds necessary for financing, nor the transfer of waiting disutility. Nor is it in the marketing system which deals specifically with the exchange of non-waiting utility in the form of funds. The interest *is* in the question of inventory holding costs and in the nature of the financing decision and its maker, who bears the costs of financing in anticipation of returns, and who does not necessarily supply the non-waiting utility from his own utility or funds.

The whole issue of the marketing function of financing arises because there exists a positive disutility to some or all members in the economy associated with waiting to acquire goods and services. In fact, the shortage cost π is greater than zero if anyone exists in the system discussed earlier to whom the cost of waiting is positive. If to someone else this cost is different from π, then some exchange of waiting will occur. The funds necessary for this exchange may be marketed or supplied by the inventory carrier himself, who, by carrying inventories, permits this exchange of waiting to be applied to that particular product. Waiting is seen here as waiting for a particular good. In effect, inventory carrying reduces the gross amount of buyer waiting, and is possible only if there is someone (a firm in the vertical market structure through which the product moves, or a firm in some other market structure which supplies this service to the first firm) who is willing to wait. Such waiting involves the supply of funds at one time in return for some other amount (probably larger) capable of use at some later date.

If the middleman in a vertical market structure incurs the responsibility of the returns to waiting and determines the total amount of waiting that is transferred by deciding on the level of inventory, then he is considered the performer of the financing function for that structure. His decision determines the level of inventory and the total costs of financing that he will incur prior to, or in anticipation of, returns from these costs. Even though he may not perform the financing function generally viewed in marketing——supplying the non-waiting time from his own funds——he makes the critical decision and hence determines, in part, total system costs. He is thus the real performer of the financing function.

Costs of holding and individual firm inventory decisions

The individual producer or middleman considered in this chapter is subject to only two basic cost sources—the cost of *holding* inventories and the cost of shortage. The individual firm faces a probabilistic demand schedule in which price is held constant. The probability distribution of demand for the individual firm stems from one or both of two basic sources:

a. probabilistic total industry demand, and

b. the probabilistic order distribution of the n buyers among the r inventory carriers.

Using the notations introduced in Chapter 3, the demand distribution for the individual firm can be expressed as:

(1)
$$f(\mu_r) = ABZ$$

where:

μ_r = number of units of product demanded of the rth firm during the production-inventory period of constant length L by the n buyers.

A = a k component row vector describing the probability distribution of orders by the n buyers during the fixed period of production-inventory.

B = a $k \times k$ transition matrix relating the number of all orders placed with any seller during the period to the total number of units ordered by the n buyers.

Z = a $k \times q$ transition matrix relating the number of orders placed by the n buyers during the production-inventory period to units of product demanded.

In this chapter, for purposes of analysis simplification, it is assumed that $q = k$ and that Z is an identity matrix, or that each order is one unit of product in size. Further, for any firm r, any element in the matrix B can be expressed as:

(2)
$$\left. \begin{aligned} b_{ij} &= \binom{j}{i}\left(\frac{1}{r}\right)^i\left(\frac{r-1}{r}\right)^{j-i}, \text{ for all } i < j \\ \text{and } b_{ij} &= 0, \text{ for all } i > j \end{aligned} \right\} i, j = 0, 1, 2, \ldots, \mu_{\max}$$

where i signifies the *columns* and j the *rows* in the matrix B. It is shown in Chapter 3 that the unit cost of shortage (π) is the same for all *sellers* in the vertical market structure, and it is now assumed that the cost of holding a unit of product in inventory for one period (ϕ) is constant and common to all sellers. As in Chapter 3, back orders are filled at the beginning of the next period.

There are two distinct ways in which the individual firm can incur inventory costs. If the units demanded of the firm exceed the firm's initial inventory, the firm will incur both holding and shortage costs. This is shown in Chart 4.1.

If, on the other hand, the firm's initial inventory exceeds the number of units demanded of it, the firm will incur only holding costs. This is illustrated in Chart 4.2.

The firm's total expected costs of inventory can be expressed as:

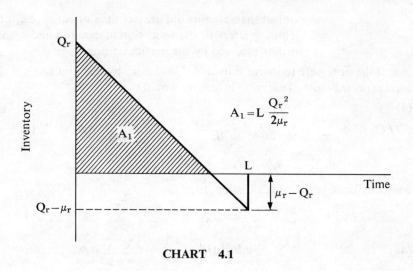

$$A_1 = L \frac{Q_r^2}{2\mu_r}$$

CHART 4.1

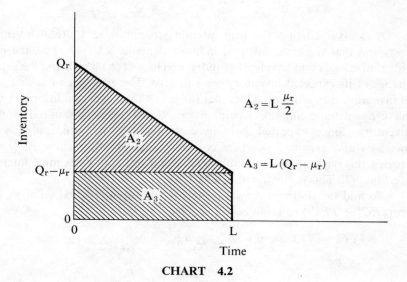

$$A_2 = L \frac{\mu_r}{2}$$

$$A_3 = L(Q_r - \mu_r)$$

CHART 4.2

(3) $$TEC_r = \phi \sum_{g=Q_r+1}^{\mu_{max}} \sum_{k=Q_r+1}^{g} a_g b_{kg} \frac{Q_r^2}{2k} + \pi \sum_{g=Q_r+1}^{\mu_{max}} \sum_{k=Q_r+1}^{g} a_g b_{kg} (k - Q_r)$$
$$+ \phi \sum_{g=0}^{\mu_{max}} \sum_{k=0}^{Q_r} a_g b_{kg} \left(Q_r - \frac{k}{2} \right)$$

where:[1]

$\sum_{g=z_1}^{\mu_{max}} \sum_{k=z_1}^{z_2} a_g b_{kg} =$ the probability that the number of units demanded of the rth firm by the n buyers during the period is equal to

77

or less than z_2 units but greater than or equal to z_1 units. Thus, g refers to the total system demand and k to the orders received by the particular firm.

If the firm were to increase its initial inventory by one unit to $Q_r + 1$ its total expected costs of carrying inventory would be:

(4)

$$TEC_r' = \phi \sum_{g=Q_r+2}^{\mu_{max}} \sum_{k=Q_r+2}^{g} a_g b_{kg} \frac{(Q_r+1)^2}{2k} + \pi \sum_{g=Q_r+2}^{\mu_{max}} \sum_{k=Q_r+2}^{g} a_g b_{kg}(k - Q_r - 1)$$

$$+ \phi \sum_{g=0}^{\mu_{max}} \sum_{k=0}^{Q_r+1} a_g b_{kg} \left(Q_r + 1 - \frac{k}{2} \right)$$

which reduces, with little distortion, to:

$$TEC_r' = \phi \sum_{g=Q_r+1}^{\mu_{max}} \sum_{k=Q_r+1}^{g} a_g b_{kg} \frac{Q_r^2}{2k} + \pi \sum_{g=Q_r+1}^{\mu_{max}} \sum_{k=Q_r+1}^{g} a_g b_{kg}(k - Q_r)$$

(4a)

$$+ \phi \sum_{g=0}^{\mu_{max}} \sum_{k=0}^{Q_r} a_g b_{kg} \left(Q_r - \frac{k}{2} \right) + \phi \sum_{g=0}^{\mu_{max}} \sum_{k=0}^{Q_r} a_g b_{kg}$$

$$+ \phi \frac{Q_r}{\bar{\mu}_r} \sum_{g=Q_r+1}^{\mu_{max}} \sum_{k=Q_r+1}^{g} a_g b_{kg} - \pi \sum_{g=Q_r+1}^{\mu_{max}} \sum_{k=Q_r+1}^{g} a_g b_{kg}$$

It is assumed that the firm attempts to minimize its total inventory costs and that the expected total industry demand is large. Thus, the individual firm must find that level of initial inventory (Q_r) which sets the rate of change of its expected inventory costs to zero. The existence of such a level of inventory is based on the fact that the firm's total expected inventory cost curve has a finite minimum point when plotted against its initial level of inventory. Since expected holding costs increase monotonically as Q_r increases and expected shortage costs decrease monotonically as Q_r increases, this is not an unreasonable assumption and both costs must intersect at a finite Q_r. This is illustrated in Chart 4.3.

To find the optimum initial inventory for any individual seller we can set $(TEC_r' - TEC_r)$ equal to zero and solve for Q_r:

$$TEC_r' - TEC_r = 0 = \phi \sum_{g=0}^{\mu_{max}} \sum_{k=0}^{Q_r} a_g b_{kg} + \phi \frac{Q_r}{\bar{\mu}_r} \sum_{g=Q_r+1}^{\mu_{max}} \sum_{k=Q_r+1}^{g} a_g b_{kg}$$

$$- \pi \sum_{g=Q_r+1}^{\mu_{max}} \sum_{k=Q_r+1}^{g} a_g b_{kg}$$

Solving for $\sum_{g=Q_r+1}^{\mu_{max}} \sum_{k=Q_r+1}^{g} a_g b_{kg}$ and noting that:

$$\sum_{g=0}^{\mu_{max}} \sum_{k=0}^{Q_r} a_g b_{kg} = 1 - \sum_{g=Q_r+1}^{\mu_{max}} \sum_{k=Q_r+1}^{g} a_g b_{kg}$$

results in the following decision rule:

(5)

$$\sum_{g=Q_r+1}^{\mu_{max}} \sum_{k=Q_r+1}^{g} a_g b_{kg} = \frac{\phi}{\pi + \phi - \phi \dfrac{Q_r}{\bar{\mu}_r}}$$

but $\bar{\mu}_r = \dfrac{\bar{\mu}}{r}$

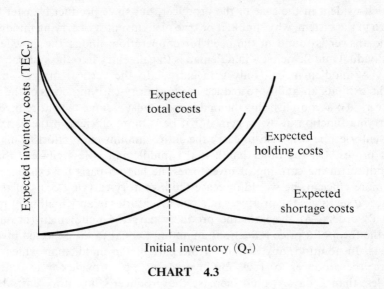

CHART 4.3

Thus:

$$\text{(5a)} \qquad \sum_{g=Q_r+1}^{\mu_{\max}} \sum_{k=Q_r+1}^{g} a_g b_{kg} = \frac{\phi}{\pi + \phi - \phi \dfrac{rQ_r}{\bar{\mu}}}$$

This decision rule states that the firm should stock Q_r units so that the probability of the firm's demand (μ_r) exceeding Q_r is equal to the ratio of unit holding cost, to the sum of unit holding and shortage costs less the product of unit holding costs, and to the ratio of initial inventories to the mean demand faced by the firm ($\bar{\mu}_r$). No *direct* solution is yielded by this decision rule. However, since the firm has full knowledge of its demand density and since Q_r is the only variable in the decision rule, a finite solution can be evolved by a trial and error process.

Since we are dealing with discrete demand densities, the solution given above is an approximation. Of course, the approximation improves as the expected demand in the industry increases, and for large expected total demand the above decision rule would be satisfactory. For relatively small expected total demand the decision rule is altered to read:

$$\text{(6)} \qquad \sum_{g=Q_r+1}^{\mu_{\max}} \sum_{k=Q_r+1}^{g} a_g b_{kg} \leqslant \frac{\phi}{\pi + \phi - \phi \dfrac{rQ_r}{\bar{\mu}}} < \sum_{g=Q_r}^{\mu_{\max}} \sum_{k=Q_r}^{g} a_g b_{kg}$$

Decision rules (5) and (6) *do not* necessarily describe the actual initial inventory holdings of the firm at the beginning of any given period. Because of the fixed production lead time of L days, the individual middleman must order one full period in advance of delivery, or the producer must begin production one full period in advance of anticipated sale. The reason for this is self-evident in the case of the producer, but since product transfer time is zero in the system, why should it be true of an inventory-carrying middleman? The answer is found in the need for cooperation among the m sellers and individual middlemen if a middleman is to gain entry into the system.

A middleman can only gain entry into the vertical market structure if he exhibits an ability to reduce the inventory-carrying costs of the m producers. To accomplish this the middleman must assume the entire inventory-carrying function in the system, for if he is more efficient in the carrying of inventories, he will wish to carry the entire amount in an effort to maximize his profits. On the other hand, if the middleman is less efficient than the producer in the carrying of inventories, he has no basis for existence. If he is more efficient, he would increase the inventory-carrying costs of the producer *if* he forces the producer to stock inventories in anticipation of middlemen's orders. At the limit the producer pays the middleman (presumably in the form of a price reduction) an amount equal to his expected inventory costs. In addition, any action on the part of the middleman which would force the producer to stock any inventories, e.g., provide for an order time of less than L days, would increase the producer's inventory costs beyond the amount he had incurred prior to the entry of middlemen. Any producer faced with this prospect would, of course, refuse to cooperate with such middlemen.

Decision rules (5) and (6) identify the *optimal initial inventory* position for the individual firm. Because of the probabilistic nature of demand, the individual firm's actual initial inventories vary from this target level or optimal initial inventory. Since expected inventory costs increase monotonically about the optimal initial inventory, the firm wishes to develop decision rules which tend to minimize these deviations. It can easily be shown that such decision rules take the form of:

a. For the individual producer

$$P_m(t) = \mu_m(t-1)$$

where:

$P_m(t) =$ optimal size of the production run for the individual producer, to be started at the beginning of the tth period for sale during the $(t+1)$th period.

$Q_m =$ optimal initial inventory position for any period for the individual producer.

$\mu_m(t-1) =$ actual sales for the individual producer during the period $t-1$.

b. For the individual middleman

$$Q_w(t) = \mu_w(t-1)$$

where:

$Q_w(t) =$ optimal order quantity for the individual middleman to be placed at the beginning of period t for delivery at the beginning of period $t+1$.

Even though we are unable to describe the actual inventories of any single firm at any point in time, we are able to state that the *expected initial inventory position* of any single firm is its optimal initial inventory (Q_r).

Comparative aggregate inventory levels

The general conclusions on aggregate inventory levels and total costs are similar to those arrived at in the previous chapter. Though the exact relationships between the total inventory level and the system's parameters differ somewhat when holding cost is substituted for overage cost, there remains the general "lack of adjustment" which comes from changes in the demand distribution. The relationship between the number of inventory-carrying firms and this "lack of adjustment" is also unchanged. The larger the number of firms in the level, the greater the absolute difference between total inventory and total expected demand, with the exception of $\pi = 2\phi$. From the proofs given below, we conclude that the system's costs increase with a larger number of firms carrying any given level of inventory. This means that even if the entry of firms into the inventory-carrying level does not change the ratio of the standard deviation to the mean of each firm's demand distribution, total system costs increase although total inventory is unchanged.

The aggregate inventories for any level of selling firms in the vertical market structure are the sum of the individual firm inventories. Since each firm employs the same decision rule regarding the size of its initial inventories and, in addition, since each firm faces the identical demand density, the expected aggregate level of inventories can be expressed as the product of the number of firms in the selling level and the expected initial inventory of any firm in the level. That is,

$$I_r = rQ_r$$

where:

I_r = expected aggregate inventories carried by the r firms in the level in question.

We now wish to determine the relation between the aggregate level of inventory, I_r, and the number of inventory-carrying firms r in the level. Assuming, for the moment, that total expected industry demand is large, a reordering of the terms of expression (**5a**) results in the following equality:

(**5b**)
$$p(\mu_r > Q_r)\left[(\pi + \phi) - \phi\frac{rQ_r}{\bar{\mu}}\right] = \phi$$
$$= p(\mu_{r+1} > Q_{r+1})\left[(\pi + \phi) - \phi\frac{(r + 1)Q_{r+1}}{\bar{\mu}}\right]$$

where:

$$p(\mu_r > Q_r) = \sum_{g=Q_r+1}^{\mu_{max}} \sum_{k=Q_r+1}^{g} a_g b_{kg}$$

therefore:

$$p(\mu_r > Q_r)\left[\left(1 + \frac{\pi}{\phi}\right)\bar{\mu} - rQ_r\right]$$

$$= p(\mu_{r+1} > Q_{r+1})\left[\left(1 + \frac{\pi}{\phi}\right)\bar{\mu} - (r + 1)Q_{r+1}\right]$$

Since our ability to reinterpret symbolically the expression $p(\mu_r > Q_r)$ in terms of Q_r and some function of μ_r is severely limited for almost all probability distributions, no direct path to the comparison of the relative magnitudes of Q_r and Q_{r+1} will be made. We can note the following, however:

a.   If $p(\mu_r > Q_r) > p(\mu_{r+1} > Q_{r+1})$

then

$$rQ_r > (r + 1)Q_{r+1}$$

b.   If $p(\mu_r > Q_r) = p(\mu_{r+1} > Q_{r+1})$

then

$$rQ_r = (r + 1)Q_{r+1}$$

c.   If $p(\mu_r > Q_r) < p(\mu_{r+1} > Q_{r+1})$

then

$$rQ_r < (r + 1)Q_{r+1}.$$

We know that when the optimal solution results in the conditions

$$Q_r = \bar{\mu}_r \quad \text{and} \quad Q_{r+1} = \bar{\mu}_{r+1}$$
$$\text{then} \quad p(\mu_r > Q_r) = p(\mu_{r+1} > Q_{r+1}) = \tfrac{1}{2}$$

This is true since, when total expected demand is large, the means of the respective probability distributions can be said to divide the probability densities in half.[2] This condition implies (from expression 5):

$$\frac{1}{2} = \frac{\phi}{\pi + \phi - \phi\dfrac{Q_r}{\bar{\mu}_r}} = \frac{\phi}{\pi + \phi - \phi\dfrac{Q_{r+1}}{\bar{\mu}_{r+1}}}$$

but

$$Q_r = \bar{\mu}_r; \quad Q_{r+1} = \bar{\mu}_{r+1}$$

Then

$$\frac{1}{2} = \frac{\phi}{\pi + \phi - \phi} = \frac{\phi}{\pi}$$

or

$$\pi = 2\phi$$

Further it can be shown that when the optimal solution for the individual firms results in the condition:

$$Q_r < \bar{\mu}_r \Rightarrow Q_{r+1} < \bar{\mu}_{r+1}$$
$$\pi < 2\phi.$$

then

By restricting ourselves to cases where total system demand is large, and by employing a normal approximation to the individual firm demand distribution it can be shown[3] that when $\pi < 2\phi$ then $p(\mu_r > Q_r) > p(\mu_{r+1} > Q_{r+1})$.

Thus the expression

$$p(\mu_r > Q_r)\left[\pi + \phi - \phi\frac{Q_r}{\bar{\mu}_r}\right] = \phi = p(\mu_{r+1} > Q_{r+1})\left[\pi + \phi - \phi\frac{Q_{r+1}}{\bar{\mu}_{r+1}}\right]$$

can be reduced to

$$\pi + \phi - \phi\frac{Q_r}{\bar{\mu}_r} < \pi + \phi - \phi\frac{Q_{r+1}}{\bar{\mu}_{r+1}}$$

or

$$\frac{Q_r}{\bar{\mu}_r} > \frac{Q_{r+1}}{\bar{\mu}_{r+1}}$$

but $\bar{\mu}_r = \dfrac{\bar{\mu}}{r}$; $\bar{\mu}_{r+1} = \dfrac{\bar{\mu}}{r+1}$

Therefore:

$$\frac{rQ_r}{\bar{\mu}} > \frac{(r+1)Q_{r+1}}{\bar{\mu}}$$

or $rQ_r > (r+1)Q_{r+1}$ for all $\pi < 2\phi$.

In a similar fashion it can be shown that when the optimal solution for the individual firm results in the condition

$$Q_r > \bar{\mu}_r \Rightarrow Q_{r+1} > \bar{\mu}_{r+1}$$

then

$$\pi > 2\phi.$$

By using the normal approximation as above it can be shown also that when $\pi > 2\phi$, then $p(\mu_r > Q_r) < p(\mu_{r+1} > Q_{r+1})$.

Thus the expression

$$p(\mu_r > Q_r)\left[\pi + \phi - \phi\frac{Q_r}{\bar{\mu}_r}\right] = \phi = p(\mu_{r+1} > Q_{r+1})\left[\pi + \phi - \phi\frac{Q_{r+1}}{\bar{\mu}_{r+1}}\right]$$

reduces to

$$\pi + \phi - \phi\frac{Q_r}{\bar{\mu}_r} > \pi + \phi - \phi\frac{Q_{r+1}}{\bar{\mu}_{r+1}}$$

or

$$\frac{Q_r}{\bar{\mu}_r} < \frac{Q_{r+1}}{\bar{\mu}_{r+1}}$$

and $rQ_r < (r+1)\,Q_{r+1}$ for all $\pi > 2\phi$.

Charts 4.4 and 4.5 illustrate these results.

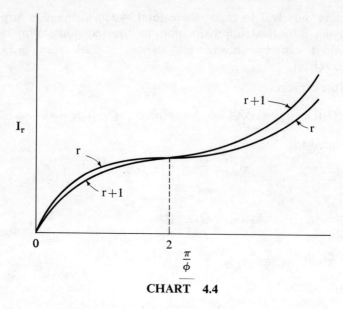

I_r

r

r+1

r+1

r

0

2

$$\frac{\pi}{\phi}$$

CHART 4.4

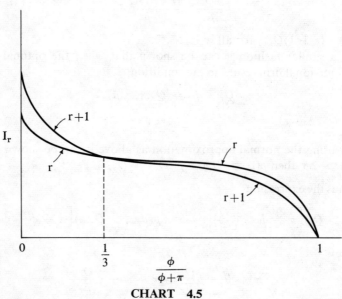

I_r

r+1

r

r

r+1

0

$\frac{1}{3}$

$$\frac{\phi}{\phi+\pi}$$

CHART 4.5

Aggregate inventory costs

Using the relationships developed in the previous section one can now examine the effect of the size of the intermediary level on total system inventory costs. Total expected inventory costs for a system of m sellers and n buyers depend upon the number of firms carrying inventory, the variance of the demand facing the individual firm, and the total level of inventory, as well as holding and shortage costs. Since all of the r firms which carry inventories are identical with respect to the nature of the inventory policy they employ, the aggregate expected inventory cost to the system is the product of the number of firms carrying inventories and the expected inventory costs for the firm:

$$\sum_{i=1}^{r} TEC_i = rTEC_r$$

From the above expression and from expression (3) the aggregate system inventory costs can be expressed as:

$$\text{(8)} \quad rTEC_r = r\left\{\phi \sum_{g=Q_r+1}^{\mu_{max}} \sum_{k=Q_r+1}^{g} a_g b_{kg} \frac{Q_r^2}{2k} + \pi \sum_{g=Q_r+1}^{\mu_{max}} \sum_{k=Q_r+1}^{g} a_g b_{kg}(k - Q_r) \right.$$
$$\left. + \phi \sum_{g=0}^{\mu_{max}} \sum_{k=0}^{Q_r} a_g b_{kg}\left(Q_r - \frac{k}{2}\right)\right\}$$

We now wish to show how the total expected system costs increase as the number of firms in the inventory-carrying level increases. In particular we wish to show that:

$$rTEC_r < (r + 1)TEC_{r+1}$$

where:

$$\text{(9)} \quad (r + 1)TEC_{r+1} = (r + 1)\left\{\phi \sum_{g=Q_{r+1}+1}^{\mu_{max}} \sum_{k=Q_{r+1}+1}^{g} a_g b'_{kg} \frac{Q_{r+1}^2}{2k} \right.$$
$$\left. + \pi \sum_{g=Q_{r+1}+1}^{\mu_{max}} \sum_{k=Q_{r+1}+1}^{g} a_g b'_{kg}(k - Q_{r+1}) + \phi \sum_{g=0}^{\mu_{max}} \sum_{k=0}^{Q_{r+1}} a_g b'_{kg}\left(Q_{r+1} - \frac{k}{2}\right)\right\}$$

and

$$b' = \binom{g}{k}\left(\frac{1}{r+1}\right)^k \left(\frac{r}{r+1}\right)^{g-k}$$

Then no serious loss of generality results if we let

$$\sum_{g=Q_r+1}^{\mu_{max}} \sum_{k=Q_r+1}^{g} a_g b_{kg} \frac{Q_r^2}{2k} = \frac{Q_r^2}{\bar{\mu}_r} \sum_{g=Q_r+1}^{\mu_{max}} \sum_{k=Q_r+1}^{g} a_g b_{kg}$$

and

$$\sum_{g=Q_{r+1}+1}^{\mu_{max}} \sum_{k=Q_{r+1}+1}^{g} a_g b'_{kg} \frac{Q_{r+1}^2}{2k} = \frac{Q_{r+1}^2}{\bar{\mu}_{r+1}} \sum_{g=Q_{r+1}+1}^{\mu_{max}} \sum_{k=Q_{r+1}+1}^{g} a_g b'_{kg}$$

Using the above approximations, and noting that:

$$\sum_{g=0}^{\mu_{max}} \sum_{k=0}^{Q_r} a_g b_{kg} = 1 - \sum_{g=Q_r+1}^{\mu_{max}} \sum_{k=Q_r+1}^{g} a_g b_{kg}$$

$$\sum_{g=0}^{\mu_{max}} \sum_{k=0}^{Q_r} a_g b_{kg} k = \bar{\mu}_r - \sum_{g=Q_r+1}^{\mu_{max}} \sum_{k=Q_r+1}^{g} a_g b_{kg} k$$

$$\sum_{g=0}^{\mu_{max}} \sum_{k=0}^{Q_{r+1}} a_g b'_{kg} = 1 - \sum_{g=Q_{r+1}+1}^{\mu_{max}} \sum_{k=Q_{r+1}+1}^{g} a_g b'_{kg}$$

and

$$\sum_{g=0}^{\mu_{max}} \sum_{k=0}^{Q_{r+1}} a_g b'_{kg} k = \bar{\mu}_{r+1} - \sum_{g=Q_{r+1}+1}^{\mu_{max}} \sum_{k=Q_{r+1}+1}^{g} a_g b'_{kg} k$$

then the proof requires that:

$$\phi(r+1)Q_{r+1} - (r+1)Q_{r+1}\left\{\pi + \phi - \phi\frac{Q_{r+1}}{\bar{\mu}_{r+1}}\right\} \sum_{g=Q_{r+1}+1}^{\mu_{max}} \sum_{k=Q_{r+1}+1}^{g} a_g b'_{kg}$$

(10) $$+(r+1)(\pi + \phi) \sum_{g=Q_{r+1}+1}^{\mu_{max}} \sum_{k=Q_{r+1}+1}^{g} a_g b'_{kg} k > \phi r Q_r$$

$$-rQ_r\left\{\pi + \phi - \phi\frac{Q_r}{\bar{\mu}_r}\right\} \sum_{g=Q_r+1}^{\mu_{max}} \sum_{k=Q_r+1}^{g} a_g b_{kg} + r(\pi + \phi) \sum_{g=Q_r+1}^{\mu_{max}} \sum_{k=Q_r+1}^{g} a_g b_{kg} k$$

From (5),

$$\sum_{g=Q_r+1}^{\mu_{max}} \sum_{k=Q_r+1}^{g} a_g b_{kg} = \frac{\phi}{\pi + \phi - \phi\frac{Q_r}{\bar{\mu}_r}}$$

and

$$\sum_{g=Q_{r+1}+1}^{\mu_{max}} \sum_{k=Q_{r+1}+1}^{g} a_g b'_{kg} = \frac{\phi}{\pi + \phi - \phi\frac{Q_{r+1}}{\bar{\mu}_{r+1}}}$$

and therefore (10) reduces to:

$$(r+1)(\pi + \phi) \sum_{g=Q_{r+1}+1}^{\mu_{max}} \sum_{k=Q_{r+1}+1}^{g} a_g b'_{kg} k > r(\pi + \phi) \sum_{g=Q_r+1}^{\mu_{max}} \sum_{k=Q_r+1}^{g} a_g b_{kg} k$$

to complete the proof normal approximations to the discrete probability densities (above) are used, i.e.,

$$\sum_{g=Q_r+1}^{\mu_{max}} \sum_{k=Q_r+1}^{g} a_g b_{kg} \simeq \int_{Q_r}^{\infty} x f(x)\, dx$$

where $f(x)$ is the normal density function. Consequently:

$$\int_{Q_r}^{\infty} x f(x)\, dx = (2\Pi)^{-\frac{1}{2}} e^{-\frac{Q_r^2}{2}}$$

Similarly,

$$\sum_{g=Q_{r+1}+1}^{\mu_{max}} \sum_{k=Q_{r+1}+1}^{g} a_g b'_{kg} \simeq \int_{Q_{r+1}}^{\infty} x f'(x)\, dx = (2\Pi)^{-\frac{1}{2}} e^{-\frac{Q_{r+1}^2}{2}}$$

Employing these normal approximations, (10) requires that:

$$(r+1)(2\Pi)^{-\frac{1}{2}} e^{-\frac{Q_{r+1}^2}{2}} > r(2\Pi)^{-\frac{1}{2}} e^{-\frac{Q_r^2}{2}}$$

This is clearly true when $Q_r > Q_{r+1}$. Since

$$\frac{\phi}{\pi + \phi - \phi\frac{Q_r}{\bar{\mu}_r}} = \frac{\phi}{\pi + \phi - \phi\frac{Q_{r+1}}{\bar{\mu}_{r+1}}}$$

then

$$\frac{Q_r}{\bar{\mu}_r} = \frac{Q_{r+1}}{\bar{\mu}_{r+1}}$$

and

$$\frac{Q_r}{Q_{r+1}} = \frac{\bar{\mu}_r}{\bar{\mu}_{r+1}} = \frac{r+1}{r} > 1$$

and the proof that $(r + 1)TEC_{r+1} > rTEC_r$ is complete when $\pi \neq 0$. The use of the normal approximation to the discrete density function is quite reasonable for large mean values. This must surely be the case in most vertical market structures. The proof without this approximation is quite tedious and would detract from the lucidity of the concepts involved.

Only two special cases exist, $\pi=0$ and $\pi=2\phi$. When $\pi=0$ there is no inducement for middlemen to carry inventories since consumers' disutility and middlemen's profits sum to zero. Hence $rTEC_r = (r + 1)TEC_{r+1}$ at $\pi = 0$.

When $\pi = 2\phi$ each firm stocks its expected demand, but as the number of firms in an inventory-carrying level is increased, expected shortages must increase and because of this, expected storage costs must also increase.[4] Hence even though $rQ_r = (r + 1)Q_{r+1}$, $rTEC_r < (r + 1)TEC_{r+1}$ at $\pi = 2\phi$.

This section can be summarized by pointing out that aggregate inventory costs for the system vary as three basic classes of factors vary. First, aggregate inventory costs vary directly with the levels of π and ϕ—the unit shortage and holding costs—and with the relative values of π and ϕ. These points are illustrated below in Chart 4.6.

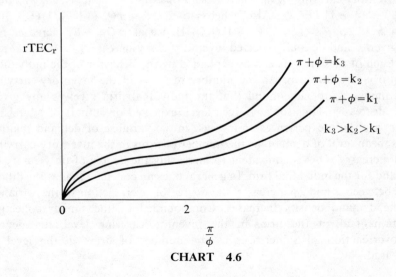

CHART 4.6

Second, aggregate inventory costs vary as the number of firms in the inventory-carrying level varies. This is shown in Chart 4.7.

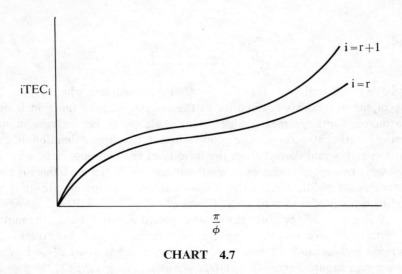

CHART 4.7

Finally, for any given π and ϕ aggregate inventory costs vary as the absolute difference between aggregate level inventories and the mean or expected demand varies. This is seen indirectly in the proof showing that aggregate inventory costs increase as the number of firms in an inventory-carrying level increases. For all $\pi > 0$ it is shown that $rTEC_r < (r + 1) TEC_{r+1}$. Also, when $\pi > 2\phi$, $\bar{\mu} < rQ_r < (r + 1)Q_{r+1}$ and when $\pi < 2\phi$, $\bar{\mu} > rQ_r > (r + 1)Q_{r+1}$. Hence as $|rQ_r - \bar{\mu}|$ increases for any given π and ϕ, total expected inventory costs increase.

Each of these results can be explained by the behavior of the individual inventory-carrying firm. As the number of firms in the inventory-carrying level increases, the likelihood that the individual firm receives any given order decreases. Thus for any given level (expected or actual) of aggregate orders each firm experiences an increase in the variance of demand relative to its mean level of demand as the number of firms in the inventory-carrying level increases. This is equivalent to increasing the degree of uncertainty of demand for the individual firm. In general one can conclude that as the difference between π and 2ϕ increases, the degree of overreaction to the variance of the demand density increases. Compounded by the similar collective reaction of all of the firms in the inventory-carrying level, the degree of overreaction also increases as the number of firms in the level is increased.

Equilibrium in the vertical market structure

Considering only inventory costs the equilibrium number of inventory-carrying middlemen in the *single level* can simply be deduced from expression (**12**). That is, we can say that for all $m > r$:

$$rTEC_r < mTEC_m$$

and for $m = r$

$$rTEC_r = mTEC_m$$

The inventory costs to the system are always lower when the number of middlemen in the system is less than the number of initial sellers m. Middlemen can only enter the system if they gain the cooperation of the m sellers and n buyers. Middlemen desiring to enter the system to perform the inventory-carrying function can do so only as long as they reduce or do not increase the inventory costs of the buyers and sellers.[5] Assuming that the entry of middlemen is dependent only on the profit possibilities in the system and that no special entry costs exist, the number of middlemen in the system will increase until the profits of individual middlemen are driven to zero by newly entering middlemen; when

$$TP_i = \frac{mTEC_m}{w} - TEC_w = 0$$

where:

$$TP_i = \text{profits of the } i\text{th middleman.}$$

Hence, the equilibrium number of middlemen in the system must be:

(**11**) $$w = \frac{mTEC_m}{TEC_w} \Rightarrow wTEC_w = mTEC_m$$

Since TEC_w increases monotonically with w, the only way that $wTEC_w$ can equal $mTEC_m$ for $\pi \neq 0$ is when[6] $w = m$. This is illustrated in Chart 4.8.

Under the conditions stated above only one level of middlemen can exist at any single point in time. Since the only basis for the existence of middlemen is the assumption of the inventory-carrying process by the entering middlemen, all inventories must be concentrated in a single level. In the absence of special strategy formulations by entering middlemen, i.e., where no rebates are allowed, entry into the system on the part of middlemen must come only in the inventory-carrying level. Entry is profitable so long as $m > w$, and when $m = w$ no further entry could be accomplished. This, however, leaves open the possibility of beginning new inventory-carrying levels as soon as profits are driven to zero in the original level. Unless we drop the assumption that inventory costs are the only relevant system costs, new inventory-carrying levels would lead to the destruction of the original

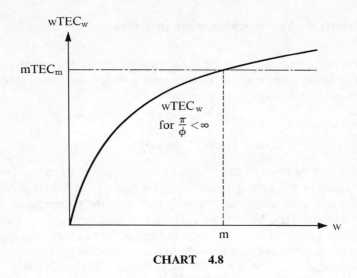

CHART 4.8

level. The firm in this level becomes completely useless if it does not carry inventories or perform any other functions.

To avoid this basic instability one must consider that middlemen incur of necessity costs other than of carrying inventories. One such is the cost of order handling. The addition of middlemen on any level increases the total number of orders placed in the system. Middlemen would then cooperate with other middlemen only if they continued to handle orders and if they are reimbursed by the members of the other entering level for this function. One can thus assume that some rebate is paid to the m for their handling of the orders of the middlemen of the first level. The middlemen's equilibrium number thus must be less than m. In turn, they demand rebates for this function from others.

Any rebate paid by entering intermediary levels alters the analysis of equilibrium somewhat. If a strategy rebate, or payment for cooperation, were added to the order handling rebate, all rebates could be treated as a single sum of some given minimum value. Once the issue of rebates is introduced there results a system containing a single inventory-carrying middleman who incurs inventory costs of TEC_1 and rebate payments to sellers and other middlemen of $(mTEC_m - TEC_1)$. This conclusion can be verified if one considers the entry of a middleman into the system who, as a condition to entry, must give a rebate of size r to each of the existing inventory-carrying firms in cooperating levels. Beginning with the case where there are no middlemen in the initial structure, the middleman has profits of:

(12) $$TP_1 = mTEC_m - mr - TEC_1$$

Given that $TP_1 > 0$, it may be possible for a second middleman to enter the system, dividing the revenues of the first middleman and assuming his proportion of the rebates to the m sellers and incurring his inventory-carrying costs. This process will continue to the point where the profits of the existing middlemen fall to zero, thereby preventing further entry[7], i.e.,

$$TP_i = \frac{mTEC_m - mr}{w_1} - TEC_{w_1} = 0$$

or

(13)
$$w_1 = \frac{m[TEC_m - r]}{TEC_{w_1}}$$

But for all $w_1 > 1$ it is possible for additional middlemen to enter the system by cooperating with the existing w_1 middlemen and by granting each of them a rebate of size, say, r_1. This process is like the one above and would continue to the point where the profits of each individual middleman in the second level fell to zero, that is, when:

$$TP_{2i} = \frac{mTEC_m - mr - w_1r_1}{w_2} - TEC_{w_2} = 0$$

or

$$w_2 = \frac{mTEC_m - mr - w_1r_1}{TEC_{w_2}}$$

This process would be repeated continuously to the point where in the last (say jth) level of middlemen only a single middleman could exist with profits of zero. At this point his profits would be described by:

$$TP_j = mTEC_m - mr - \sum_{i=1}^{j-1} w_ir_i - TEC_1 = 0$$

or

$$TEC_1 = mTEC_m - \left[mr + \sum_{i=1}^{j-1} w_ir_i \right]$$

where

$$mr + \sum_{i=1}^{j-1} w_ir_i = \text{total rebates granted to middlemen and sellers}$$

in the system.

Under these conditions a stable equilibrium having the minimum possible

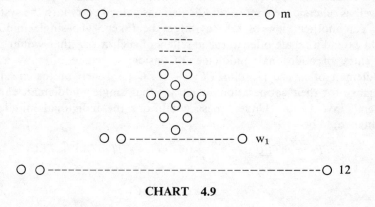

CHART 4.9

inventory costs to the system of TEC_1 would result. But total rebates would be equivalent to the sum of the savings generated by having a single middleman carry the system's inventories, including the increase in costs which results from increased order handling which the entry of every middleman causes. The system is illustrated in Chart 4.9.

Cooperation and rebates strategies

Since rebates are required as a condition for the stability of the system's equilibrium, reasons other than order handling should be considered for firms demanding rebates greater than zero in exchange for their relinquishing the inventory-carrying function. The general reasons given in Chapter 2 on contact and communication functions in vertical market structures apply here.[8] In addition, however, the notion that shortage costs might be viewed as a policy parameter for the individual firms forms a basis for rebate demands. In effect, the derivation of an optimal inventory policy depends in part upon the level of the firm's unit shortage costs. Conversely, the inventory policy of any profit-maximizing firm of the type we are dealing with here reflects the view of shortage costs. Since the inventory policy determines expected shortages, it is possible that expected shortages, or rather the lack of shortages, may be treated as a competitive element much as price or advertising.

The possibility in our system of treating the level of shortages as an inter-firm competitive element exists when the buyer's repurchase behavior is related to his experience with the shortages of the individual firm. This line of argument is expanded and more rigorously developed in the succeeding chapters. Suffice it to note at this point that one possible reason for rebate demands by sellers for cooperating in determining the location in the system of the inventory-carrying function can stem from their differing policy statements of unit shortage costs. The argument, of course, extends to middlemen as well as sellers once a set of middlemen has gained entry into the system.

Yet another view of rebates might be taken. The single middleman could extend a rebate offer to the m sellers of such a size that would *prevent* the entry of additional middlemen. Consider a rebate offer by a single middleman of a size $(1/m)[mTEC_m - 2TEC_2]$ to each of the m sellers in exchange for their cooperation in letting that single middleman carry the system's inventories. Under these conditions the individual middleman's profits would be

$$TP_1 = mTEC_m - m\left[\frac{1}{m}(mTEC_m - 2TEC_2)\right] - TEC_1$$

or

$$TP_1 = 2TEC_2 - TEC_1 > 0$$

A second middleman attempting to enter the system would find that he could gain only zero profits by competing in the same level as the first middleman. That is:

$$TP_2 = \frac{mTEC_m - m\left[\frac{1}{m}(mTEC_m - 2TEC_2)\right]}{2} - TEC_2 = 0$$

Of course, middlemen could bid for the single position as the inventory carrier for the system. The highest possible rebate bid by any middleman would be $\frac{1}{m}(mTEC_m - TEC_1)$ since this rebate, granted to each of the m sellers, would result in zero profits for the middleman. In less than perfect competition one could expect the actual rebate prevailing in the system to be located between these two extremes. Profits on inventories would be divided among the m sellers and a single middleman. The m sellers receive a minimum profit when the rebate is $\frac{1}{m}[mTEC_m - 2TEC_2]$ and the single middleman makes zero profits when the rebate is $\frac{1}{m}[mTEC_m - TEC_1]$. In any event, the use of rebates as competitive elements among middlemen would result in a stable or unstable equilibrium position of a single middleman in the system where expected inventory costs are minimized and total profits for the m sellers and the single middleman equal $(mTEC_m - TEC_1)$. In the event that the single middleman's profits are zero, the equilibrium is stable.

Contact costs combined with inventory requirements

By combining the performance of the contactual and inventory-carrying functions, the equilibrium number of all middlemen in the system differs from the equilibrium number when each is considered separately. In the absence of rebates the equilibrium number of middlemen in the primary level lies between the equilibrium number when contact is considered alone and that when inventory is considered alone. The general nature of the equilibrium structure is similar to that which emerges in the case of contact considered by itself.

Allow middlemen to assume both the contactual and inventory-carrying functions in the system. The equilibrium of middlemen in the primary level in the vertical market structure is that number w_1, which equates the sums of contactual and expected inventory costs for the m sellers and n buyers and the contactual and expected inventory costs of the w_1 middlemen, i.e., when

$$mTEC_m + C_1mn = w_1TEC_{w_1} + C_1w_1(m + n)$$

where
$$C_1 = \text{unit cost of contact.}$$

Hence:
$$w_1 = \frac{mTEC_m + C_1 mn}{TEC_{w_1} + C_1(m + n)}$$

It is known that:
$$\frac{C_1 mn}{C_1(m + n)} < m$$

and that at $w_1 = m$
$$\frac{mTEC_m}{TEC_{w_1}} = m$$

Thus, independent of the relative magnitudes of expected inventory and contactual costs in the system, the equilibrium number of middlemen in the primary level of the system will be:
$$\frac{mn}{m + n} < w_1 < m$$

This is illustrated in Chart 4.10.

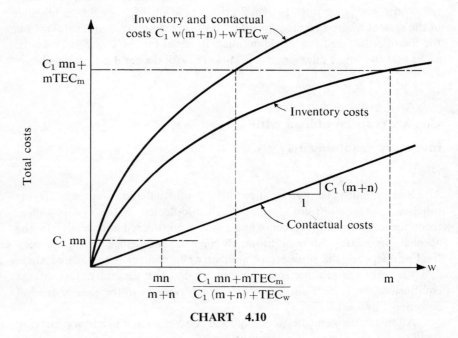

CHART 4.10

It is known that when middlemen do not incur rebates and contactual costs, their assumption of the inventory-carrying function does not lead to further expansion of the system, since assumption of these responsibilities by middlemen in other levels results in the disbanding of the previous level.

Adding contactual responsibilities, however, provides a basis for the existence of middlemen quite independent of their inventory-carrying responsibilities. Hence, one would not expect levels of middlemen performing only contactual functions to exist in the system, while at the same time, they might be the most efficient level for the carrying of inventories. The basis for creating such additional levels has already been established by the creation of the primary level of middlemen, and for all $w_1 > 2$, at least two additional levels of middlemen would find entry into the structure profitable based on contactual operations only.

Given this structure of middlemen based on contactual operations, the inventory function would be performed by that level which most efficiently performs it for the system; that is, where only a single firm carries inventories. One would not expect a primary level of middlemen containing two or more firms to carry the system's inventories. The expected equilibrium structure takes the form shown in Chapter 2 where:

$$w_1 = \frac{mn}{m + n}$$

$$w_2 = \frac{mw_1}{m + w_1}; \quad w_3 = \frac{nw_1}{n + w_1}$$

$$\cdot \quad \cdot \quad \cdot \quad \cdot \quad \cdot \quad \cdot \quad \cdot$$

$$w_{2n} = \frac{mw_{2n-2}}{m + w_{2n-2}} = 1; \quad w_{2n-1} = \frac{nw_{2n-3}}{n + w_{2n-3}} = 1$$

In addition to the contactual function performed by all firms, one firm would carry inventories.

Expected profits from contactual functions for all firms in equilibrium are zero. The inventory costs of the individual firm (TEC_1) are lower than those of the m sellers ($mTEC_m$), so that the single inventory-carrying firm in the system makes profits of $mTEC_m - TEC_1$. Since it is assumed that no rebates are granted, and since all firms seek to attain the single profit position in the structure, the resulting equilibrium is highly unstable.

Even in the absence of rebate demands in exchange for the cooperation needed for entry of middlemen, the middlemen seeking the single profit position in the system would bid for the spot by offering rebates to the m sellers and n buyers. Under these conditions the firm seeking to maximize its profits would be forced to grant a *total* rebate to the m sellers and n buyers of at least R to prevent the entry of additional competing middlemen, where:

$$R = (mTEC_m - 2TEC_2) + C_1(mn - 2m - 2n)$$

Therefore, a second middleman seeking to enter the system in competition with the first would be faced with profits of:

$$TP_2 = \frac{mTEC_m + C_1mn - (mTEC_m - 2TEC_2) - C_1(mn - 2m - 2n)}{2}$$

$$- C_1(m + n) - TEC_2 = 0$$

which provide no motivation for entry into the system as a competitor.

Of course the maximum rebate that could be offered by a profit-maximizing middleman is $[mTEC_m + C_1(mn) - TEC_1 - C_1(m + n)]$ since any larger total rebate by the middleman would result in negative profits. The actual rebate granted by the middleman is a function of the nature of the competitive and cooperative bargaining positions of the m sellers, n buyers, and the middlemen seeking entry into the system.

One final view of rebates is of importance. To this point the granting of rebates and the size granted have taken either of two forms. First, rebates are considered minimum demands by existing firms in the structure—designed to offset some loss of utility, or to cover order-handling costs the firms would suffer if additional firms were allowed to enter the structure. Secondly, rebates are considered as a competitive instrument—one which allows a middleman to gain a monopolist's position in the structure. Both of these views treat rebates as endogenously determined variables. It might well be that rebates could be determined exogenously. For example, consider the government's position as a possible price administrator. In such a case, the government could limit the maximum size of rebates and thereby prevent the existence of a monopolist in the structure. Since all of our analyses treat the system's output as a constant, any rebate granted can only mean a price reduction at the same volume.

As an illustration, assume that the maximum rebate grant is fixed at $100\,r\%$ of the cost ($0 \leq r < 1$) of the level's inventory and contactual acitivities.[9] Hence a middleman desiring to enter a structure composed of the m sellers and n buyers could offer total rebates as large as $r[mTEC_m + C_1mn]$, resulting in profits of:

$$TP_1 = (1 - r)\,[mTEC_m + C_1mn] - [C_1(m + n) + TEC_1]$$

So long as $TP_1 > 0$, the possibility of further entry by middlemen exists and given that entry continues until profits fall to zero, the primary level of middlemen would contain w_1 firms where:

$$\textbf{(14)} \qquad w_1 = (1 - r)\frac{mTEC_m + C_1mn}{TEC_{w_1} + C_1(m + n)}$$

The existence of w_1 firms in the primary level provides a basis for the entry of additional middlemen since both contactual and inventory costs can be reduced. Thus a middleman desiring to intervene between the m sellers and w_1 middlemen in the primary level by granting the maximum allowable rebates would have profits of:

$$TP_2 = (1 - r)[w_1TEC_{w_1} + C_1mw_1] - [TEC_1 + C_1(m + w_1)]$$

This level could be expanded to the point where individual firm profits would fall to zero. At this point the level would contain w_2 firms where:

$$w_2 = (1 - r)\frac{w_1TEC_{w_1} + C_1mw_1}{TEC_{w_2} + C_1(m + w_1)}$$

The equilibrium number of middlemen w_1 is greater than the equilibrium number w_2, since the only basis for reduction in contactual costs by the w_2 middlemen in the second level with respect to contacts among the m sellers and w_1 primary middlemen can occur when $w_2 \leq \dfrac{mw_1}{m + w_1} < w_1$. Similarly reductions in inventory costs can come if $w_2 < w_1$. The combined costs of w_2 can thus be less than those of w_1 if and *only* if $w_2 < w_1$.

Given that $w_2 > 2$, further reductions in costs could occur if additional middlemen enter the structure. Thus, the process of cost-reducing entries continues to the point where only a single middleman can find it profitable to enter the system. A mapping of the resulting equilibrium structure would appear similar to the one shown in Chart 1 of Chapter 2. Note that the equilibrium structure resulting from granting the maximum allowable rebate by entering middlemen is one in which only a single firm carries inventories and all firms perform the contactual function. This results in a division of the system's aggregate rebate of size[10] $[mTEC_m + C_1mn - TEC_1 - C_1K]$ among all the middlemen and the m sellers in the system[11]. The size of r will determine the allocation of the total rebate among the m sellers and the middlemen. In particular, the m sellers receive a total rebate of $r[mTEC_m + C_1mn]$. For all $r > 0$ middlemen's profits under conditions of perfect competition are expected to be zero.[12] Finally the number of middlemen in the equilibrium structure is in part dependent upon the size of the rebate r. As r increases the number of middlemen falls, and the converse also is true. This can be verified by examining expression (**14**) and noting that as r increases, w_1 falls. Since all other levels are dependent upon the size of the primary level, as the size of the primary level is reduced all other levels and numbers of levels are reduced in size.

The only restriction on rebate grants by middlemen imposed in this model is on the maximum size of the grant. Thus we must consider the effect of rebate grants of less than the allowable maximum. The only effect of this behavior, of course, would be to expand the system, i.e., to increase the number and levels of middlemen in the system beyond those which would result from a rebate grant of the maximum allowable size.

Given that the maximum allowable rebate grant is less than $[(mTEC_m - 2TEC_2) + C_1(mn - 2m - 2n)]$—the minimum grant needed to prevent the entry of more than one middleman into the system—rebate grants no longer represent an effective competition-eliminating variable for the individual middleman unless the rebate can be used to secure a stronger cooperative relationship between the middleman and the m sellers and n buyers. (This possibility is the subject matter of the next section.) Hence, the actual rebate grant, in this system, would approach the minimum rebate *necessary* to gain the cooperation of the existing firms in the structure rather than the maximum possible since no competitive, or profit-producing, advantage can be gained by giving any more than is necessary to enter the system.

The static equilibrium condition of this system is the state where there is no incentive for profit-maximizing firms to enter or exit from the vertical market structure. The profit incentive is assumed to exist for all non-negative profits. If this were not true, and if there existed some minimum acceptable profits, the system would be only slightly altered but would be one where no firms would secure profits greater than the acceptable minimum. The larger the minimum acceptable profit point, the smaller would be the number of middlemen and the number of levels of middlemen in the equilibrium structure.

Reducing uncertainty of demand

It has been shown that the reduction in the number of inventory-carrying firms in the vertical market structure leads to lower total system inventory costs. This is turn leads to potentially greater profits for each middleman (the actual change in profits being a function of the bargaining for rebates.) One strategy, therefore, the middlemen may employ is that which leads to the reduction in the number of middlemen. Another is that which leads to the reduction in the uncertainty of demand facing him without necessarily reducing the total number of middlemen. If a middleman in the primary level could devise some means to attain such a goal, then his total inventory-carrying costs would be reduced and the expected value of his output need not be reduced as a consequence.[13] The resulting expected cost savings is then potential profit for the middlemen to be divided with the $m + n$ initial firms in some fashion determined by bargaining and the competitive conditions of each level in the system.

Consider the situation where a vertical market structure has some given number of middlemen in the primary level. Under such conditions the middleman, in order to reduce the uncertainty of demand facing him, contracts with a given number of the buyers. If all the buyers were identical, he could contract to supply all the needs for a given product of some segment of the buyers equal to n/w_1. This would mean that his total expected demand would remain unchanged, but he now is certain that once an order is generated by a member of this group for the product in question he would receive that order. The new expected inventory costs under these conditions of reduced uncertainty would be *lower* than they had been prior to the contract.

Such a strategy entails a level of cooperation greater than that needed merely to satisfy the conditions that are necessary for exchange. It involves a *guarantee* on the part of the buyer to purchase exclusively from that particular middleman once he has decided to purchase. In return, the buyer is to receive some gains in one form or another. This strategy of increased cooperation differs from that designed to reduce the number of middlemen in some respects although both lead to reduced demand uncertainty.

It must be shown that:

a. Such a contract between an individual middleman and $\frac{n}{w_1}$ buyers would leave the expected demand facing him unchanged. (Here w_1 is the number of middlemen in the system's primary level at the time of strategy formulation.)

b. Such a contract reduces the uncertainty of demand which the middleman faces.

We assume that the n buyers have identical probability distributions of orders in a given time period, and that each order is of size one unit. We also assume that each buyer's demand is independent of that of any other buyer. Then if the ith buyer among the n has an order distribution with mean $\bar{\mu}_i$ and a variance of $\sigma^2_{\mu_i}$, it follows that the mean of the order distribution of all buyers is:

$$\bar{\mu} = \sum_{i=1}^{n} \bar{\mu}_i$$

The mean of the aggregate demand distribution is the sum of the means of *independent* random variables. Also, the variance of the aggregate demand distribution is equal to the sum of variances of these independent random variables. Thus:

$$\sigma^2_\mu = \sum_{i=1}^{n} \sigma^2_{\mu_i}$$

It follows, since all buyers are assumed to be identical, that:

$$\bar{\mu} = n\bar{\mu}_i \qquad (i = 1. \ldots n)$$

and

$$\sigma^2_\mu = n\sigma^2_{\mu_i} \qquad (i = 1. \ldots n)$$

Consider some sub-set of k firms in the set of n firms, such that $k = \frac{n}{w_1} < n$. Then:

$$\bar{\mu}_k = \sum_{i=1}^{k} \bar{\mu}_i = k\bar{\mu}_i = \frac{\bar{\mu}}{k}$$

and

$$\sigma^2_{\mu_k} = \sum_{i=1}^{k} \sigma^2_{\mu_i} = k\sigma^2_{\mu_i} = \frac{\sigma^2_\mu}{k}$$

Therefore

$$\frac{\bar{\mu}_1}{\sigma^2_{\mu_1}} = \frac{\bar{\mu}_k}{\sigma^2_{\mu_k}} = \frac{\bar{\mu}}{\sigma^2_\mu}$$

Where no contracts exist between any of the r middlemen and any of the n buyers, each middleman faces a demand distribution $f(\mu_r) = AB$.

Let A' be the demand distribution the middleman faces when he contracts to supply all the orders for the product generated by a group of $\frac{n}{w_1}$ buyers. In order to show that the uncertainty of demand falls following the creation of such an agreement, it is necessary to show that

$$\text{Var}(AB) > \text{Var}(A') \quad \text{for all} \quad w_1 > 1$$

and that

$$E(AB) = E(A').$$

The variance of (AB) is

$$\sigma_{AB}^2 = E[\text{Var}(AB\,|\,A)] + \text{Var}E(AB\,|\,A)$$

where

$$E[\text{Var}(AB\,|\,A)] = pqE(A) = pq\bar{\mu}, \text{ and}$$
$$\text{Var}E(AB\,|\,A) = p\text{Var}(A) = p\sigma_\mu^2$$

Thus $\sigma_{AB}^2 = pq\bar{\mu} + p\sigma_\mu^2$.

It has been shown that,

$$\frac{\bar{\mu}}{\sigma_\mu^2} = \frac{\bar{\mu}_k}{\sigma_{\mu_k}^2} \text{ (Where } k = \frac{n}{w_1} \text{ and hence } \sigma_{\mu_k}^2 \text{ is the variance of } A';$$

and where $\bar{\mu}_k$ is the mean of A').

In Chapter 3 it is shown that the mean of AB is equal to $\bar{\mu}/w_1$. Therefore the mean of AB is equal to $\dfrac{n}{w_1}\bar{\mu}_k$ where $\bar{\mu}_k$ is the mean of A'. Using this fact and returning to the relation of the variance of AB to the variance of A', the proof that the former exceeds the latter reduces to showing that:

$$pq\bar{\mu} + p\sigma_\mu^2 > \sigma_{\mu_k}^2$$

Substituting $\dfrac{1}{w_1}$ for p, $\dfrac{w_1 - 1}{w_1}$ for q, and $\dfrac{\bar{\mu}_k}{\bar{\mu}}\sigma_\mu^2$ for $\sigma_{\mu_k}^2$ results in the necessary condition that:

$$\frac{1}{w_1}\left(\frac{w_1 - 1}{w_1}\right)\bar{\mu} + \frac{1}{w_1}\sigma_\mu^2 > \frac{\bar{\mu}_k}{\bar{\mu}}\sigma_\mu^2$$

But

$$\frac{\bar{\mu}_k}{\bar{\mu}} = \frac{k}{n} = \frac{1}{w_1}$$

Hence we must show:

$$\left(\frac{w_1 - 1}{w_1^2}\right)\bar{\mu} + \frac{1}{w_1}\sigma_\mu^2 > \frac{1}{w_1}\sigma_\mu^2$$

or

$$\left(\frac{w_1 - 1}{w_1^2}\right)\bar{\mu} > 0$$

which is true for all $w_1 > 1$, $\bar{\mu} > 0$. Therefore, when $w_1 > 1$ and $\bar{\mu} > 0$,

$$\sigma_{AB}^2 > \sigma_{\mu_k}^2 = \sigma_{A'}^2$$

In summary, when the middleman, by contracting with a group of $k = \dfrac{n}{w_1}$ buyers, shifts the distribution of demand facing him from AB to A', he leaves his expected demand unchanged but reduces the variance of the demand distribution facing him. This reduction in uncertainty in turn reduces his expected inventory costs, as shown earlier. The exact portion of these savings that a middleman retains will in turn depend upon the competition of actual and potential middlemen and on the economic power of the initial buyers and sellers.

Once a middleman is allowed the use of this cooperation strategy in the model, all others must be allowed it also. If all middlemen entered into such contracts and bid for the buyers by offering greater proportions of their expected savings in inventory costs, then the competition would drive the middleman's share of these to zero.[14] The equilibrium number of middlemen would be w_1, and the equilibrium segment of the buyers which each has under contract must be $\frac{n}{w_1}$. This assumes of course that the group of n buyers are well organized and do not compete among themselves for the middlemen who might be offering contracts of varying rebate levels. The equilibrium distribution of the expected inventory cost savings will fall between the two extremes, but exactly where is not determinable in the model.[15] Finally, if the equilibrium distribution between the existing middlemen and the n buyers leads to positive profits for the middlemen, such profits would attract new middlemen. Their freedom of entry would determine finally the equilibrium number of w_1 and their equilibrium profit levels. Since the nature of competition among the buyers is not treated as an endogenous variable, it must be stated that free entry of middlemen would again lead to a new equilibrium number $\hat{w}_1$ which is greater than w_1, to expected zero profits for each, and to a system where each middleman is guaranteed the orders of a segment $\frac{n}{\hat{w}_1}$ buyers, a segment smaller than $\frac{n}{w_1}$.

If the middlemen in the primary level should choose the strategy of segmenting the buying market with each contracting for all the purchases of a single group, the equilibrium vertical market structure differs from that which would exist if no such strategy were employed. Considering the performance of the contact and communication function first, the system's total output in terms of information would remain unchanged since it is assumed that each middleman continues to contact all sellers. Furthermore, there is no need for each buyer to contact all middlemen, since each buyer now no longer considers purchasing from any but one middleman. Since this middleman contacts all sellers, each buyer is still in contact with each seller. In short, middlemen will contact only possible buyers, or that group under contract. The result is now a total number of contacts in the system of

$$\hat{w}_1\left(m + \frac{n}{\hat{w}_1}\right) = \hat{w}_1 m + n.$$

The total revenue from contact is still equal to mn. The equilibrium number of middlemen in the primary level considering only contact would be that which, with no rebates, would set $mn - \hat{w}_1 m - n = 0$

or

$$\hat{w}_1 = \frac{mn - n}{m}$$

This is greater[16] than $\frac{mn}{m + n}$, which existed prior to contract strategy. Since the equilibrium number of middlemen, when both contact and inventory are considered separately, is greater than in the absence of contract strategy, the equilibrium number for both functions considered simultaneously also must be greater. Modification to this analysis may be easily made to introduce communication costs and other market imperfections.

For any given number of middlemen w_1 the net profits for each from contact alone is greater when the buyers are segmented and rebates are zero. That is, whereas profits would have been $\frac{mn}{w_1} - (m + n)$ per individual, they now would be $\frac{mn}{w_1} - (m + \frac{n}{w_1})$. Thus greater rebates are possible, and also, the equilibrium number of middlemen in the second case, $\hat{w}_1$, will exceed the one in the first case, w_1, by an amount that depends directly on the rebate given. If rebates increase in order to compensate buyers for a loss of freedom of choice, then the new system will have a total contactual cost that is smaller than that of the old system. The total reduction in cost, given free entry into the middleman level, will be greater with the greater increase in rebates.

When a contract exists between a seller and a number of buyers, a market imperfection can be said to exist. Under such circumstances the entry of new levels of middlemen between each middleman and the buyers under contract to him could not reduce total contact costs. An entry of one middleman would now increase the total costs between the middleman and his buyers from $\frac{n}{\hat{w}_1}$ to $\frac{n + 1}{\hat{w}_1}$. Expected inventory costs also could not fall since the number of inventory-carrying firms could not fall below the *one* middleman in the primary level serving the $\frac{n}{\hat{w}_1}$ buyers. The only new levels of middlemen would exist between the m sellers and the $\hat{w}_1$ middlemen, and all conditions of rebates mentioned earlier as necessary for equilibrium must also hold. Thus the equilibrium vertical market structure would contain multiple levels only between the primary level of middlemen and the m sellers.

The special contractual relations between middlemen in the primary level and the n buyers have a very clear empirical counterpart in today's "voluntary chains." In voluntary chains, a middleman contracts to be the exclusive supplier for a given group of retailers of an agreed-upon product or group of products. To repay the retailer for losing his choice of source of supply, the middleman supplies him with a number of services.[17] These services are only supplied by middlemen who are part of a voluntary chain and certainly involve the middleman who supplies them in added costs. Such added costs must be adequately covered from the gains of membership in a voluntary chain or no such chain would be created. From the above it is clear that such costs are covered, at least in part, from the middlemen's lower inventory-carrying costs which result from the reduction in the uncertainty of demand that comes with the agreement creating a voluntary chain. They are also partly covered by lower contact costs.

1   The multiplication, under the summation signs, of the term $a_g b_{kg}$ by the element k merely results in the *expectations*, in units of product, of the rth firm rather than the probability as described above.

2   See Chapter 3 about why this last condition can be safely assumed.

3   This follows from an examination of expression (5b) for the case k_r, $k_{r+1} < 0$ and is dependent upon the assumption that $\bar{\mu}_r/\sigma_r > \bar{\mu}_{r+1}/\sigma_{r+1}$. For example assume that $k_r = k_{r+1} < 0$. Such an assumption contradicts the requirement that $\bar{\mu}_r/\sigma_r > \bar{\mu}_{r+1}/\sigma_{r+1}$. Only when $0 > k_{r+1} > k_r$ is it possible to satisfy (5b) and the relationship $\bar{\mu}_r/\sigma_r > \bar{\mu}_{r+1}/\sigma_{r+1}$. By further employing a normal approximation to the individual firm demand density it follows that $\rho(\mu_r > Q_r = \bar{\mu}_r + k_r\sigma_r) > \rho(\mu_{r+1} > Q_{r+1} = \bar{\mu}_{r+1} + k_{r+1}\sigma_{r+1})$.

4   The reader may verify this mathematically by returning to expressions (8) and (9) and comparing the second terms of each, keeping in mind that as r increases the degree of negative skewness of the individual firm's demand density also increases.

5   This implies that the m sellers and n buyers are indifferent to the existence of middlemen in the channel so long as their *previous* costs are not increased with respect to inventory carrying alone.

6   For the case of $\pi = 0$ no inventories will be carried in the system and, therefore, efficiency of inventory carrying cannot serve as a basis for the existence of middlemen.

7   It should be clear that $TEC_w = f(w)$ and for this reason one might question the value of expression (13). It should be noted, however, that while it is virtually impossible to find the functional form $w = f(TEC_w)$ the expression can be numerically evaluated for any w given m, n, π, ϕ, and the vector $\{a_1, a_2, \ldots, a_{\mu_{max}}\}$.

8   Those listed in Chapter 2 are:

   a. Loss of direct contact.
   b. The realization that bargaining could increase profits.

9   Because system output is fixed, as is the original price of output (determined among the m sellers and n buyers), a limiting of rebate size as a proportion of the original (fixed) costs of the system is equivalent to limiting the size of the price reduction as a proportion of the original system price.

10   K is the total number of contacts made in the system by middlemen. This number K, as is shown earlier, is determined as an equilibrium value by competitive conditions and inventory costs, C_1, and the rebate r.

11   While the rebate grant is given to the m sellers, this rebate must also result in a lowering of the price to the n buyers, since their cooperation is necessary for the entry of middlemen into the structure. The actual division of the rebate among the m sellers and n buyers is a matter of the cooperative relationship which exists among themselves as well as the competitive behavior of the firms in each of these basic levels. Since this is a matter of little concern to the analysis now, no attempt will be made to specify this division of the rebate grants from the system's middlemen.

12   Since only whole firms can exist because w_1 is not continuous, this condition can only be *approached* and no guarantee of achievement can be made.

13   Allowing backorders makes the average level of output of the system independent of the number of middlemen. The individual middleman's output from the performance of the financing and storing functions is just the total system output so identified divided by the total number of middlemen.

14   There could be some question regarding the loss of freedom suffered by the middleman when he contracts to serve a sub-set of buyers on an exclusive basis. It is known that while the expected demand of the middleman does not change, the maximum possible demand does change, but this is offset by a reduction in the uncertainty of demand. How these offsetting effects are viewed by the middleman is a matter of individual preferences regarding risk, and for this reason a zero profit state might not result in equilibrium.

15   These two extremes would be zero in the case of total indifference on the part of the n buyers, and $w_1[TEC_{w_1} - TEC_1]$ in the case where the middlemen must yield the maximum rebate.

16
$$\frac{mn - n}{m} > \frac{nm}{m + n}$$
$$(m + n)(m - 1)\frac{n}{m} > mn$$
$$m^2 - m - n + mn > m^2$$
$$mn > m + n$$

which is true for all $m, n > 2$ the necessary condition for this system.

17   For an example of the contents of such a contract see Phillips, Charles F, and Delbert J. Duncan, *Marketing: Principles and Methods*, 4th Edition (Homewood, Ill.: Richard D. Irwin, Inc., 1960), pp. 164–167.

5

Exchange Transactions

A system of waiting lines

A vertical market structure can be characterized as a system of waiting lines. The system is made up of buyers who are serviced in some fashion by sets of selling units. The buyer firms in the system require service in the form of filled orders or completed transactions. The seller firms invest resources to perform this service thereby making it possible to bring the goods exchanged under the required control of the buyer, hence generating revenues. The structure is a system by virtue of the existence of these order-service relationships among the buying and selling firms. One form the system takes is that for which queuing models have been developed. It is useful to employ the concepts of these models to analyze the efficiency of this order-filling aspect of the vertical market structure.

The structure viewed as a system of waiting lines involves two basic types of costs. The first is the cost to the system which results from the time that elapses between the buyer firms' order placements and the filling of orders. The second cost is that of resource employment by the seller firms to fill orders. Given the efficient use of resources, the elapsed time between arrival of an order and its required filling will be less when greater resources are employed in performing the services. There is thus some optimum point for the speed of performing this service, or in other words, for the capacity of the service unit.

It is obvious, furthermore, that structures with or without various levels of middlemen affect the total optimum time-plus-service costs of the structure differently. Thus, one object of what follows is to show precisely how total system costs vary as the structure varies. The exact functions performed by different levels in the structure are also shown to affect these costs, and hence, so does the allocation of the system's required order-filling function to levels and firms in the structure. The proof of these general conclusions and their restatement in more specific terms are the objectives of this and the next chapter.

Processing exchange agreements

If two members of a vertical market structure enter into an exchange agreement, then only one condition out of a number necessary to an exchange transaction is met. Such a transaction occurs if and only if each of the two members has attained the goal which prompted the agreement. The exchange agreement is thus turned into a completed transaction by a process that involves either or both parties in the use of economic resources and the incurring of costs. In essence, one could view this process as a production process whereby, given the agreement of the terms of exchange, inputs are used to bring about the fulfillment of the agreement. The implementation of exchange is the output of the activities identifying this production process.

Inventory, one input to this process, has already been discussed. Inventory carrying involves certain costs and the use of resources, and in turn may make exchange more profitable. Having the product on hand at the instant of agreement on the terms of exchange may not be necessary to the production process leading to the fulfillment of the agreement. However, the previous analysis shows that, other activities included in the production process being totally ignored, the allocation of resources to the input of inventory carrying may indeed render the process more profitable and efficient. Some of the other activities of the process differ from inventory carrying in that they are elements in the execution of the process and not merely determinants of its efficiency. Thus, whereas the process can have a positive output without positive levels of inventory, it cannot have a positive output without positive levels of some other inputs. There are, in fact, minimum constraints on the levels of these inputs if the exchange agreement is to be transformed into an exchange transaction.

From agreement to an actually completed transaction the necessary activities could be given any number of names. The important point is, of course, not the definition of activities but their costs and the relation of outputs to inputs. In order to identify the models employed, however, some definition of these activities should be made. The three main types of activities making up the production process are those of order processing, order filling, and transportation between the parties to the exchange. Of course, each of these could be broken down into component activities and further into jobs and ultimately into tasks. The individual firm must in fact solve the problem of organizing these activities and of determining the levels of inputs employed in them. Given the organization of facilities, different combinations of inputs may be employed to produce a given output. Finally, all decisions on the level of inputs and on organization will include as a variable the cost of waiting for the output of the process.

The firm's decision on process inputs

The models developed are aimed at identifying optimum and equilibrium allocations and organization of the activities involved in the exchange process within the vertical market structure. That is, the optimum total cost of performing these activities, or any others that increase the efficiency of the system and of waiting for the output, are compared for different vertical market structures. The determination of this optimum cost essentially depends on the allocation of the performance of these activities to different levels in the structure and on the individual efficiency of the firm. In order, therefore, to make a comparison of structure efficiency, optimizing decisions of individual firms are considered.

For any given selling firm, the output capacity of the process permitting the effecting of sale and purchase can be viewed as the number of exchange agreements which can be turned into actual transactions in any given time period. Thus, given the supply of agreements (orders), the decision must be made by the firm on the number of these that it is to be capable of processing into transactions per unit of time. This decision involves the resources to be allocated to permit a firm to become an actual operating member in a vertical market structure, the organization of these resources, and the choice, if any, of the services performed on orders.

The decision presents a problem for two reasons. In the first place, revenues and hence profits in any given period are a function of the number of transactions completed. The relationship is dependent, in turn, on the value of time to both buyers and sellers. Even if buyers are willing to wait indefinitely for the agreement to be turned into a transaction, with no return to them for waiting, they are not simultaneously willing to pay for their agreed-upon purchases at the time of agreement. In fact, it may be assumed that waiting is costly to the buyer since the present value of utility or profit resulting from the completed transaction falls as the instant of completion lies further from that of agreement. The shorter the time during which an agreement is processed into a transaction, the lower the waiting cost is to both buyer and seller. The cost to the seller is reflected by his having to wait for his returns from the transaction, or by the lower revenues received at the time of agreement.

To the firm the problem is then to balance the costs of decreasing the time needed to process an agreement against the increases in revenues derived from such time reductions. In other words, it must balance the cost of increasing the output capacity of the process for any given period, and the *cost of waiting*. Of interest here are the costs associated with the *scale* of the process, not those associated with *actual* output which is assumed to have a *fixed expected value* over time. The decision to be made by the firm relates to the scale of a specific segment of its marketing operation. It does not refer to the decision on actual output, which is viewed as being dependent in part on the probabilistic supply of exchange agreements and in part on the scale of operations in a probabilistic manner.

The cost of the output capacity level of the process depends upon the levels of the inputs used. It depends on the capacity levels of activities available to operate on agreements to turn them into transactions. When resources allocated to the performance of these activities are increased, the capacity of the process in terms of output per time period can be expected to increase, at least within some ranges. This means, as is shown below, that the expected waiting costs can be expected to decrease since any agreement now can be processed in a shorter time span. The increases and decreases in these costs also will depend on the manner in which the firm organizes these activities. One reason, therefore, for the existence of a decision problem on the scale of the process is that the organization in terms of sequencing, division of work, the relation of men to machines, etc., will determine in part the output capacity of the process which is made up of these activities.

The firm is partly comprised of a limited and simplified set of activities defining those marketing operations which are involved in the processing of orders. Suppose that these activities were identified as: order receipt and recording; location and counting of items; collection of items; transfer of ordered items to point of shipment; recording transactions; preparation of bill; receipt of money; and transportation and delivery of ordered items. Excluding the last activity, the case might be, in effect, a non-self-service cash-and-carry wholesale or retail operation organized so that the buyer merely orders, receives goods and bill, and makes payment. The firm could organize the activities and sequence them in a number of ways, one of which involves the use of a single employee performing in some sequence all these activities. The single employee is probably capable of producing the completed set of activities a given number of times in a given time period. Two employees may be hired and the work each does determined in some given way. The capacity of the process may then be expected to increase, with such an increase being determined by the decision on how to allocate the activities between the two employees.

For purposes of the analysis in this and the next chapter it is assumed that the organization and determination of the proportions of the man and machine inputs are optimized by the firm for every level of total costs incurred in any given period.[1] The only decision which remains is that of determining the capacity of the process per time period. Though this assumption is rather vast in its implications, its removal would complicate tremendously the models developed below but would not change their basic nature.

Demand and service patterns

As it is realistic to view the demand generated by all the firms in the group of n buyers as probabilistic, so is it realistic to view the timing of the generation of orders by this same group as being probabilistic. It is postulated that in any given time period of fixed length T the n firms order any given number of times with some probability. Furthermore, the emission of the orders in the same period is now considered to occur at intervals, the length of which is probabilistically distributed. In terms of the inventory models, depletion of stock is no longer evenly distributed throughout the period. Its rate of depletion is probabilistically distributed because both the arrival pattern of the orders over time and the rate of filling these orders are probabilistic.

Consider now the n buyers, each generating a stream of orders over time, and ignore for the moment the destination of these orders. If we assume now that each buyer orders at instants in time independently of the orders of all other buyers and all previous orders by the same buyer then all orders generated will be distributed in a Poisson fashion. In turn, if these orders are allocated randomly among the m sellers, for example, then each such seller is faced with an arrival pattern of orders which is also characterized by a Poisson distribution. The mean and variance of the individual firm order arrival Poisson distribution will be $(1/m)$th of those of the total distribution.[2]

Each seller in the structure determines the capacity of his own process of filling orders. We will view the inputs which are employed in the process as determining the probability distribution of the capacity of the process. It is assumed that any given order will take a time to be processed, the length of which is characterized by an exponential probability distribution. The two characterizations, the capacity distribution and the service time (order-filling time) distribution are two ways of characterizing the same process.[3]

It may be argued that if some buyer happens to have a series of experiences with one seller, all of which involve a very lengthy waiting time, that the buyer eventually would prefer to go elsewhere. That is, any series of events may be used by buyers to develop opinions on the expected waiting times for orders placed with different sellers. Realistically, this would be a very reasonable hypothesis, which would mean that arrival patterns may or may not reach the stable point, and if they did there would no longer be a perfectly random coupling of buyers and sellers. In developing the model, however, this possibility for learning from experiences is eliminated by a number of assumptions and by the particular form of the costs to sellers of having buyers wait for service. The possibility that the inputs are not optimally combined by each firm, and hence the possibility for learning and improvement, are assumed away. In short, the arrival and service time distributions are assumed to be stationary.

The assumption of the stability of arrivals implies the assumptions that all seller firms are identical in efficiency, in ability to optimize the process input combinations, and in their competitive strengths. Every seller firm, therefore, has no advantage from any competitive strategy; any action on its part can be matched by all other firms. In turn, whatever the cost of the buyer's waiting time to the sellers, it is the same per unit of such time for all firms. The firm, by varying this cost in an attempt to introduce preference among buyers for it over other sellers, will not be successful.[4] Given a waiting cost to buyers, any buying firm will seek that seller whose operations minimize this cost or who is willing to incur it.

If one seller were not to incur this cost, and every other seller did, then preference by buyers for this firm's *competitors* would develop. All selling firms, therefore, incur on the average equal proportions of the waiting costs of buyers. Also by assumption the sellers assume this entire cost.[5] The exact amount of the cost of waiting to buyers per unit of time is a parameter in the system dependent on exogenous demand variables.

Intermediaries as coordinators in
vertical market structures

Both in the analysis of contact and communication costs and the analysis of inventory costs, changes in vertical market structures are related to the system's efficiency. Such changes are basically those which involve the existence of intermediaries. From the proofs and explanations given for the effects of structure on the efficiency of performing say, the inventory function, one can conclude that the more efficient structures are in general better coordinated than the less efficient ones. With one middleman the total system's inventory problem is solved optimally, whereas with no middleman, a number of inventory problems, one for each m, are solved *independently* of one another. The difference in the two cases is, surely, one of coordination.

The concept of coordination requires a somewhat more detailed exposition, since analyses of the costs of the time and of the process of filling orders involve the discussion of intermediaries that may operate in a special manner. It is shown in the analysis below that a single intermediary, considering only these two kinds of costs in the system, would increase the system's efficiency if he were to perform the complete functions which generate these costs. The intermediary would increase efficiency by the same means as he did in the inventory cases, by taking over the performance of a function.

In addition, the introduction of an intermediary who performs only a purely coordinative function is possible. In this latter case an entirely new kind of problem, and hence entirely new decision, is created. The decision is one involving the manner in which the original sellers and buyers are paired off for completed transactions. This new and purely coordinative function performed by a middleman, in turn, leads to changes in the decision on process capacity by each of the original m sellers. The reduction in waiting and process costs which an optimum decision to this new problem brings about is coupled with increased costs of communication.

Coordination is best defined in terms of the lack of independence in the formulation of the problems of sub-systems within a system. Coordination is at its maximum possible level when all the variables making up the system, or all sub-systems within it, are treated simultaneously within a single formulation of the problem. For this definition to be meaningful, one must be capable of measuring various levels of coordination. However, to do so in terms of units of independence in problem formulation is obviously extremely difficult, since such units of measurement are unfortunately vague. Comparison of degrees of coordination within and among systems using such units ignores the magnitude of the decision problems to be formulated. Consequently, a more meaningful measure for coordination based on units of the *output* of coordination is now devised.

Coordination has an output and incurs a cost. For purposes of our analysis, the output to coordination is the total reduction in all costs of a vertical market structure, the total output of which is held constant.[6] The cost of obtaining a given level of output with no coordination can be, for example, Y. Coordinating the system by varying the structure in some fashion, and holding its output in terms of average orders serviced per unit time constant, leads to total system costs net of coordinating costs of, for example, X. The output to coordination is given by $(Y-X)$. This value is always non-negative because of the definition of coordination. The value is used as the basis for measuring the amount of coordination, but not until a number of conditions are clearly stated.

The first condition refers to the existence of a random element in the value of $(Y-X)$. It is possible that optimization of sub-systems independently of one another would produce a total system cost figure (for constant output) which equals the total system costs in the case of coordination. Each sub-system may make certain assumptions about all others, and these assumptions may by pure chance produce a total system cost as low as that obtained by simultaneous treatment of all sub-systems, i. e., by conscious coordination. For this reason the *value* of the output of coordination is characterized by the expected value of $(Y-X)$. It is obvious from the definition of coordination that $E(Y-X)$ for nontrivial decisions increases monotonically with coordination, up to some given maximum, and is hence used as a measure of such coordination.

A second condition for using this measure of coordination is that, as stated, we hold the total system's total average output constant throughout the models. The third and final condition is that we apply the concept of coordination only to *systems*, since the whole issue of coordination is irrelevant if the simultaneous treatment of the variables will conceptually never give a different result from their independent treatment; that is, if the variables do not form a *system*. Systems, therefore, are indeed the things which are coordinated. They are made up of *dependent* input and output variables. This dependence gives coordination meaning and a logically feasible output.

Achieving any level of coordination involves some cost. The costs of coordination are those associated with the removal of independent decision-making. It costs more to treat the system as a whole than it would to treat sub-systems independently since the information needed in the former case is greater than in the latter. In essence, by treating sub-systems independently, the costs of the information on the exact nature of the dependence of the sub-systems is avoided. Since, therefore, coordination involves some costs, the optimum amount of coordination must be solved for only after the costs of dependence are considered. In general the costs of coordination come from two sources: the need for information which increases as the number of independently treated sub-systems is reduced, and the development of more complex decision criteria which are needed as more variables are treated simultaneously.[7]

Consider the problem which each of the m sellers faces with respect to the decision on order-processing capacity. Assume a structure with no intermediaries, a constant output in terms of orders processed per unit time, and totally random arrivals of orders from the n buyers. Ignore for the moment the issues of contact and communication and inventory carrying. Each seller among the m optimizes the expected capacity of the order-processing function. If all the m firms are identical and order arrivals are perfectly random (no preference), then all will have the same optimum solution. Given such independent behavior, what is the structure's total cost of order processing and waiting by the n buyers?

The structure just described will include situations where some sellers have orders waiting to be filled and others are without orders to process at all. Since waiting involves cost it is possible that something might be done to reduce profitably this unnecessary waiting. A possible solution is, of course, to find out at some cost just which firms are free and to direct those waiting buyers to them. Doing something to avoid the possibility of such waiting could actually reduce the cost of the order-filling process, at the same time holding constant the total output of the system. A structure of this type is in effect one in which each m solves optimally only for a sub-system, including himself and the n sellers. The combination of such sub-system optima is far different from the total system's optimum solution.

In a vertical market structure it is possible to introduce an intermediary who could coordinate the entire system profitably. Given the costs of the information needed to coordinate the behavior of the m sellers and the n buyers, it is possible for a single intermediary to reduce the probability of an order's waiting at a particular seller while at least one other seller is free. It is in fact possible that the probability of such an event's occurring be reduced to zero. The cost of such a reduction must, of course, be balanced against the gain to the entire system resulting from the intermediaries' behavior. The presence of an intermediary between the m and the n could turn m independent sellers into the *equivalent* of a single firm with m processing units, and hence could increase the efficiency of the total system.

To perform this purely coordinative function the intermediary incurs costs of gathering information on the status of the m processing units (occupied-free). In return he reduces the time an unfilled order spends in the system and the optimum expected capacity of each process unit, thereby reducing both the cost of time for all orders in the system and the cost of all processing capacity. If the cost of attaining this coordination is exceeded by the coordination derived (defined as an increase in output, or reduction in this case of the two other costs) then a vertical market structure with one intermediary would be more efficient than an uncoordinated one without an intermediary. It may also be the case that coordination is less costly to obtain in a vertical market structure with an intermediary than in another without one. If this were also true, then the former structure would be more efficient than the latter in implementing exchange transactions.

The firm's decision on expected process capacity

In a vertical market structure that has no intermediaries the arrival of orders from the n buyers to the individual seller among the m is assumed to be distributed in a Poisson fashion. The number of orders which can be processed in any time period of length T by a given order-filling process is also characterized by a Poisson distribution. This distribution has a mean which is uniquely related to the amount of resources invested in the process capacity and the length of the time period (T). If we define the relevant time period to be of unit length, then the individual seller is faced by a mean arrival rate (λ_m), and must decide on the process mean service rate (v_m) or the amount of resources he is to invest in a process with a given mean service rate.

It is assumed that the mean arrival rate is fixed over time. The functional relationship between the mean service rate and the cost incurred, or resources committed to the attainment of such a rate, are also assumed constant over time. The firm's problem is to minimize its expected costs of operating the service unit or process, plus the costs it incurs as a result of the time an order spends in the firm's system. It does so by choosing a particular service rate, v_m, or an average order-filling capacity per unit time. If we now assume that the firm's lead time for altering the service rate v_m is very lengthy and much greater than the unit period, it will be shown that the firm determines the optimum mean process capacity by setting the average service rate v_m at a level such that:

$$(1) \qquad v_m = \sqrt{\frac{C_1 \lambda_m}{C_2}} + \lambda_m$$

In this equation the terms are identified as follows:

C_1 = cost to the selling firm of having an order in its system per unit time, i. e., from the instant of its arrival to the instant it is filled. (Dollars per order per unit time an order spends in the m's system.)

C_2 = cost of maintaining and operating a service unit of mean service rate (mean capacity per unit time) of one order per unit of time. A service unit of mean service rate of orders v_m per unit time costs $C_2 v_m$ dollars per unit time to operate and maintain. (Dollars per unit of service rate.)

λ = average number of orders generated by the n buyers per unit time; it is the mean of the Poisson distribution of orders generated by the n buyers per unit time.

$\lambda_m = \dfrac{\lambda}{m}$ = mean order arrival rate at the service unit of the single seller among the m sellers per unit time; it is the mean of the Poisson distribution of order arrivals per unit time for the selling firm.

The minimum total expected cost to the firm per unit time for the performance of the order-filling function occurs when the firm chooses the optimum service rate $v_m = \sqrt{\dfrac{C_1 \lambda_m}{C_2}} + \lambda_m$ and is:

$$(2) \qquad TEC_m^* = 2\sqrt{C_1 C_2 \lambda_m} + C_2 \lambda_m.$$

In order to arrive at these two equations, the total order-filling cost function for the individual seller among the m must be obtained in terms of the decision variable v_m. To do so the individual seller system's states, in terms of the probability of various numbers of orders in the system at instants in time, must be derived. Let P_x be the probability that there are x orders in the individual seller system at any *instant* in time. In the Appendix it is shown that:

$$P_x = \left(\frac{n\alpha}{v_m r}\right)^x P_0$$

where,

n = number of buyers.
α = expected orders generated by an individual buyer per unit time
v_m = seller's service rate per unit time.
r = number of competing sellers, $r = m$ in this case.
P_o = probability that there are zero units in the system of the single seller at an instant of time.

Since, as it is shown in the Appendix, the mean order generation rate by the n buyers per unit time is $n\alpha = \lambda$, and since $\frac{\lambda}{m}$ is the mean arrival rate for the individual seller among the m, the equation can be rewritten as:

(3) $\qquad P_x = \left(\frac{\lambda_m}{v_m}\right)^x P_0$, where $P_0 = 1 - \frac{\lambda_m}{v_m}$.

The average number of orders in a single seller's system at any instant in time is designated by A_m and is defined as:

(4) $\qquad A_m = \sum_{x=0}^{\infty} x P_x$

or, $\qquad A_m = P_0 \sum_{x=0}^{\infty} x \left(\frac{\lambda_m}{v_m}\right)^x = P_0 \sum_{x=0}^{\infty} x \rho^x$

where $\qquad \rho = \frac{\lambda_m}{v_m}$

Substituting for P_0

$$A_m = \lim_{g \to \infty} (1 - \rho)\rho[1 + 2\rho + 3\rho^2 + \cdots + g\rho^{g-1}], \text{ and}$$

$$\frac{A_m}{\rho(1 - \rho)} = K_m = \lim_{g \to \infty} [1 + 2\rho + 3\rho^2 + \cdots + g\rho^{g-1}]$$

Let,

$$L_m = \int_0^{\infty} K_m d\rho = \lim_{g \to \infty} [\rho + \rho^2 + \cdots + \rho^g]$$

This reduces to,

$$L_m = \frac{\rho}{1 - \rho}$$

In addition, in order to obtain K_m,

$$\frac{d}{d\rho} L_m = K_m = \rho(1 - \rho)^{-2} + (1 - \rho)^{-1}$$

and hence,

$$K_m = \frac{1}{(1 - \rho)^2}$$

Since,

$$K_m = \frac{A_m}{\rho(1 - \rho)}$$

then, the average number of orders in a seller's system is

$$A_m = \frac{\rho}{(1 - \rho)}$$

Since $\rho = \frac{\lambda_m}{v_m}$

(5)
$$A_m = \frac{\lambda_m}{v_m - \lambda_m}$$

The average time an order spends in the system of the single seller is the product of the average number of units in the system and the average time between the departing or filled orders, i.e.,

$$\varphi_m = A_m \frac{1}{\lambda_m} = \frac{\lambda_m}{\lambda_m(v_m - \lambda_m)}, \text{ or}$$

(6)
$$\varphi_m = \frac{1}{v_m - \lambda_m}$$

The basic reasoning behind equation (6) is that an order which arrives at the single seller's process unit expects to be in the system for a time period which depends on the average number of orders in the system and the average rate at which the process unit fills these orders. This rate, however, is made up of two parts. When the system is not empty the service rate is v_m. When the system is empty it is, of course, zero. The mean departure rate of orders is thus, v_m multiplied by the probability that the system is not empty, plus zero multiplied by the probability that the system is empty. It is thus:

$$v_m(1 - P_o) + oP_o = v_m(1 - P_o).$$

The average time it takes to service an order is thus $\frac{1}{v_m(1 - P_o)}$. Since the system is in steady state and $P_o = 1 - \lambda_m/v_m$ it is clear that $v_m(1 - P_o) = \lambda_m$. Substituting for A_m from (5):

$$\varphi_m = \left(\frac{\lambda_m}{v_m - \lambda_m}\right)\left(\frac{1}{\lambda_m}\right), \text{ or}$$

$$\varphi_m = \frac{1}{v_m - \lambda_m}$$

The sum total of the times which all orders are expected to spend in the single seller's system determines the total expected waiting costs for the seller. This total is given by the expected arrival rate multiplied by the expected time each spends in the system $\left(\dfrac{\lambda_m}{v_m - \lambda_m}\right)$ and surprisingly, is equal to the average number of orders in the firm's system at any instant in time, A_m.

Total expected costs for the single seller's performance of the order-filling function can now obtained. If C_1 is the cost of having an order in the system per unit time, and C_2 is the cost of maintaining and operating a process unit with a mean service capacity of one order per unit time, the total expected costs per unit time for the single seller are

$$TEC_m = C_1 A_m + C_2 v_m$$

or,

(7)
$$TEC_m = C_1 \frac{\lambda_m}{v_m - \lambda_m} + C_2 v_m$$

Since for the single seller and all m sellers, λ_m, C_1, and C_2 are parameters by assumption, minimizing TEC_m involves only the choice of v_m. Thus the seller to minimize TEC_m sets

$$\frac{d}{dv_m} TEC_m = 0 = -C_1 \lambda_m (v_m - \lambda_m)^{-2} + C_2$$

Solving for v_m the optimum is as given in equation (1), or

$$v_m^* = \sqrt{\frac{C_1 \lambda_m}{C_2}} + \lambda_m$$

Substituting the optimum v_m in equation (7), the minimum total expected costs per unit time are:

$$TEC_m^* = C_1 \frac{\lambda_m}{\sqrt{\dfrac{C_1 \lambda_m}{C_2}} + \lambda_m - \lambda_m} + C_2 \left(\sqrt{\frac{C_1 \lambda_m}{C_2}} + \lambda_m\right)$$

This reduces to equation (2), viz.,

$$TEC_m^* = 2\sqrt{C_1 C_2 \lambda_m} + C_2 \lambda_m$$

Total system costs with no intermediaries

The model to this point incorporates a number of minor assumptions. Work on filling an order by the individual seller's process unit starts the instant the previous order's filling process is completed, provided the new order is present in the system at that instant. There is no time lost by a single process unit in shifting from servicing one order completely to starting service on another if it is available. Each seller is assumed to have a single processing unit which operates on only one single order at a time. It can be easily shown that if there are no diseconomies or economies of scale of the process unit's capacity, it is always preferable for the seller to have a single unit capable of operating on only one order at a time with expected capacity of v_m, than it is to have any other number of process units k (for k greater than 1) with expected capacities of $\frac{v_m}{k}$ each. In the former case the expected waiting time, that is the expected time in system, for the same total cost associated with a total v_m, given constant returns to scale, is always less than it is in the latter.[8] The assumption is therefore reasonable.

Implicit in the constant cost per order per unit time are a number of assumptions. Buyers do not incur disproportionate disutilities as the time they wait increases. They do not differentiate between the time spent in waiting for the order-filling to start and the time it takes to fill the order once the process does start. Both assumptions can be easily relaxed without altering the essence of the analysis. The parameter C_1 can be made a function of the time in the queue and the time in service. The total cost for any given time spent in the system is just the sum of the two functions at the appropriate values of these two variables. In this case, the possibility that many service units, under the same assumption on returns to scale, are more profitable than a single station (which by definition works on only one order at a time) will exist and must be accounted for either by assumption or by analysis. Finally it is assumed that the servicing unit is incapable of instantaneous adjustment of its service capacity rate to the number of people actually in the system.

In the model of the vertical market structure with no intermediaries, the total minimum expected system costs of waiting and order-filling process capacity per unit time are made up of the sum of these costs to each individual seller. Since all sellers among the m are identical with respect to the relevant variables, the total minimum expected costs are the product of the number m and the individual seller's costs. Thus, from equation (2) the *system's* minimum expected costs per unit time are:

$$SEC = m(2\sqrt{C_1 C_2 \lambda_m} + C_2 \lambda_m)$$

Since λ_m is defined as λ/m, this reduces to:

(8)
$$SEC = 2\sqrt{C_1 C_2 m \lambda} + C_2 \lambda$$

Middlemen as order fillers

Consider a structure with m sellers, n buyers, and a single middleman or intermediary. In such a structure, just what does the middleman do? What are the characteristics of the bonds between the middleman and the original sellers and buyers which permit this intermediary to be a member of the system? In the case of contact and communication the middleman operates as the supplier and receiver of information. In the case of inventory the middleman determines and generally assumes all the risks and requirements of the decision on inventory levels.

The costs that are presently under consideration are only those associated with the resources necessary to implement exchange transactions and those associated with the time an order spends in the system. The single middleman's operations obviously must have something to do with the performance of the order-filling function of exchange. Suppose the middleman were to set up an order-processing unit and, upon receipt of the orders from the n buyers, would fill these orders. Thus the middleman would perform on the orders from the group of n buyers the functions that would have been performed by the m sellers. Unless the middleman also takes over all the producing functions of the initial group of sellers (in which case the structure would be without intermediaries and not that structure which we would wish to consider) he would need to have the cooperation of the m firms which now must invest in some resources to fill the orders of the middleman. Given then that the middleman's presence in the structure is predicated upon his requiring some form of service from the m sellers in order that he might be capable of completely filling the orders from the n buyers, is such a structure possible? That is, given that the middleman operates in this manner, could he improve, or not decrease, the efficiency of the system, so that he could leave unaffected or improved the profits that would have accrued to the m sellers and n buyers in his absence and still find it possible to make positive profits?

The vertical market structure with one intermediary involves two costs. One is the cost to the middleman of servicing the buyer group's orders. The other is the cost to the system of filling the orders that must be generated by the single middleman. The cost to the intermediary of servicing the orders from the n buyers must be obtained. Assuming an organization of services identical to that of each of the m sellers, a single intermediary would expect to incur order servicing and waiting costs per unit time of

$$TEC_w = C_1 A_w + C_2 v_w; \text{ for } w = 1$$

Given that the arrival rate of orders to the single middleman is $\lambda_w = \lambda$, for $w = 1$, and that v_w is the middleman's mean order servicing rate per unit time, the total expected cost figure (as in the case of single seller) is:

(9) $$TEC_w = C_1 \frac{\lambda}{v_w - \lambda} + C_2 v_w; \text{ for } w = 1$$

To obtain the optimum service rate for the single middleman we set

$$\frac{d}{dv_w} TEC_w = 0 = -C_1 \lambda (v_w - \lambda)^{-2} + C_2$$

and, solving, obtain the optimum service rate,

$$v_w^* = \sqrt{\frac{C_1\lambda}{C_2}} + \lambda$$

Substituting this value of v_w into equation (9) we obtain the minimum total expected cost of servicing orders in the system for the single middleman in the structure per unit time;

(10) $$TEC_w^* = 2\sqrt{C_1C_2\lambda} + C_2\lambda$$

The minimum total expected cost in the absence of any intermediaries for all m sellers is given in equation (8):

(8) $$SEC = 2\sqrt{C_1C_2m\lambda} + C_2\lambda$$

The single middleman can gain the cooperation of the m sellers and n buyers and exist as part of the structure when he operates in the fashion described, only if the costs to the system of having the *middleman's orders serviced* equal, or are less, than the difference $SEC - TEC_w^*$ per unit time. If the middleman's orders are not serviced, then, of course, he cannot fill the orders of the group of buyers and meet the condition that the system's output remain unchanged. As is postulated, the middleman cannot operate in the form of an original seller and replace them all. The costs to the system of servicing the middleman's orders thus are needed before the two vertical market structures are compared.

Suppose that in his ordering process the middleman merely ordered from the m sellers as he filled orders for the n buyers. That is, every order he fills generates an order from him to one of the m sellers. Suppose also that the middleman allocated his orders to the m sellers in a random fashion. Under these conditions the arrival rate of orders from the single middleman to each individual seller is λ_m. That is, since the middleman generates orders at the *average rate* at which he services them, and since in steady state he services an average of λ orders per unit of time, the expected number of orders received from him by each seller is merely $\frac{\lambda}{m} = \lambda_m$ per unit of time. The cost to each seller of servicing the middleman's orders when the seller's service unit is at optimum capacity is:

$$TEC_m^* = 2\sqrt{C_1C_2\lambda_m} + C_2\lambda_m$$

and the cost to all m sellers combined is

(11) $$mTEC_m^* = 2\sqrt{C_1C_2m\lambda} + C_2\lambda$$

This assumes that the cost to the individual seller of having a middleman's order in the system per unit time is the same as that of having an order from the n buyers. The time a middleman's order remains in the selling group's system determines in part the expected time that a buyer's order will remain in the middleman's system. The middleman must maintain a buffer inventory to be able to fill the orders from the initial buying group. The rate at which he depletes this buffer must be matched by the rate at which the selling firms add to it. If this is not the case the buffer level will go to infinity or to zero. With zero buffer inventories, the middleman cannot service any orders, and the time which orders from the buyers spend in his system mounts rapidly. By allowing the compensation for waiting of an order in the system to be equal to that required of him by the n buyers, the middleman assures himself of a level of buffer inventories with a constant average. He also does not alter the profit to the buyers and sellers by so doing.

The total cost of the system without intermediaries can be viewed as the total revenue of the single middleman when he is in the system. Equation (11) is thus the middleman's total revenue. Total costs to the middleman are made up of those expressed in equation (10), i.e., the costs of servicing the n group's orders and the costs of the service units at the m level. This latter is merely $mC_2v_m^*$, where v_m^* is the optimum expected capacity of each seller among the m group, under the conditions of randomly allocated arrivals from the middleman at the average rate λ_m. Total expected profits per unit time can thus be defined as the difference between total revenue and total expected costs or:

$$(12) \quad TEP_w = 2\sqrt{C_1 C_2 m\lambda} + C_2\lambda - 2\sqrt{C_1 C_2 \lambda} - C_2\lambda$$
$$- mC_2\left[\sqrt{\frac{C_1\lambda_m}{C_2}} + \lambda_m\right]$$

where $\left(\sqrt{\dfrac{C_1\lambda_m}{C_2}} + \lambda_m\right)$ is the value of the optimum expected service rate capacity v_m^* of each of the m sellers.

Since $\lambda_m = \dfrac{\lambda}{m}$, the last term in equation (12) becomes

$$\sqrt{C_1 C_2 m\lambda} + C_2\lambda,$$

and the equation reduces to

$$TEP_w = \sqrt{C_1 C_2 m\lambda} - 2\sqrt{C_1 C_2 \lambda} - C_2\lambda \quad \text{for} \quad w = 1$$

For the middleman to be capable of remaining a member of the system, his total expected profits per unit time must be greater than or equal to zero. Thus, the condition for his existence is,

$$\sqrt{C_1 C_2 m\lambda} - 2\sqrt{C_1 C_2 \lambda} - C_2\lambda > 0$$

This reduces to

$$\sqrt{m} - 2 \geq \sqrt{\frac{C_2\lambda}{C_1}}$$

and finally to

$$(13) \quad m \geq \frac{C_2\lambda}{C_1} + 2\sqrt{\frac{C_2\lambda}{C_1}} + 4$$

It can be shown, however, that a middleman operating in this fashion does not maximize his profits. The middleman could still operate by filling the orders of the n buyers and weaken the condition for his membership in the system as given in equation (13). Instead of generating orders randomly to the m sellers at the rate of λ, the rate at which he services the orders, the middleman could leave a standing order with each of the m sellers. The order states that the service capacity of each process unit (each of the m sellers) be set at λ_m and that each seller is to operate the facility *continuously* and not wait for each order before starting to process. Each of the m sellers would thus be servicing an average of λ_m orders per unit time for the middleman. This is the rate at which they actually serviced under the middleman's procedure of generating orders only on their receipt from the n buyers. The middleman's total cost per unit of time of having his orders serviced would be $mC_2v_m^*$ where v_m^* is equal to λ_m instead of being equal to $\sqrt{C_1\lambda_m/C_2} + \lambda_m$. Total expected profits per unit time would now become

(14) $\qquad TEP_w = 2\sqrt{C_1C_2m\lambda} + C_2\lambda - 2\sqrt{C_1C_2\lambda} - C_2\lambda - mC_2\lambda_m$

Again, the condition of the middleman's membership in the system, since $\lambda_m = \dfrac{\lambda}{m}$, is that:

$$2\sqrt{C_1C_2m\lambda} - 2\sqrt{C_1C_2\lambda} - C_2\lambda \geq 0$$

which finally reduces to

(15) $\qquad\qquad m \geq \dfrac{C_2\lambda}{4C_1} + \sqrt{\dfrac{C_2\lambda}{C_1}} + 1$

In comparing the two conditions for the two procedures for the middleman, it is obvious that equation (15) is less stringent than equation (13) since:

$$\dfrac{C_2\lambda}{C_1} + 2\sqrt{\dfrac{C_2\lambda}{C_1}} + 4 > \dfrac{C_2\lambda}{4C_1} + \sqrt{\dfrac{C_2\lambda}{C_1}} + 1$$

or $\qquad \sqrt{\dfrac{C_2\lambda}{C_1}} + \dfrac{3C_2\lambda}{4C_1} + 3 > 0$ which is true for all $C_1, C_2, \lambda > 0$

In both conditions it is interesting to note a number of factors. In the first place, for any given λ, C_1, and C_2, the middleman's profits per unit time increase as m increases. The larger m is, the more likely it is that the middleman could become a member of a vertical market structure for any values of the other variables. In the second place it also appears that products with larger waiting costs in the system (a larger C_1) increase the possibility of positive profits for a middleman.

Both conditions are derived on the basis that costs of buffer inventories for the middleman are totally ignored, and that costs of placing orders are in effect equal to zero. Relaxation of the first assumption occurs below in the discussion of multi-functional middlemen. The second assumption is a minor one and easily handled by assigning some cost parameter, say C_3, to be greater than 0 per unit time, to the contact facility between any two firms, or to the placing of an order.

The middleman as a pure coordinator

The middleman can operate as a pure coordinator within the system. He receives and holds, if necessary, the orders of the buyers in a queue, and on a first come–first served basis, directs each to a process unit as these become free. He would in fact operate as would a decision maker who had a single firm of m distinct process units, each with some expected service capacity v_m. The middleman would not have the costs of maintaining an order-filling process unit as a part of his operation of capacity v_w. It is assumed for the moment that there are no costs of facilities for the middleman to operate in this manner, except those relating to the necessary information costs.

The middleman therefore operates as matcher of buyer and seller. He receives the orders from the n buyers, and gathers, at some cost, information which permits him to know which of the m sellers are processing an order and which are not. On receipt of the order, one of two situations would occur: there is a seller with a "free" process unit, one in which the service unit is not presently filling an order; and there is no free seller. In the first case it is assumed that the order is sent instantly, with no loss in time at all, to one of the free sellers for filling. The sellers are chosen on the basis of the length of time they have been free to this point. Of the free sellers the one which has been free the longest time gets the order. In the second case the middleman holds the orders from the n buyers. He releases them instantaneously by the rank of their arrival to his operation as each seller becomes free.

In order to operate in this manner, the middleman must have continuous knowledge of the state of each seller. Thus it is visualized that a system of contacts is developed whereby the instant a seller is free he informs the middleman, a communication involving an infinitesimally small period of time which can be safely ignored. It is also visualized that the middleman records the names of sellers who report themselves free and places each one at the bottom of the list of sellers who are still free. The process is again instantaneous (or takes a negligibly small period of time which can thus be ignored.) On the arrival of an order, it is sent immediately to the seller at the top of the list, and the list is updated. If on the report of a seller that he is free, an order from one of the n buyers is waiting at the middleman, this order is sent on for processing, and the seller is left in the list of busy seller process units.

With this form of operation can a middleman exist in a structure, that is, be a member of the system and make total expected profits per unit time of zero or more? To answer one must first characterize the steady-state conditions for the entire vertical market structure with one intermediary. It may be recalled that the system operates as if it were made up of a single seller firm with m process units. Using the queuing models for such firms to characterize the vertical market structure, it can be shown from the system's steady-state equation that[9]

$$(16) \qquad \sum_{x=0}^{\infty} P_x = \sum_{x=m}^{\infty} \frac{\left(\dfrac{\lambda}{v_m}\right)^x}{m! \, m^{x-m}} P_0 + \sum_{x=0}^{m-1} \frac{\left(\dfrac{\lambda}{v_m}\right)^x}{x!} P_0$$

where

P_x = the probability that there are x orders in the system of m selling firms (service stations) and the middleman's queue.

Since $\sum_{x=0}^{\infty} P_x = 1$, it can be shown that the probability that the system is empty is:

$$(17) \qquad P_0 = \cfrac{1}{\displaystyle\sum_{x=0}^{m-1} \frac{\left(\dfrac{\lambda}{v_m}\right)^x}{x!} + \frac{\left(\dfrac{\lambda}{v_m}\right)^m}{m!} \left(\dfrac{m}{m - \dfrac{\lambda}{v_m}}\right)}$$

where:

m = number of service units or individual sellers in the vertical market structure.

λ = arrival rate of orders at the single middleman's operation per unit time for the whole system.

v_m = the expected service capacity per unit time of *each* process unit or seller firm.

$\dfrac{\lambda}{mv_m} = \dfrac{\lambda_m}{v_m} < 1$ (the stability of queue length condition)

The costs to the system are again made up of the costs of the time which orders spend in the system and those of the service or process unit. In addition, system costs involve the costs of obtaining the knowledge on the status of each seller (occupied or free) in order to operate in this manner. Ignoring for the moment this last cost, the total expected costs per unit time for the system, with one middleman operating, are

$$SEC'_w = \lambda C_1 \varphi_m + m C_2 v_m$$

where φ_m is the average time an order spends in the system.

Again φ_m can be obtained in terms of λ, v_m and m, and this equation becomes

$$(18) \qquad SEC'_w = C_1 \left(\frac{\lambda v_m \left(\dfrac{\lambda}{v_m}\right)^m}{(m-1)! \, (mv_m - \lambda)^2} P_0 + \frac{\lambda}{v_m} \right) + m C_2 v_m$$

The optimum service rate of each process unit must be obtained. To solve *simultaneously* for all the m sellers we can view the problem as that of the middleman who undertakes all costs of the system, and who is constrained by the fact that the system must have m process units or sellers. The const-straint stems from the requirement that structures compared for efficiency must have the identical number of sellers and the identical number of buyers. A middleman cannot exist unless he obtains the cooperation of all the m sellers and n buyers. To obtain the optimal v_m we first must differentiate equation (18) with respect to v_m. The complexity of this step can be tremend-ously reduced with very little cost to the nature of the analysis if it is assumed that the number of process units or sellers m is large.

Under this assumption the total expected cost equation for the system is simplified, since the average time an arrival spends in the system is simpli-fied. As m increases, P_o approaches rapidly the value $e^{-\lambda/v_m}$. Similarly the term $\dfrac{\lambda v_m \left(\dfrac{\lambda}{v_m}\right)^m}{(m-1)!\,(mv_m - \lambda)^2}$ approaches zero rapidly as m increases. Thus under the assumption of a fairly large number of sellers, the total expected costs (per unit time) of the vertical market structure with one middleman approach

(19) $$SEC'_w = C_1\left(\frac{\lambda}{v_m}\right) + mC_2 v_m$$

The middleman, to minimize these costs, must set $\dfrac{d}{dv_m} SEC'_w = 0$. Solving, he obtains the optimum v_m^* as:

$$v_m^* = \sqrt{\frac{C_1\lambda_m}{C_2}}.$$

Minimum total expected costs to the system are obtained by substituting this value of v_m^* into equation (19), and are:

$$SEC'^*_w = \frac{C_1\lambda}{\sqrt{\dfrac{C_1\lambda}{C_2 m}}} + C_2 m\sqrt{\frac{C_1\lambda}{C_2 m}}$$

or

(20) $$SEC'^*_w = 2\sqrt{C_1 C_2 m\lambda}.$$

In order for the middleman to operate in the manner of a single firm with m process units and to attain this cost figure of equation (20), he requires continuous knowlege of the status of each of the m sellers. Obtaining know-ledge of this constantly-changing status involves the middleman in some cost. This cost must be added to SEC'^*_w in order to obtain all the relevant costs of the system and to compare these with the cost of the system without the middleman and without coordination.

Suppose that the middleman stores information on the occupied-free status of each seller. At the instant that a seller m becomes free he calls the middleman at a cost of C_3 to inform him of his change of status. Assuming that the call takes an infinitesimally small amount of time, the total number of calls received by the middleman per unit time is λ. This is the average rate at which orders are completed by the m sellers in the steady state and hence the average rate at which they become free. Total costs per unit time of obtaining this information, necessary for the operation which permits maximum coordination, are $C_3\lambda$. The middleman is also involved in costs of entering this information into records, that is, maintaining a list of the free sellers and their identity, updating the list by removing the sellers to whom he sends an order, and maintaining the rank of the free sellers by order of the arrival of this information from each that he is free. Assuming this cost per unit time is C_4, the system's minimum total expected cost per unit time when it operates with one middleman and attains maximum coordination is:

(25) $$SEC^*_w = 2\sqrt{C_1 C_2 m\lambda} + C_3\lambda + C_4$$

The system's total expected cost per unit time without the middleman and without coordination is given in equation **(8)** as:

(8) $$SEC = 2\sqrt{C_1 C_2 m\lambda} + C_2\lambda$$

The middleman can exist if his absence does not permit the m sellers and n buyers to make greater profits and only if he can make zero or positive expected profits per unit time. Thus $SEC^*_w \leqslant SEC$, for the middleman to exist in a vertical market structure. This condition is given by

(26) $$C_3\lambda + C_4 \leq C_2\lambda$$

or

$$C_2 - C_3 \geq \frac{C_4}{\lambda}$$

It is now also possible to identify the manner of operations of the single middleman which maximizes his profits (positive or negative) by comparing the conditions for his existence in the case of both types of operations. By identifying C_1, C_2, C_3, C_4, λ, and m, one could determine the optimum type of operation for the middleman in the structure, considering only the order-filling function. One also could determine whether it is possible for a middleman to exist at all by operating in an optimal manner.

---

1   This subject is too vast to be fully explored here. A particular form of the problem is discussed in Chapters 8 and 9.

2   This is known as the reproductive property of the Poisson distribution.

3   For a proof see Churchman, C.W., et al., *Operations Research* (New York: John Wiley and Sons, Inc., 1957) p. 400.

4   When strategy formulation is permitted by removing the assumptions on similarity, this cost element would become an important means for the granting of rebates as discussed in Chapter 2.

5   Realistically the costs of waiting are shared by buyer and seller according to elasticities of demand and supply. The introduction of prices into the analysis must be kept until a later point, for it is a very complex subject and would only obscure this analysis.

6   The definition of all costs excludes the costs of coordination.

7   See for an excellent simplified exposition of coordination and of the costs thereof, Marschak, Jacob, "Efficient and Viable Organizational Forms" *in* Mason Haire, ed, *Organizations* (New York: John Wiley and Sons, Inc., 1959).

8   When the firm's system is less than completely full (but not empty) the multiple service station firm must incur greater service time than a similar firm with only a single service station of the same ultimate capacity.

9   For proof see Morse, Philip M., *Queues, Inventories and Maintenance* (New York: John Wiley and Sons, Inc., 1958) pp. 29–55.

6

Equilibrium Structures Implementing Exchange Transactions

Methods of coordinating the systems

The single middleman in a vertical market structure could serve as an order filler and undertake to perform all the functions necessary to the implementation of exchange transactions for the n buyers. On the other hand, he could serve as a pure coordinator, directing the buyers' orders to the sellers not occupied in filling an order. In each case the middleman's relationship to the buyers and sellers is different, and since it is assumed that he is a profit maximizer, the middleman will choose that form of operation which attains this goal. It is not obvious which set of relationships is the more profitable, since in both cases profits depend upon the values of the system's parameters. In consequence the determination of the equilibrium number of middlemen in the primery level and the equilibrium number of levels of middlemen must be made for both sets of middleman behavior patterns.

A structure with order-filling intermediaries is one in which the middle-man must perform more than one function. He must of necessity, for example, decide on the level of inventory he is to carry. This decision, in turn, affects the decisions on inventory carried by each of the m sellers. Both types of decisions are closely related to the equilibrium conditions for the entire structure. In order, therefore, to obtain these conditions for structures involving such multi-function middlemen, functions and sources of costs must be treated simultaneously. For the case of the order-filling middleman, therefore, problems of equilibrium are taken up only after those of the structure with single-function middlemen.

A middleman does not necessarily set out to "coordinate" the system, but rather to maximize profits. The fact that he does find it possible to achieve his goal stems from the effects his behavior has on total system costs. These effects are discussed in detail for the model of the structure developed and are the effects of the coordination which the middleman's behavior introduces into the system. The very concept of coordination is of course a general one applicable to all types of system operations. It is not the term "coordination" as such that is of value to the analysis of vertical market structures, but the concept of the economic phenomenon wherein outcomes are dependent upon the simultaneity of the selection of the values of decision variables. A vertical market structure is indeed a particular case of such a phenomenon.

The general concept of coordination involves simultaneity of: choice of values of decision variables, information, and decision criteria. The degree of simultaneity determines the closeness with which maximum system output is attained. This is the basic concept of system and sub-system optimality relations already discussed. Information collection and transfer, and the creation of decision criteria, are the cost-incurring inputs which permit the attainment of this simultaneity. Thus, a conceptual model of the phenomenon first must be developed before these relationships can be identified.

The general model which develops the concept of the value of information and of the relationship between the amount of information and the decision rules as related to the system's output, is given in a rigorous axiomatic form by Marschak.[1] In this form, Marschak's model develops the conditions under which a system's output becomes related to the information available to the decision makers, and identifies the role played by decision rules in this relationship.

A simultaneous determination of the optimal values of decision variables of the vertical market structure permits a reduction in the total system's waiting and service capacity costs. Complete simultaneity is possible only if perfect information is available to the middleman on the status of the m sellers. However, various alternatives to perfect information may be available. For every level of the amount of relevant information available to the middle-man, there is some set of decision rules which will maximize coordination. Substituting decision criteria for information implies of necessity a lower output and hence less coordination. But if decision rules are less costly to devise than is the information they replace, then the reduction in coordination caused by the substitution may be worthwhile. The vertical market structure case is a particular one in which this possibly is to be found.

The obvious advantage of the use of decision criteria by the middleman to obtain some measure of coordination for the vertical market structure is the elimination of costly and continuous information transfer. One decision criterion which the single middleman might employ is that which allocates arriving orders from the buyers to the m sellers so that each seller receives every mth order. The middleman would in this fashion eliminate the *need* to receive and store any information on the status of each of the m sellers. However, by operating in this manner a lower level of coordination is attained than that which stems from the use of full information transfer.

The decision criterion eliminates the probability that any two or more (up to m) consecutively generated orders will arrive at a single seller operation. In the purely uncoordinated system this probability is not zero. Orders may now be in a queue at the individual seller's operation if the previous order is still in service while m following orders have been generated, or if the order prior to that one is still in service while $2m$ following orders have arrived, one of which is in the queue, and so on. The middleman in fact holds no queues but merely serves to even out the flow of arriving orders. Each seller still receives $\frac{\lambda}{m}$ orders. Given that it receives the $(i-1)$th order, the probability that it receives the ith and $(i+1)$th $\cdots$ $(i+(m-1))$th order is zero. The expected time an order spends in the system for a given total order-servicing capacity is less than it would be with no coordination at all. It is, however, greater than that for perfect coordination since the probability of waiting at a seller's operation while others are free is greater than zero unless coordination is perfect. Without incurring any cost of information on the status of the sellers, a certain level of coordination is achieved by the application of a decision rule. The cost of using the rule is the necessary cost of maintaining the records of ranking of the order priorities of the m sellers.

The question which the middleman needs to have answered is whether maximum coordination at the cost of full information on the occupied-free status of the sellers is more profitable than some alternative sets of decision rules. The answer must depend upon the information necessary to employing decision rules, and its costs. It must depend upon the exact nature of the relationship of coordination (system output) to the level of information and degree of sub-optimization. The value of information[2] to any decision maker depends uniquely upon the nature of the problem. To the middleman the problem does not permit an easy identification of this relationship.

The purpose of showing that different vertical market structures have different levels of efficiency is attained by knowing that some are more coordinated than others without any resort to collusion among would-be competing firms. The middleman provides the cooperative relationships which permit such coordination and which define a particular structure.

Multiple middlemen forms of operations

Unless the multiple middlemen in the primary intermediate level cooperate among themselves, no single intermediary can succeed in coordinating perfectly the total system. If more than one middleman exists in the primary intermediate level, and there are no other intermediary levels, then the system for each middleman contains at least one element that is by definition non-cooperative and hence non-coordinatable. One such element is the competing middleman. No middleman may therefore solve for all relevant decision variables for the total system optimally. In fact such a solution can occur only when there is just one middleman. That system, barring rebate strategies, is not within the power of the single middleman.

If middlemen would cooperate, perfect system coordination *would be possible*, though the information costs necessary to its attainment would be higher by an amount which would depend upon the method of cooperation chosen. Such cooperation would involve the pooling of information on the exact ranking of all orders in all middlemen queues and on the status of all m sellers. It may take the form of information transfer among the w middlemen or the creation of a single middleman in a new level operated jointly by all the middlemen in the primary level. This new operation would be the only holder of orders in queue and the sole system coordinator. But such cooperation is in effect collusion and hence of no interest here. The question remains: how will the middleman operate if he is to be a pure coordinator and yet is unable to attain perfect coordination of the operations of all m sellers and all w middlemen in the unique primary intermediate level?

With multiple middlemen in the level, the same information transfer which permitted the single middleman to attain perfect system coordination will no longer permit the individual firm to do so. Each firm, in addition, has lower expected revenues with the larger the number of middlemen in the level, since each scale of operations in terms of orders handled is $\frac{1}{w}$ of all orders generated. Thus the same information costs are now coupled with revenues that are smaller because the scale of operations is smaller, and because the total system coordination is less. This method of operation, with multiple middlemen, may not be the optimal even if it were the optimal for the middleman who is unique in the level. Different patterns of middleman behavior, that is, different structure forms, may well have different optimum cost levels. The possibility of strategy decision rules involving search by the *m* sellers for orders with the *w* middlemen and by the middlemen for free *m* sellers may now gain a relative advantage over the system of full information transfer on a continuous basis.

Generally the many possible structure forms are extremely complex and difficult to characterize algebraically. Each structure would involve its own particular equilibrium number and levels of middlemen. Few structures would have identical cost functions or identical equilibrium states. To isolate the differences in structural efficiency and to solve analytically for the equilibrium state of the *most* efficient structure requires that all structures *not* obviously less efficient be characterized algebraically and equations derived for their relevant states. However, complex interdependencies of the probabilities of particular system states render this characterization inordinately complicated, involved, and lengthy. It is best, therefore, to settle on only one structural form and to derive its equilibrium algebraically. One can then indicate some measures of the variations that would occur in these conditions as variations in the structural form are permitted. Complex structural forms can be considered less formally with the conditions determining their relative efficiency indicated. Since the object is to analyze vertical market structures and not to develop new and more complex queuing models, there is no alternative to this decision.

Equilibrium conditions for the primary level

Consider the vertical market structure in which every middleman assures himself, by agreement with some of the *m* sellers, that a given set of sellers will always call only on him for orders to fill. In competitive circumstances this number will be $\frac{m}{w}$. The result is that the midlemen firms segment the vertical market structure just as they did in the performance of the inventory function to create what are essentially voluntary chains. Thus instead of middlemen receiving a call from one of the *m* sellers whenever that seller becomes free with a probability of $\frac{1}{w}$, a middleman now receives a call with a probability of *one* from every one of $\frac{m}{w}$ sellers whenever a seller in this group becomes free. Such segmentation is essentially in the realm of strategy formulation by middlemen. It is resorted to here, but much of the potential middleman strategy is ignored because of the complexity of the problem. It is hoped that when the analysis is complete, segmentation clearly can be shown *not* to be an advantageous strategy for sellers and middlemen in this case.

In the primary intermediate level individual middlemen have an arrival rate of $\frac{\lambda}{w}$ orders where λ is the rate at which the n buyers collectively emit orders which are then randomly allocated among the w middlemen. Each middleman contracts with a given number of sellers, equal to $\frac{m}{w}$, who now assure him that he and he alone will be the source of orders for them to fill. The entire vertical market structure is thus made up of w sub-structures, each with one middleman and $\frac{m}{w}$ sellers, who in turn have an order arrival rate of $\frac{\lambda}{w}$. Each sub-structure is thus similar to the single middleman vertical market structure. The chief difference is that in a single middleman structure the middleman is guaranteed an order once it is emitted from the n buyers, whereas in this case the probability of his receiving it is $\frac{1}{w}$. However, since the emission of orders is distributed in a Poisson fashion, with mean λ, the modified distribution of a single middleman sub-structure is also a Poisson with a mean $\frac{\lambda}{w}$.

The total cost of waiting in all sub-structures of this form will increase as their number increases, given a number of sellers, m; a total order-filling capacity, mv_m; and a total number of buyers, n, emitting orders at the aggregate rate of λ. These costs increase even when order service capacity costs are held constant for the entire vertical market structure because the expected time an order spends in the sub-structure will be longer the more sub-structures there are. This is again obvious since with more than one sub-structure, the probability is greater than zero that at any instant in time some sellers will be idle in some sub-structures while orders are waiting in other sub-structures. Positive probabilities also exist for combinations of sub-structures in this and other different sets of conditions. Such situations lead to longer expected waiting times for any order in the system.

It is intuitively obvious that the greater the number of sub-structures, the higher the probabilities of those system states that lead to longer waiting times. This point is apparent in the comparison between a structure with one middleman and structures with more than one middleman, and is shown in the model. The models therefore must show that expected waiting time increases monotonically with the number of middlemen who operate in a designated manner. They also must show the existence of an equilibrium number of middlemen in the primary intermediate level, and hence must derive the equations which permit the derivation of this number in terms of the system's parameters, namely λ, v_m, C_1, C_2, and C_3.

Using the same notation as in the previous chapter we have the following definitions:

w = number of middlemen in the primary intermediate level.
λ = average rate of order emission by the n sellers.

v_m = average rate at which a single seller is capable of implementing exchange agreements.

φ_m = average time an order spends in the system.

C_1 = cost to a sub-structure of having an order in its sub-structure per unit time.

C_2 = cost to a sub-structure of maintaining and operating a service unit of mean service rate of one order per unit time.

C_3 = cost to the sub-structure of transferring the information on the status of a seller to the middleman.

C_4 = cost to the sub-structure of maintaining the records on sellers' status and ranking if they are idle and hence in queue.

The types of costs C_1, C_2, C_3, and C_4 are borne by the sub-structure's middleman and $\frac{m}{w}$ sellers, in some proportion. If one should make the assumptions of Chapter 2, one would make these sellers indifferent to the presence of a middleman, given that their profits are equal to what they would be in the absence of all middlemen. If we assume that no rebates are given by middlemen, then any savings introduced by the existence of a primary intermediate level are shared as profits by the w middlemen in that level. Who actually incurs these costs in a sub-structure is now irrelevant. We can assume for purposes of simplicity that it is the middleman who incurs all these costs and receives as profit his share of the difference between the total cost of the entire system with no intermediaries, and the costs to all w sub-structures when there are w middlemen in the primary intermediate level.

For any number (w) of middlemen in the primary intermediate level, there exist w sub-structures, each with one middleman and $\frac{m}{w}$ sellers who receive orders only from this middleman and cooperate only with him. For every sub-structure, then, the arrival rate of orders is $\frac{\lambda}{w}$. The probability that there are x units in a sub-structure at an instant in time (P_x) is obtained in a similar manner as that for the vertical market structure with one middleman.[3]

(a) When $x \geqslant \dfrac{m}{w}$,

$$P_x = \left(\left(\frac{m}{w}\right)! \left(\frac{m}{w}\right)^{\left(x-\frac{m}{w}\right)} \right)^{-1} \left(\frac{\lambda}{w v_m}\right)^x P_0$$

where P_0 = probability that there are no units in the sub-structure.

(b) When $x < \dfrac{m}{w}$,

$$P_x = \frac{1}{x!}\left(\frac{\lambda}{w v_m}\right)^x P_0$$

From these two equations it can be shown that the expected time an order spends in the sub-structure is:

$$(1) \qquad \varphi_m = \left(\frac{v_m \left(\frac{\lambda}{w v_m} \right)^{\frac{m}{w}}}{\left(\frac{m}{w} - 1 \right)! \left(\frac{m v_m}{w} - \frac{\lambda}{w} \right)^2} \right) P_0 + \frac{1}{v_m}$$

It can also be shown that the probability that there are no units in the sub-structure is:

$$(2) \qquad P_0 = \frac{1}{\left[\sum_{x=0}^{\frac{m}{w}-1} \frac{1}{x!} \left(\frac{\lambda}{w v_m} \right)^x \right] + \left[\left(\frac{m}{w} \right)! \right]^{-1} \left(\frac{\lambda}{w v_m} \right)^{\frac{m}{w}} \left(\frac{\frac{m}{w}}{\frac{m}{w} - \frac{\lambda}{w v_m}} \right)}$$

The expected time an order spends in the sub-structure reaches a value of great interest when $w = m$. At this point there are m sub-structures, just as there were m sub-structures when the total system had no middlemen at all, with each sub-structure having *one* queue and *one* service unit. Evaluating equation (1) for the case of $\frac{m}{w} = 1$ we obtain:

$$(3) \qquad \varphi_m = \frac{\frac{\lambda}{m}}{\left(v_m - \frac{\lambda}{m} \right)^2} P_0 + \frac{1}{v_m} \quad \text{(i.e., for } w = m)$$

To obtain the value of P_0 for $m = w$ we have

$$(4) \qquad P_0 = \frac{1}{1 + \frac{\lambda}{m v_m} \frac{v_m}{\left(v_m - \frac{\lambda}{m} \right)}}$$

which reduces to:

$$P_0 = 1 - \frac{\lambda}{m v_m}$$

Substituting this value for P_0 into equation (3) and simplifying, we have the expected time an order spends in the system when $w = m$:

$$(5) \qquad \varphi_m = \frac{1}{\left(v_m - \frac{\lambda}{m} \right)}$$

The expected time in the system is now identical to that in the case of no middlemen in the system, provided that the service capacity of each of the m seller stations is the same in both cases. When the number of middlemen equals m, each middleman, with his attached seller, has an arrival rate $\frac{\lambda}{m}$, and his total cost of operation in terms only of the variables to be decided (waiting time costs and service time costs) is given by

(6)
$$TEC_{w=m} = C_1 \lambda_m \varphi_m + C_2 v_m$$

$$TEC_{w=m} = C_1 \frac{\lambda_m}{\left(v_m - \dfrac{\lambda}{m}\right)} + C_2 v_m$$

To optimize, the middleman can only control (by assumption) the value of v_m. Since equation (6) is identical to equation (7) of the previous chapter, the optimum v_m is the same in both the cases of no middleman and $w = m$ middlemen, and is $v_m^* = \sqrt{\dfrac{C_1 \lambda_m}{C_2}} + \lambda_m$. Substituting this value of v_m into equation (6), simplifying, and summing for all $w = m$ sub-systems gives us the minimum expected total costs for the whole system, ignoring all but waiting and service capacity costs:

$$SEC_{w=m} = m(2\sqrt{C_1 C_2 \lambda_m} + C_2 \lambda_m)$$

or since $\quad \lambda_m = \dfrac{\lambda}{m}$,

(7)
$$SEC_{w=m} = 2\sqrt{C_1 C_2 m \lambda} + C_2 \lambda$$

This equation is identical to equation (8) of the previous chapter. The absolute limit on the number of middlemen in the primary intermediate level occurs when $w = m$. Here all contact and record-keeping costs have been ignored, so that the limit on the equilibrium w would be, in effect, smaller than m were these costs considered.

It has already been shown that obtaining the optimal v_m when $w = 1$ is extremely complex unless m is assumed to be large. It cannot be assumed that the number of sellers in sub-systems for all w is large. Let us assume therefore that the value of v_m remains unchanged for all values of w ranging from 0 to m. It is set at the optimized value for $w = 0$ and $w = m$. If it is now found that waiting time is reduced for $w = 1$ and $w < m$, then the system costs would be even lower if v_m is optimized for values of $w = 1$ and $1 < w < m$. That is, by assuming v_m to be held the same for all values of w, one can show total system expected costs of waiting and service to be higher for $w = m$ than for $1 < w < m$ and that these in turn are higher than when $w = 1$.

Assuming, therefore, a constant v_m, one can obtain the total expected system costs of waiting and service capacity and then consider other system costs. Having obtained equation (7), we now need to show that $SEC_{w=1} < SEC_{w=0} = SEC_{w=m}$. For $w = 1$ it can be shown that:

(8)
$$SEC_{w=1} = C_1 \left(\frac{\lambda v_m \left(\dfrac{\lambda}{v_m}\right)^m}{(m-1)!\,(m v_m - \lambda)^2} P_0 + \frac{\lambda}{v_m} \right) + C_2 m v_m$$

Since m is relatively large, the value for P_0 can be approximated by $e^{-\frac{\lambda}{v_m}}$ and expression (8) reduces to:

(8a) $\qquad SEC_{w=1} = C_1\left(\dfrac{\lambda v_m\left(\dfrac{\lambda}{v_m}\right)^m e^{-\lambda/v_m}}{(m-1)!\,(mv_m - \lambda)^2} + \dfrac{\lambda}{v_m}\right) + C_2 m v_m$

Similarly the relevant expected costs of the system can be obtained for $m > w > 1$, and for $\dfrac{m}{w}$ relatively large. The expected costs of waiting and service for the *system's* entire group of sub-systems is:

(9) $\qquad SEC_{m>w>1} = C_1\left(\dfrac{\lambda v_m\left(\dfrac{\lambda}{wv_m}\right)^{\frac{m}{w}}}{\left(\dfrac{m}{w}-1\right)!\left(\dfrac{m}{w}v_m - \dfrac{\lambda}{w}\right)^2} P_0 + \dfrac{\lambda}{v_m}\right) + C_2 m v_m$

Since $\dfrac{m}{w}$ is large, the value of P_0 can be approximated with very little loss of accuracy by $e^{-\lambda/wv_m}$ and equation (9) becomes:

(9a) $\qquad SEC_{m>w>1} = C_1\left(\dfrac{\lambda v_m\left(\dfrac{\lambda}{wv_m}\right)^{\frac{m}{w}} e^{-\lambda/wv_m}}{\left(\dfrac{m}{w}-1\right)!\left(\dfrac{m}{w}v_m - \dfrac{\lambda}{w}\right)^2} + \dfrac{\lambda}{v_m}\right) + C_2 m v_m$

To show that the expected system costs of waiting and service are higher for $w = m$ than they are for $w < m$, and that these latter are higher than the costs for $w = 1$ we shall write out in extensive form the system costs for $w = m$. These costs are obtained directly from equation (1). In addition, of course, the costs of the service capacity must be added. Thus:

(10) $\qquad SEC_{w=m} = C_1\left(\dfrac{\lambda v_m\left(\dfrac{\lambda}{mv_m}\right)}{\left(\dfrac{m}{m}-1\right)!\left(\dfrac{m}{m}v_m - \dfrac{\lambda}{m}\right)^2} P_0 + \dfrac{\lambda}{v_m}\right) + C_2 m v_m$

If the total expected costs of the system increase as the number of middlemen in the primary intermediate level increases, then an equilibrium number of middlemen would exist. It is required to show that expression (9a) is larger than expression (8a). Reducing the two expressions it is necessary to show that:

(11) $\qquad \dfrac{w^2\left(\dfrac{\lambda}{wv_m}\right)^{\frac{m}{w}} e^{-\lambda/wv_m}}{\left(\dfrac{m}{w}-1\right)!} > \dfrac{\left(\dfrac{\lambda}{v_m}\right)^m e^{-\lambda/v_m}}{(m-1)!}$

By further reduction it becomes sufficient to show that:

(12) $\qquad w(m-1)! - \left(\dfrac{m-w}{w}\right)!\,w^{(m-w)/w} > 0$

By inspection this can be seen to be true. Furthermore, as w increases, the left hand side of the inequality increases. This means that system costs of waiting and service increase as the number of middlemen increase. The maximum system costs which permit middlemen to exist are attained when $w = m$. If, in addition, the cost of the information which middlemen need to coordinate the system increases with the number of middlemen, the equilibrium number of these will occur at some value less than m. In conclusion, if the costs of coordinating the system do not exceed the reduction in waiting and service costs brought about by the existence of a single primary level of coordinating middlemen, then an equilibrium number of such middlemen will exist. This number will be some number greater than one and less than m.

Alternative structure forms

An alternative structure form to that modeled is one in which the middlemen in the primary intermediate level operate in a manner that precludes any segmenting of the m sellers. Each middleman incurs the costs of having every seller inform him the instant the seller becomes free or if his status should change from that of being free to that of being occupied in filling an order. Every middleman thus keeps an up-to-date record on the status of all the m sellers. This form of the structure involves as in all cases a completely random choice of the middleman by the arriving orders from the n buyers. When a seller finishes filling an order and instantly informs all middlemen of the fact, he would find middlemen in one of two possible states. There are either one or more orders from the n buyers waiting at the operation of one or more of the w middlemen in the single level, or there is no order waiting anywhere. Similarly, when an order arrives at a middleman operation it either finds a free seller or none at all. If a seller is waiting, the order goes immediately into service. If there is no seller waiting, then the order joins the other waiting orders in that middleman's queue and is ranked on the basis of its arrival time in this queue. (It is not ranked on the basis of its arrival at the middleman level because the middlemen act independently.)

Since every middleman keeps records on the status of all m sellers, an order from a buyer has to wait at the middleman's operation only if all sellers are occupied at the instant of its arrival. At any instant in time there cannot be both orders and sellers waiting for service at the primary intermediate level. Suppose that an order from one of the n buyers finds no free seller upon its arrival. Suppose also that no other orders are waiting in a queue at the middleman's operation to which this order has come. The order must wait, therefore, until a seller becomes free. The first seller who becomes free instantly informs all middlemen, and it is assumed as usual that the probability that two sellers finish filling an order at the same instant is zero.

Since the order in question is at the head of a middleman's queue, it is sent to be serviced by this seller. However, all other middlemen who have one or more orders waiting will send the one at the head of their queues. On arriving at the seller's operation the order may find itself either alone or with other orders. It may be one of 1, 2, 3, . . . or at most w orders arriving virtually simultaneously at this level, and since the seller can only, by assumption, fill one order at a time, the order may now have to wait before service on it starts. If orders are picked randomly then there is a nonzero probability that when the order is one among many, it will wait before the seller can start filling it. Orders in effect now have a positive probability of waiting at the intermediate level and at the seller level.

When the system operates in this manner every order can expect not to wait at the seller level if there is at least one seller free when it arrives, which means that no orders are waiting anywhere in the intermediate level. It can also expect not to wait at the seller level if, when at the instant the next seller becomes free, it is at the head of a queue at a middleman's operation, and no other middleman has an order in his queue. On the other hand, a seller can now expect to get a single order under only two circumstances. The first is when only one middleman in the intermediate level has any orders at all in his queue when the seller becomes free. The second is when the seller finds no orders at the intermediate level at the instant it becomes free and has to wait, i.e., join a queue of sellers of lengths 0, 1, $\cdots$, $m - 1$ sellers already waiting. The probability, therefore, of a seller's getting more than one order in a batch, from one message to all middlemen that he has become free, is positive. This probability was, of course, zero in the structure form which was solved explicitly in the previous section.

From this operation it is possible to derive some general conclusions on the total system cost of waiting and order-filling capacity. If we maintain the same expected capacity to service orders of all m sellers at the level that is optimum for the case of a single middleman, we leave unaltered this cost of the system. What then happens to the expected time an order spends in the system and total system waiting cost? The answer is that they must go up. The reason is that in this structure, with more than one middleman, there is a nonzero probability that some sellers will be idle and waiting for orders while there are orders waiting in a queue at the operation of some one or more sellers. There is a positive probability that the system could, at an instant in time, be in a state where r orders are waiting in queues at r different middleman operations (r is less than or equal to w). This means that all m sellers are occupied. The first seller who becomes free receives all of the r orders. This results in the likely state that some or all of the remaining $m - 1$ sellers will incur idle facility time while the first seller is incurring (excessive) waiting time.

If the system permits some sellers to be idle and orders to wait simultaneously, then the expected time any order would spend in the system is higher than when the probability that this occurs is zero, that is, of course, given that the total order-servicing capacity is the same for the two systems. The system with one middleman has a lower expected cost for the time an order is in the system than the system with more than one middleman.

An increase in the number of middlemen will also increase the cost of information gathering. Each seller must now inform w middlemen, instead of just one, that he is free or that he has just become occupied. Record-keeping costs on the status of the seller are now incurred by w middlemen instead of one. Decentralizing coordination leads in this case to less coordination at greater cost. There should be, in effect, a finite equilibrium number of middlemen in the primary intermediate level, namely, that at which the total increase in system waiting and information costs equals the total profit of the single middleman, given of course that this was positive.[4] This equilibrium number will be a function of the system's parameters—waiting costs, capacity costs, information costs, and the expected time an order spends in the system. It is this latter that is impossible to derive analytically because of the complex interrelationships between the system's state probabilities which are evident from the preceeding descriptions. One can, however, prove that if one middleman could exist in the structure, the entry of others would increase costs and that a finite equilibrium number of middlemen exists. Exactly what the equation for this number is, it is not possible to ascertain.

Other structural forms could be studied in a similar fashion. In general such structure forms cannot be approached analytically for general algebraic solutions. Simulation and mathematical programming may provide explicit solutions.

Multiple levels of middlemen

There is no possibility that the discussion of *purely coordinating middlemen* as developed will permit the derivation of a finite equilibrium number of levels of middlemen in the system. There are no costs considered which increase with the addition of a new level, except the costs of information gathering in the case of the introduction of the primary intermediate level. When a new level of middlemen is created, if the coordination needs to be done at only one level, these costs will be transferred from level to level as they develop. In consequence, no finite number of levels can be identified as the equilibrium one, unless we resort to the concept of rebates, including the costs of order handling which increases with the number of levels and number of middlemen.

Identify the number of middlemen in the primary intermediate level to be $\hat{w}_1$. Consider now the entry of a middleman in the level between this number $\hat{w}_1$ and the m sellers. The queue of the arriving orders is obviously (from the considerations leading to the inference of the existence of the first level) best held at this new level. If such is the case, there is no need for the $\hat{w}_1$ middlemen to hold any information on the occupied-free status of the m sellers. All coordination is transferred to the middlemen in the level between the m and the $\hat{w}_1$. However, as more middlemen enter this new level, the ones in the primary level will need information on the status of the queues held by those in the new level. As these continue to increase in number, the costs of coordination to the $\hat{w}_2$ middlemen, those in the second level, will continue to increase. Coordinating, waiting, and service costs also continue to increase for the $\hat{w}_2$ middlemen in the new level. This new level finally has an equilibrium number $\hat{w}_2 < \hat{w}_1$. Their costs of coordination now involve keeping records on the status of some of the m sellers and involve the $\hat{w}_1$ middlemen in keeping records on some of the $\hat{w}_2$ middlemen.

Another level is now logically possible between the $\hat{w}_2$ middlemen and the m sellers, provided that $\hat{w}_2 > 1$. In this context the $\hat{w}_1$ middlemen no longer incur any costs of coordination since the $\hat{w}_2$ middlemen no longer hold any queues. The system's costs of coordination fall as a result, but the fall is balanced in part by the costs of coordination incurred by this new level. The net effect will be a decrease in total costs since $\hat{w}_1 > \hat{w}_2$. There is thus a possibility that the new level containing $\hat{w}_3$ middlemen will be larger than $\hat{w}_2$ but still smaller than $\hat{w}_1$ because now the system can incur larger waiting and service costs than it did with $\hat{w}_1$ and $\hat{w}_2$. As $\hat{w}_3$ increases in number, a new level between it and the m would become possible and the whole argument repeats itself. There is in fact no guarantee that the system's equilibrium number of levels can be derived. The simplified concept of the system may not permit the existence of such an equilibrium. However, if the routing of orders through successively increasing levels of middlemen is considered to lead to increasing costs, such an equilibrium would be easily shown to exist. The analysis of such a cost in terms of rebates would parallel very closely that of Chapter 4. Furthermore, the issue of an equilibrium number of levels also can be quickly resolved when multi-function middlemen systems are developed more fully. Once one conceptualizes a system (more realistically) as requiring multi-functions to be performed, the equilibrium number of levels of middlemen is easily derived. The costs of performing the contact function, of physical distribution, of removing buyers from the source of supply, of entry, and of cooperation which are considered in Chapter 2 and Chapter 4 guarantee this. It remains true, nonetheless, that the concept of the system in which middlemen are pure coordinators is a useful simplifying device which bares some fundamental relations making up one aspect of vertical market structures.

Equilibrium conditions for
multi-function middlemen

The order-filling middleman serves as an excellent basis for the analysis of vertical market structures where middlemen perform various combinations of the cost-incurring functions already considered. This middleman is by the very nature of the definition of his operations one who must make the decisions on the resources he is to allocate to implementing exchange transactions. Also filling orders with an aim to maximize profits is not possible without a decision on the inventory which is to be carried to permit such order filling. The first combination of functions then to be considered simultaneously for intermediaries is that which includes inventory carrying and the servicing of orders.

In a vertical market structure with no intermediaries, the individual seller among the m sellers can be characterized in terms of two dimensions. The selling firm is made up of a production sector and a marketing sector. Part of its resources must be allocated to the production of the physical good, and part allocated to the handling of the orders for this physical good. For the firm, one problem is thus to determine the capacity of its physical production facilities, or the costs it is to incur in order that it may be capable of producing the good at some maximum average rate. The other problem is to determine the rate at which it can handle the orders it receives. The handling of an order does not necessarily imply filling it, but involves satisfying the customer in a manner clearly defined below.

The distinction between the firm which does not carry any inventory of the finished good and one which does is one between a "custom order" firm and a firm selling a "standardized" product from inventory. There are of course firms which lie between these two extremes, firms which carry the product in some degree of finished form and then engage in some physical production activities to suit the particular order. For the purely custom firm the problem is to determine the capacity of the order-filling facility, which in this case involves the entire operation of the firm, excluding only the decision on raw material inventory. Firms that carry some form of the finished product use inventory, i.e., raw materials that had been operated on by their physical production facilities, because they find it profitable to do so. They are in essence trading off the cost of the customers' *waiting* for costs of *holding* the product in some degree of finished form. The historical development of the artisan's workshop into a productive facility and a store, and later the separation of these two segments, illustrates this point. Firms in some form of this intermediate stage are those which we now designate as the m sellers, and the introduction of the intermediaries characterizes vertical structures which develop in the manner of the last-mentioned stage.

Each of the m sellers recognizes the possibility that inventory carrying may allow more profits. The possibility exists for distinguishing between the problems of physical production facilities and marketing facilities. Such a distinction at this point does not necessarily permit the independent solution of the two problems. It merely serves as a useful devide for exploring the nature of the firm's operation and the essential relationships that make up the problems. Eventually both problems may require simultaneous solution for the firm's optimal decisions. For the moment each segment of the firm's operation is characterized separately.

The selling firm wishes to employ its physical production facilities fully at all times and hence to produce at some given rate on a continuous basis. Any given level of resources allocated to physical production facilities and their continuously planned use determines uniquely the distribution of the firm's output of the physical product per unit of time. The mean rate of production is a *measure* of the capacity of the firm's physical production facility. The costs of production per unit of output are in turn uniquely related to this mean capacity, and for our purposes this relation is assumed to be a linear one. All costs of operation are assumed to be incurred by the selling firm, and these costs are:

$C_1 =$ cost of holding one unit of the physical product in finished form in inventory per unit time.

$C_2 =$ cost of running short one unit of the physical product in finished form.

$C_3 =$ cost per unit time of maintaining and operating a physical production facility with an average output capacity of one unit per unit time.

$C_4 =$ cost of having an order in the firm's system per unit time. An order is in the system from the moment it arrives until the moment it is filled, or released unfilled but compensated for being unfilled (the shortage cost element) for the time it is in the system.

$C_5 =$ cost per unit of time of maintaining and operating an order-filling facillity with an average output capacity of one per unit time.

The seller firm's system involves two decision variables and a parameter which is not a cost as such. The variables are:

$\mu_m =$ capacity of the physical production facilities, i.e., the mean rate at which the facilities produce the finished good.

$v_m =$ capacity of the order-filling sector (marketing) of the firm, or, the average rate at which the facility is capable of handling orders.

It is assumed that the rate at which orders are serviced is independent of the fact that an order may or may not be capable of being filled from inventories. On the average an order will take the same time to be filled once its turn for service arrives as it does to leave the system unfilled once its turn for service arrives, but serviced in the sense of being compensated for not being filled. An order is not filled only if there are no finished goods in inventory when the order's time for service starts.

The parameter which remains is:

λ_m = rate at which orders from the n buyers arrive at the single seller's system.

It is assumed that $\frac{1}{\mu_m}$ and $\frac{1}{v_m}$ are the means of exponential distributions and λ_m is the mean of a Poisson distribution. It may also be noted once more that the firm's productive facility produces continuously at the average rate μ_m, whereas its order-filling facility services orders at the average rate v_m only if such orders are available. Since the mean order arrival rate is λ_m, the actual average rate at which orders are serviced is λ_m, while its potential mean service rate is v_m. The physical production facility operates at its potential capacity, but the order-filling facility operates at some level below its potential capacity, so that $\lambda_m < v_m$.

One can describe the operations of the firm in two queuing models. Products arrive into inventory at some average rate μ_m. Orders arrive from buyers at some average rate λ_m. Inventory, when its level is not zero, is depleted at a mean rate of λ_m, and orders leave the system filled or unfilled but serviced at an average rate of λ_m. In diagramatic terms the firm's operations can be characterized as follows:

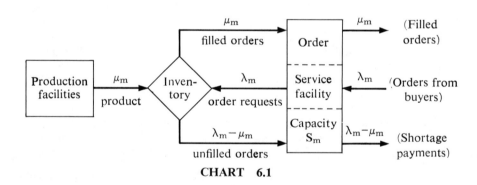

CHART 6.1

One can now characterize the firm's problem as two queuing problems, one with an arrival rate μ_m and a service capacity rate λ_m, the other with an arrival rate λ_m and a service capacity rate v_m. With respect then to the physical production facilities problem, these cost elements can be defined as making up the total cost of *this* section of the firm's operation. The first is the shortage cost element. The firm is short if its inventory level is zero. In terms of the firm's queuing model there are no units in inventory when the system is empty of its arrival units. With an arrival rate of μ_m, and a potential departure rate of λ_m, the system is empty of finished goods $\left(1 - \frac{\mu_m}{\lambda_m}\right)$ of the time—providing of course, that $\lambda_m > \mu_m$. If $\mu_m > \lambda_m$, the queue of finished products in inventory would increase to infinity.

If the production section of the firm is empty of units of product $\left(\dfrac{\lambda_m - \mu_m}{\lambda_m}\right)$ of the time, and if the average rate of order arrivals is λ_m, then the average number of orders per unit of time that does not find a unit of product in inventory is $\lambda_m\left(\dfrac{\lambda_m - \mu_m}{\lambda_m}\right)$. The firm's expected shortage costs per unit time are:

$$(13) \qquad C_2(\lambda_m - \mu_m)$$

The production sector's inventory holding costs are obtained by deriving the average number of units of product in inventory. In terms of the queuing model where the units of product are the arrivals, this number is equivalent to the average number of arrivals to be found in the queue. In other terms, the average inventory level is given by the expression, $\dfrac{\mu_m^2}{\lambda_m(\lambda_m - \mu_m)}$. There are on the average μ_m orders arriving per unit time, and the cost of holding each is C_1 per unit time. In addition there is the cost of holding all products while each is in process of production which is a unit average time equal to $\dfrac{1}{\mu_m}$, giving a total cost of $\dfrac{\mu_m}{\mu_m}C_1$ or merely C_1. The cost to this sector of holding inventory per unit time is:

$$(14) \qquad C_1\left(1 + \frac{\mu_m^2}{\lambda_m(\lambda_m - \mu_m)}\right)$$

Finally the cost of operating and maintaining a physical production facility which produces at the mean rate of μ_m is:

$$(15) \qquad C_3\mu_m$$

Expressions (13), (14), and (15) give us the total cost of the firm's physical production sector, not including the raw material cost of the product. The order-filling (marketing) sector's costs are similarly obtained. The average time an order spends in the marketing sector of the firm is given by the expression $\left(\dfrac{1}{v_m - \lambda_m}\right)$. This is under the conditions that each order is handled completely by the order-filling facility before any other order is operated upon. In essence, the system is one with a single service station which has a mean service rate capacity of $v_m > \lambda_m$. Some orders are filled by this system, but some are not. Those not filled are such because no product is in inventory at the time their turn arrives. Nonetheless, the order-filling facility must handle the order in the sense that it must compensate the buyer for its being out of stock and for the buyer's waiting. The time it takes to handle an order is thus assumed to be distributed in an exponential manner with mean $\dfrac{1}{v_m}$ for all orders that are handled. The total expected cost of time spent in the system for this section of the firm is given by the average time an order spends in the system multiplied by the average number of orders arriving multiplied by the cost per order, namely,

(16)
$$C_4\left(\frac{\lambda_m}{v_m - \lambda_m}\right)$$

The cost of maintaining and operating the order-filling facility of the firm per unit time is directly related to the facility's service rate potential and the constant (by assumption) cost per unit of service rate, or:

(17)
$$C_5 v_m$$

Finally, there is a cost of holding the product after it leaves the inventory in the production sector and enters the order-filling sector to permit the servicing of an order. If one assumes that the instant service on an order starts, the physical product is removed from the inventory, then that product will still be held by the firm until it leaves with the completely serviced order. Since it takes $\frac{1}{v_m}$ units of time to service an order, the product must be considered to be held in the inventory of the order-filling section this length of time after it leaves the inventory in the production sector. The expected cost per unit time of holding inventory in the marketing sector is $\frac{\mu_m}{v_m}$, or an average of μ_m units each held on the average $\frac{1}{v_m}$, times the holding cost C_1, or:

(18)
$$C_1 \frac{\mu_m}{v_m}$$

The total expected cost for the firm's operation per unit time is the sum of the costs in expressions (13) through (18). Thus:

(19)
$$TEC_m = C_2(\lambda_m - \mu_m) + C_1\left(1 + \frac{\mu_m^2}{\lambda_m(\lambda_m - \mu_m)}\right) + C_3\mu_m$$
$$+ C_4\left(\frac{\lambda_m}{v_m - \lambda_m}\right) + C_5 v_m + C_1\frac{\mu_m}{v_m}$$

It is postulated that each seller among the m firms wishes to minimize this total cost function. The two control variables the firm has are μ_m and v_m. To minimize the cost function its partial derivatives with respect to these two variables are set equal to zero, and the variables' optimal values then determined. If we let $\frac{\mu_m}{\lambda_m} = \rho_1$, and $\frac{\lambda_m}{v_m} = \rho_2$, the expected cost equation for the firm becomes:

(20)
$$TEC_m = C_1\left[(1 - \rho_1) + \frac{\rho_1}{1 - \rho_1}\right] + C_1\rho_1\rho_2$$
$$+ C_3\lambda_m\rho_1 + C_2\lambda_m(1 - \rho_1) + C_4\left(\frac{\rho_2}{1 - \rho_2}\right) + \frac{C_5\lambda_m}{\rho_2}$$

To minimize this function with respect to ρ_1 and ρ_2 we have:[5]

$$\frac{\partial}{\partial \rho_1}TEC_m = -C_1 + \frac{C_1\rho_1}{(1-\rho_1)^2} + \frac{C_1(1-\rho_1)}{(1-\rho_1)^2} + C_1\rho_2 + C_3\lambda_m - C_2\lambda_m = 0$$

and

$$\frac{\partial}{\partial \rho_2}TEC_m = C_1\rho_1 + \frac{C_4\rho_2 + C_4(1-\rho_2)}{(1-\rho_2)^2} - \frac{\lambda_m C_5}{\rho_2^2} = 0$$

These two equations can now be solved for the two unknowns, namely, the optimal ρ_1 and ρ_2. However, obtaining a general "neat" solution for these variables in terms of the parameters C_1, C_2, C_3, C_4, C_5, and λ_m is impossible. Since our purpose is to compare total system costs for different kinds of vertical market structures with and without intermediaries, the complexity of this formulation tends to obscure the analysis. One can, as is done below, show that a single comparison of the total system costs for two structures, say, one without intermediaries and one with intermediaries, would show a reduction in costs provided that (a) $w < m$ for the structure with w middlemen in a primary level and no others; (b) $mv_m = wv_w$, i.e., total system order-filling capacity is unchanged; and (c) $m\mu_m = w\mu_w$. Thus one system always costs less to meet the *same* output level requirement than the other when the values of mv_m and $m\mu_m$ remain unchanged. This implies that the *optimum value* for the two variables will involve system costs that are lower for one than for the other. The advantage in being able to compare the optimum states of different systems to uncover which involves lower expected costs is the clarity and detail that this brings to the conclusions on the manner in which the introduction of middlemen affects the system's efficiency. If the cost of this clarity and detail were too high in the case of the system characterized by equation (20), it is not too high in the case of a slightly more simple characterization of the system. The simplification involves the assumption that the value of $(\rho_1\rho_2)$ in equation (20) is negligible. It is, for example, extremely small if C_4 is tremendously large in comparison to C_1 and the optimum v_m is large. Making this assumption, therefore, the single seller among the m, in a vertical market structure with no intermediaries in it, has total expected costs of:

(21) $$TEC_m = C_1\left[(1-\rho_1) + \frac{\rho_1}{1-\rho_1}\right] + C_3\lambda_m\rho_1 + C_2\lambda_m(1-\rho_1)$$
$$+ C_4\left(\frac{\rho_2}{1-\rho_2}\right) + \frac{C_5\lambda_m}{\rho_2}$$

To minimize its costs the firm sets:

(22) $$\frac{\partial}{\partial \rho_1}TEC_m = 0 = (C_3 - C_2)\lambda_m - C_1 + \frac{C_1}{(1-\rho_1)^2}$$

and

(23) $$\frac{\partial}{\partial \rho_2}TEC_m = 0 = \frac{C_4}{(1-\rho_2)^2} - \frac{C_5\lambda_m}{\rho_2^2}$$

Equations (22) and (23) are now capable of solution independently of one another. Solving (22) for the optimum ρ_1 we have:

$$\rho_1 = 1 - \sqrt{\frac{C_1}{C_1 + (C_2 - C_3)\lambda_m}}$$

Substituting $\frac{\mu_m}{\lambda_m}$ for ρ_1, this identifies the optimum μ_m as:

(24)
$$\hat{\mu}_m = \lambda_m\left[1 - \sqrt{\frac{C_1}{C_1 + (C_2 - C_3)\lambda_m}}\right]$$

This expression would be meaningful only if $(C_2 - C_3)\lambda$ were not a negative number; since $0 < \rho_1 < 1$, however, $C_2 > C_3$, and $(C_2 - C_3) > 0$. The whole concept of the system would be meaningless unless $0 < \rho_1 < 1$ and $C_2 > C_3$.

Solving equation (23) for the optimum ρ_2 we have:

$$\rho_2 = \frac{\sqrt{\dfrac{\lambda_m C_5}{C_4}}}{1 + \sqrt{\dfrac{\lambda_m C_5}{C_4}}} = \frac{\sqrt{\lambda_m C_5}}{\sqrt{C_4} + \sqrt{\lambda_m C_5}}$$

Substituting $\frac{\lambda_m}{v_m}$ for ρ_2 the optimum v_m for the single seller would be:

(25)
$$\hat{v}_m = \lambda_m\left(1 + \sqrt{\frac{C_4}{\lambda_m C_5}}\right)$$

The minimum total cost of operating both the physical production and the order-filling facilities making up any firm among the m sellers is that into which the optimum values for μ_m and v_m are substituted. The minimum expected total cost for the single seller's operation is:

(26)
$$TEC_m = \lambda_m C_5 - C_1 + 2\sqrt{C_4\lambda_m C_5} + C_3\lambda_m$$
$$+ 2\sqrt{C_1^2 + C_1(C_2 - C_3)\lambda_m}$$

The total cost of the operation of the entire vertical market structure with no intermediaries and with m sellers is m times TEC_m. The system's minimum total expected costs are thus:

(27)
$$SEC_m = m[\lambda_m C_5 - C_1 + 2\sqrt{C_4\lambda_m C_5}]$$
$$+ C_3\lambda + 2\sqrt{(C_1 m)^2 + C_1(C_2 - C_3)m\lambda}$$

In the vertical market structure with intermediaries in a single primary level it is postulated that all decisions are made by these intermediaries and all costs incurred by them. Each middleman in the primary intermediate level carries inventories of the product which arrives at the rate of μ_w. Each middleman also has an order-filling facility with a mean potential rate of v_w orders serviced per unit of time. The product is produced by the m sellers at the rate $\frac{w\mu_w}{m}$. The middlemen are allowed to enter if they leave the profits of the m sellers and utility (or profits) of the n buyers unchanged. Each middleman must now solve for the optimum values of μ_w and v_w.

The optimal value of μ_w is obtained in a manner similar to that of μ_m. Thus the optimal μ_w is:

$$\text{(28)} \qquad \hat{\mu}_w = \lambda_w \left[1 - \sqrt{\frac{C_1}{C_1 + (C_2 - C_3)\lambda_w}} \right]$$

The entry of middlemen increases the total output rate for the entire system over what it was for the system without middlemen, when each decision-making firm optimizes its output rate (for each m) or its purchase rate (for each w), provided that $w < m$. Thus we wish to show that $w\hat{\mu}_w > m\hat{\mu}_m$, or that:

$$\hat{\mu}_w > \frac{m}{w}\lambda_m \left[1 - \sqrt{\frac{C_1}{C_1 + (C_2 - C_3)\lambda_m}} \right]$$

Since $\dfrac{m}{w}\lambda_m = \lambda_w$,

then,

$$\hat{\mu}_w > \lambda_w \left[1 - \sqrt{\frac{C_1}{C_1 + (C_2 - C_3)\lambda_m}} \right]$$

which is true since,

$$\hat{\mu}_w = \lambda_w \left[1 - \sqrt{\frac{C_1}{C_1 + (C_2 - C_3)\lambda_w}} \right]$$

The denominator in the square root sign in this equation contains λ_w which is greater than λ_m for all $w < m$, making the term in the bracket in the equation larger than that in the inequality. The system with intermediaries thus incurs smaller total shortage costs but incurs greater costs of physical production.

When the optimum v_w is obtained, the system's expected cost for the single middleman is[6]:

$$\text{(29)} \qquad TEC_w = \lambda_w C_5 - C_1 + 2\sqrt{C_4 \lambda_w C_5} + C_3 \lambda_w$$
$$+ 2\sqrt{C_1^2 + C_1(C_2 - C_3)\lambda_w}$$

The total system's minimum expected costs are in turn:

$$\text{(30)} \qquad SEC_w = w[\lambda_w C_5 - C_1 + 2\sqrt{C_4 \lambda_w C_5}] + C_3 \lambda$$
$$+ 2\sqrt{(C_1 w)^2 + C_1(C_2 - C_3)w\lambda}$$

In comparing SEC_m and SEC_w it can be shown that total expected system costs are lower in the vertical market structures with intermediaries in a single primary level, and nowhere else, then they are with no intermediaries at all provided, of course, that the number of middlemen is smaller than m. Comparing equations (27) and (30) shows that this conclusion is true since

(31)
$$2\sqrt{C_4 \lambda C_5 m} + 2\sqrt{(C_1 m)^2 + C_1(C_2 - C_3)m\lambda} - mC_1 >$$
$$2\sqrt{C_4 \lambda C_5 w} + 2\sqrt{(C_1 w)^2 + C_1(C_2 - C_3)w\lambda} - wC_1$$

The first term on the left hand side exceeds the first term on the right hand side for $w < m$. The second term on the left hand side must be some value greater than $2C_1 m$ since the term $(C_1 m)^2$ lies within the square root sign and $C_1(C_2 - C_3)m\lambda$ must be positive, as shown earlier. The second term on the left is thus of some positive value of $2C_1 m + E_m$. The second term on the right hand side is similarly $2C_1 w + E_w$, and $E_m > E_w$ since $C_1(C_2 - C_3)w\lambda$ is always smaller than $C_1(C_2 - C_3)m\lambda$ for $w < m$. The inequality (31) must thus hold if $2C_1 m - mC_1 > 2C_1 w - wC_1$ or $C_1 m > C_1 w$, which is true for all $w < m$. System costs with different numbers of middlemen in the primary intermediate level can be compared in the same manner and easily shown to increase with the number w.

Middlemen in the primary intermediate level who operate as order fillers in the system described by the model can be members of the vertical market structure. The vertical market structure's costs of the three types considered are reduced by the entry of such middlemen, and these costs increase as the number of middlemen in the primary intermediate level increases.[7] When the number of such middlemen reaches m, no middleman could make a positive profit since system costs are at a level equal to that of a vertical market structure with no middlemen. The equilibrium number of middlemen in this level is thus equal to m.

In developing these conclusions, it is assumed that the two sectors, the physical production and the marketing or order-filling sectors, of the firm could be optimized independently. Thus, it was assumed that the term $C_1 \rho_1 \rho_2$ was negligible and could be ignored. If we do not ignore this element, then middlemen could exist in the primary intermediate level if m times equation (19) were shown to be greater than w times the total cost of operation for each middleman when: total system production $(m\mu_m)$ is the same in both systems; mv_m is the same in both systems; and $w < m$. It must be shown that $SEC_m^* < SEC_w$ or that:

(32)
$$m\left[C_2(\lambda_m - \mu_m) + C_1 + C_1\left(\frac{\mu_m^2}{\lambda_m(\lambda_m - \mu_m)}\right) + C_3 \mu_m \right.$$

$$\left. + C_4\left(\frac{\lambda_m}{v_m - \lambda_m}\right) + C_5 v_m + C_1 \frac{\mu_m}{v_m} \right] > w\left[C_2\left(\frac{m}{w}\lambda_m - \frac{m}{w}\mu_m\right) \right.$$

$$+ C_1 + C_1\left(\frac{\frac{m}{w}\mu_m^2}{\frac{m}{w}\lambda_m(\lambda_m - \mu_m)}\right) + \frac{m}{w}C_3 \mu_m$$

$$\left. + C_4\left(\frac{\frac{m}{w}\lambda_m}{\frac{m}{w}v_m - \frac{m}{w}\lambda_m}\right) + C_5\left(\frac{m}{w}v_m\right) + C_1\left(\frac{\frac{m}{w}\mu_m}{\frac{m}{w}v_m}\right) \right]$$

It is assumed here that the arrival rate for a middleman is $\frac{\lambda}{w}$ which is equal to $\frac{m}{w}\lambda_m$ since $\lambda_m = \frac{\lambda}{m}$. Thus this reduces to showing that:

$$mC_1 + mC_1\left(\frac{\mu_m^2}{\lambda_m(\lambda_m - \mu_m)}\right) + mC_4\left(\frac{\lambda_m}{v_m - \lambda_m}\right) + \frac{mC_1\mu_m}{v_m} > wC_1$$

$$+ wC_1\left(\frac{\mu_m^2}{\lambda_m(\lambda_m - \mu_m)}\right) + wC_4\left(\frac{\lambda_m}{v_m - \lambda_m}\right) + \frac{wC_1\mu_m}{v_m}$$

This is obviously true for all values of $w < m$, since all terms are positive, and $\mu_m < \lambda_m < v_m$. In fact, system costs increase linearly with w. The conclusion is that whatever μ_m and v_m happen to be, leaving them unchanged and introducing middlemen in a primary level reduces system costs if the number of middlemen is less than the number of sellers m. If the middlemen and the m now optimize, the system costs when the middlemen exist are obviously lower than when they do not, and the two systems have equal costs only when $w = m$, giving m as the equilibrium number of w.

Combining the contact and communication and order-handling functions with the inventory and order-filling coordinating functions will cause the equilibrium number of middlemen in the primary intermediate level to exceed $\frac{mn}{m + n}$ but fall short of m. The market imperfections and the element of rebates (including order-handling costs that reduce the equilibrium number of middlemen in the discussion of Chapters 2 and 4) will similarly reduce the equilibrium number here to one somewhere between $\frac{mn}{m + n}$ and m. This in turn will reduce the equilibrium number of levels and middlemen in the levels in the total system.

The model which ignores these added elements does not permit the identification of the equilibrium number of levels of middlemen in the vertical market structure. The problems emerge because any increases in system costs accompanying the entry of middlemen are totally excluded from the model. If w_1 is the equilibrium number of middlemen in the primary level and is equal to m, then another level of middlemen could exist between w_1 and m and also be equal to m in equilibrium. This could continue indefinitely unless some costs increase with the creation of levels. One such cost is that of the loss of contact between the producers and the n buyers, and another is the cost of order handling. Yet another cost is that of contact, which would lead to an equilibrium structure similar to that of Chapter 2 with the single middleman closest to the n buyers carrying the inventory and filling the orders. Costs which increase with the creation of levels of inventory, including the primary intermediate level, are discussed throughout this work. The conclusion still remains true, however, that the order-filling coordinating middleman who also performs the contact function can exist in a vertical market structure. It is also true that an equilibrium number of

EQUILIBRIUM STRUCTURES

such levels of middlemen, with each level containing an equilibrium number of middlemen, exists.

1   Marschak, Jacob, "Towards an Economic Theory of Organization and Information," in Thrall, Robert A., et al., *Decision Processes* (New York: John Wiley and Sons, Inc., 1954); and Marschak, Jacob, "Problems in Information Economics," in Bonini, Charles P., et al., *Management Controls* (New York: McGraw-Hill Book Company, 1964).

2   *Ibid.*

3   Saaty, Thomas L., *Mathematical Methods of Operations Research*, (New York: McGraw Hill Book Company, Inc., 1959). This is but one of many possible references wherein the multi-service station queuing models are developed to give the solutions to the system states given here.

4   The details are given in Chapter 5.

5   This is possible because TEC_m is single-valued in μ_m and v_m and hence in $\frac{\mu_m}{\lambda_m}$ and $\frac{\lambda_m}{v_m}$.

6   The optimum $\hat{v}_w$ is obtained in a similar manner to that of $\hat{v}_m$ and is:

$$\hat{v}_w = \lambda_w\left[1 + \sqrt{\frac{C_4}{C_5\lambda_w}}\right]$$

7   The three types of middlemen are (a) the pure coordinator with segemented sellers, (b) the pure coodinator without segemented sellers, and (c) the order-filling middleman.

7

Production Decisions

Extending the generality of the partial analysis

That economic system—the vertical market structure—which forms the subject of analysis is defined earlier in terms of firms (or consumers) and the various cooperative relationships between them. The cooperative relationships which are relevant are those which are either essential to the conclusion of exchange agreements and the completion of transactions, or those which affect the efficiency of such exchange activities. In Chapter 1, the set of firms $\{A_1, \ldots, A_m, X_1, \ldots, X_n\}$ is defined as a vertical market structure, when every A_i has at least one such cooperative relationship with one or more X_j, and conversely for each X_j. Further, the sub-sets of firms $\{A_1, \ldots, A_m\}$ and $\{X_1, \ldots, X_n\}$ form two levels within the structure if the firms in each sub-set compete among themselves for the sales or purchases of the firms in the other sub-set.

Using this general definition of a vertical market structure, it is impossible not to include within it every single firm and consumer in the economy, every kind of cooperative relationship, and every kind of product. To develop a model of such a system would be to capture reality, but it would also be to hide the phenomenon's essential and important characteristics in a mass of irrelevant detail. On the other hand, more restricted definitions of what constitutes a vertical market structure permit the development of models that reveal its essential features. Such models are furthermore solvable, comprehensible, form building blocks for more realistic models, and permit generalized conclusions. Every model developed to this point, therefore, contains within itself a strict definition of what constitutes a vertical market structure. Each model constitutes a partial analysis of the real world phenomenon. The conclusions on equilibrium derived from each model and its combinations refer to sub-systems within the total economy. Nonetheless, the conclusions are general and refer to any vertical market structure, including the total economy, providing that the system does not include important variables *not* included in the partial analysis. The less partial the analysis the larger the number of different kinds of vertical market structures to which its conclusions apply.

There are three basic dimensions of vertical market structures which the partial analysis models consider in varying degrees of completeness. The dimensions are clear from the general definition and are (a) the kinds of cooperative relationships and the functions involved in these relationships among firms in the structure, (b) the number of products exchanged in the structure, and (c) the starting points of the initial levels of m sellers and n buyers. The three dimensions are not completely unrelated but form a basis for developing partial models. Thus one model may discuss only the cooperative relationship exemplified by the particular configuration of the performance of the contact function in a structure. One model may assume the existence of a single product exchanged (for money) throughout the structure in the same physical form, independent of the number of levels in the structure. The limits on the initial levels of m sellers and n buyers, the equilibrium numbers of which are exogenously determined, may be arbitrary or tied in closely with the product's physical form.

The limitations on the variables considered by a model may be removed by combining the single function models and thereby removing the limitation on the generality of the conclusions. One limitation now to be removed is that of the physical form of the product. Intermediaries may now engage in physical production. The removal of the restriction on production has an interesting side effect on the generality of the conclusions of partial analysis. It permits generality in a hitherto unattainable direction.

For purposes of analysis, it is useful to make the distinction between physical production functions and marketing functions, although the real world distinction is not always clear. All models to this point derive equilibrium structures in which the functions performed by the middlemen levels do not involve changing the physical form of the product. The models' conclusions therefore apply to structures in which any physical production is performed by either or both of the initial buying and selling levels only. Since in these models, the variables and parameters determining the equilibrium of the structure, given an exogenously determined number of initial sellers and initial buyers, do not include those of physical production, all conclusions are limited to vertical market structures in which no intermediary level performs such functions. If the m initial sellers are in fact producers, then the model which ignores production cannot apply to the vertical market structure in which this level is viewed as lying below some other level which is now considered the initial level of sellers. Unless physical production variables are considered as determinants of the equilibrium states of vertical market structures, the sub-systems in the economy to which the models apply are sharply limited.

It is useful therefore to develop models which involve physical production decisions and functions as variables, and which solve for the equilibrium locations of such decisions and functions within the vertical market structure. In these models the choice of the initial levels of m sellers and n buyers still may be arbitrary or pragmatically determined by empirical requirements. It is no longer, however, limited to those levels between which no intermediary levels perform physical production functions, given, that is, that the conclusions of the theoretical analysis do refer to and apply to some real world phenomena. If the initial level of m sellers includes producing firms, then no basic distinction between their operations and those of intermediaries exists in the analysis. The equilibrium of levels of producing firms is now within the realm of solution of the model and not necessarily the upper and lower bounds on the levels of the vertical market structure being analyzed. Any model which accepts as exogenously determined variables the number of initial sellers and buyers may now obtain conclusions applicable to a structure where these numbers are variables. The two initial levels now become intermediary levels and two other levels of sellers to, and buyers from, these become the parameters. The model's conclusions are no longer inapplicable to vertical market structures in which the product changes form, such as an entire economy.

One model developed in this chapter also increases the generality of the analysis by allowing a given product to be demanded in a form with one or more variable characteristics. Thus, not only can the product change form within the structure as it heads for a unique form in which it is demanded, but it also arrives in a form that is not unique. In other words, a product may be demanded by the initial buyers in various forms. Though the same product, it may be that some initial buyer firms require one characteristic, and others require some other. The analysis is thus a modest relaxation of the assumption that within the vertical market structure only one unique form of the product is purchased by the n initial buyers. As is clear from the model, the analysis is still a partial one since it is not generalized completely to multiple products. It is generalized to a single product with one or more characteristics taking on a continuum of measurable values. The product demanded by the n initial sellers may be, for example, paint of a given chemical form and at a constant price, the shade of gray—from pure white to pure black—in which it is demanded being a variable.

Variations in the product's physical form

The problem of the location of the production processes within a vertical market structure is discussed in varying forms by Alderson[1] and by Bucklin[2], among others. Generally speaking the problem is to locate as part of a given channel, or vertical market structure, the forms of a product. That is, given a particular product which starts as some raw material, the question is to identify the particular form in which it is purchased and sold by every *level* in a vertical market structure and to compare total structure costs for different configurations.

The "principle of postponement" as elaborated by Alderson[3] states that at the last possible level in the channel, the product should take on the form in which it is used by the consumer or user. The gains from such postponement are associated with the cost of "sorting" and the reduction in risk which comes about from settling on a form required by only a small segment of the users. Thus, if the production process involves costs which limit the capacity of a product to take any desired final form, the more of the process that follows the placing of an order, the less the "risk" that the product will not meet the needs of the buyer. This principle when not balanced by any other would suggest that all physical production involving the use of resources be done by the final user. To avoid this conclusion, Alderson sees rising with this postponement some costs which are associated with economies of scale in production. Thus he states, "Fabrication cannot be postponed beyond the point in the marketing process at which the necessary plant equipment and labor skills are available."[4] Bucklin further works at balancing the principle of postponement by reference to the "principle of speculation." This principle states that costs of ordering, transportation, and stockouts, among others, fall as the process of changing form is moved to the "earliest point" in the channel.[5]

The authors cited indicate the possibility of the existence of a relationship between the vertical market structure and the optimum location of production points within it. The purpose of this analysis is to relate in a rigorous manner the total costs of production and order filling to the vertical market structure. The problem involves the determination of the exact relations, and the conditions under which they hold, between the manner in which pre-order and post-order production are located within the structure and within any given firm in any given level.

Suppose that there were only two levels in a vertical market structure. The question then is to solve for the optimum amount of pre-order production in which the firm in the level of the initial sellers is engaged. Given one level of intermediaries which is made up of order-filling firms, we must ascertain the optimum pre-order production by the firm in the initial level of sellers, and the optimum pre- and post-order production by any firm in the intermediary level. The optimum decisions for both kinds of firms must be determined simultaneously, and the costs for both kinds of vertical market structures compared.

Pre- and post-order production

In the analysis there are two given levels in all vertical market structures characterized by models in which the number of firms is considered to be an exogenously determined variable. The level of m initial sellers is made up of firms which receive the product or products in some physical form, and then by operating physical production facilities, obtain a product in some other form which they exchange with firms in the next level. It is assumed that the forms in which these firms receive the products or raw materials are exogenously determined variables. The firms in the initial level of buyers always purchase the product in a given form. This form is also considered to be a parameter totally independent of the vertical market structure. It is in effect postulated that any and all production or marketing (selling) activities of these firms lie outside the area of analysis. The *form* in which the m firms in the initial selling level sell the product is a variable for which the models give a solution, since it depends upon the vertical market structure. The total amount of physical production performed (though not the cost of production) by firms in all the levels of a market structure except that of the initial buyers is thus given. That is, the total amount of physical transformation performed in the vertical market structure on a product is assumed to be independent of that structure.

Since the form of the product when it first enters the structure and the form in which it enters the final level of buyers in the structure are set, the problem becomes one of locating its form as it enters and leaves all other levels in the structure. A companion problem is to determine for any given firm in the structure the amount of transformation in the product's form which it is to perform prior to the arrival of an order from the next level, and the amount that is performed after the order arrives. The decision will, of course, affect the costs of inventory carrying and the time it takes to fill an order completely.

In the last model of the previous chapter the firm is conceptually divided into a production and a marketing sector. The distinction is based on the concept that some functions of the firm could not (at less than infinite cost) be performed prior to the arrival of an order. This simplifying assumption permits the characterization of the problem of determining the capacities of the facilities designed to perform those functions which can and those which cannot precede the arrival of an order. The model is also simplified by the assumption that all functions which could precede the arrival of an order would be performed prior to its arrival. These are the functions which determine the physical chacteristics of the product, or, in general, are the physcial production functions. In the following models there is still a distinction made between the two kinds of functions. All those which can precede an order are termed physical production functions, and those that cannot are termed marketing, or order-filling, functions. However, two basic assumptions are relaxed in these models.

In Chapter 6 two particular assumptions made are (a) there is only one form in which the product is demanded by the initial level of n buyers and (b) all physical production operations are to be performed prior to the order's arrival. In turn, this leads to the conclusion that these operations would always remain in the level of the initial sellers. The first model drops the second assumption and keeps the first, while the second model drops the first assumption and keeps the second. When either assumption is dropped, it becomes possible for the structure to split the total amount of physical production between levels in the structure.

In relation to the "principle of postponement," the statement of the two assumptions permits a dual interpretation. In the first place the problem is to determine the amount of production which is to occur in the various levels and the allocation of this amount by each firm in the level to pre- and post-order production. Part of this problem is comparing the total costs of various market structures, given that there is a single form in terms of all the characteristics which the product can take. Secondly, we must determine the optimum set of different values of a measurable characteristic of the finished product which each level must produce. In addition, the optimum amount of physical production which is to be allocated by firms in each level to obtain any value not in this set is determined.

The solution to this second problem assumes that there is a probability that any value of the characteristic will be demanded by the n initial buyers, and that any such value can be derived by combining and operating on two particular products in the set of available products. Also vertical market structures are compared for efficiency and equilibrium states. It is possible, therefore, to view the whole issue of postponement as a problem even though there is no issue of matching the final buyer's preferences without added costs. Though the form in which the next buyer requires the product is known, it is not necessarily true that the optimum decision is to have the product in inventory in that form.

The issue of production in vertical market structures depends upon one's concept of the production process. In the models, the nature of the production process and the concept of pre- and post-order production are somewhat simple. There is no discussion of any length of the different kinds of such processes, their physical constraints, or the manner in which any given product is produced. The internal organization of the firm's production process is assumed to be given. The same is assumed of the internal organization of the firm's processes of filling orders. The models permit one to solve for the productive capacity of the firm, the order-filling capacity of the firm, the amount of total production a firm engages in, and the allocation of this amount to pre- and post-order production (the form in which the product is to be carried in inventory). Not all firms in a vertical market structure's different levels need necessarily be confronted with all these problems. The concepts of intermediaries and cooperation between levels permit the simultaneous allocation of the production and marketing functions to different levels. The simultaneous solution of all these problems for firms in more than one level is a meaningful object of search. It is quite possible that the conclusion should be that no inventory be carried in more than one level, or that no more than one level engage in physical production.

It is possible that for any two given vertical market structures the amount of production done by the level which receives the order from the n buyers will be less in one structure, and yet this structure is more efficient that the other. The existence of intermediaries efficiently removes production further, in terms of the number of levels, from the level of the initial buyers. The existence of intermediaries may not be explained in terms of the greater postponement in production which they allow, but rather by the reduction in total costs of production and marketing. These reductions in turn mean that the optimum postponement of production is smaller than it would have been without intermediaries. Thus, not only is there the possibility that structure costs will vary with the location of production in the structure, but there is also the effect of the structure itself on the relative gains and losses obtained from moving the location of production to levels nearer to the initial level of n buyers.

One product form and variable
extent of completeness

In a vertical market structure with m sellers and n buyers and no intermediaries there is assumed to be one single product exchanged for money. The m sellers obtain the product in some form and the n buyers demand the product in some other form. The exact amount of transformation in the product form obtained through the use of physical production resources is given and fixed. In fact, this amount is assumed to be fixed for all vertical market structures considered in this chapter. The buyers' orders generally are assumed to follow the Poisson distribution with mean rate λ. Each firm among the m sellers is thus faced with a Possion order arrival probability distribution with mean $\lambda_m = \dfrac{\lambda}{m}$.

Each seller, as in the last model in Chapter 6, most perform two broad sets of functions; those of physical production and those of order filling. The firm produces the product at some rate in which the average time of production is distributed in an exponential manner with a mean $\frac{1}{\mu_m}$. It also invests resources in a marketing sector which is capable of servicing orders at some average time interval also characterized by an exponential distribution with a mean $\frac{1}{v_m}$. The firm's production sector turns out the product in some form. Then the product is carried in inventory. The marketing sector, upon the arrival of an order, performs any of the remaining amount of transformation in the product's form to bring it to that single form desired by all the buyers, and additionally performs the marketing activities which fill the order. The only difference between this type of operation and that characterized by the last model of Chapter 6 is that the form in which the product leaves the production sector and goes into inventory is *not* given as that form in which it is demanded. The decision on how close to its final form the product is to be brought prior to the order is now a variable to be optimized. The firm must also optimize the values for μ_m and v_m.

Quite clearly, the closer the product is to the final form in which it is demanded when it goes into inventory, the higher the level of resources which are invested in it. This means that the costs incurred per unit of product when it enters inventory rise with the extent of its completeness when it leaves the production sector. Hence for the same level of inventory, the holding costs must also increase. On the other hand, the more complete the product, the less time an order will spend between the time of arrival and the time of its satisfaction, for any given amount of resources expended on the firm's marketing sector. Furthermore, the higher the average output rate μ_m, the higher the average level of inventory and therefore the higher the expected holding costs. A higher mean rate μ_m implies fewer shortages. Finally, a higher v_m involves greater expected costs in the capacity of the marketing sector but also lower expected costs resulting from a shorter average order-filling time. The decision variables μ_m and v_m have the same dimensions they have in the last model of Chapter 6. The dimensions of the third variable—the extent of completeness of the product—require some discussion.

Products are altered from one form into another in a great variety of ways. If one product requires heating for y units of time at $z°$ centigrade to turn it from form A to form B, then the work of transforming it can be said to be half complete if it is heated for $\frac{y}{2}$ units of time at $z°$ centigrade. The extent of its completeness measured from A as the zero point is measureable in terms of units of time, given the required temperature. However, in what units can one measure the completeness of an automobile from some given form to its final form of sale but without the required radio? In order, therefore, to obtain some broad unit of measure applicable to all products, the concept of extent of completeness is related directly to the incurring of costs. That is, if it costs C_0 dollars to operate the physical production facilities in the producing sector to transform the product from form A to form B, then with A as the zero point, the product is half complete if $\frac{C_0}{2}$ dollars have been incurred as costs in the transformation process. Though the concept is somewhat simple, it is a general one and relevant to the problem of inventory costs which are closely (and by assumption in the model, uniquely) related to the amount of money invested in the product prior to its entry into inventory.

For our purposes, therefore, the extent of a product's completeness x_m is defined as the ratio of the costs incurred by the production sector of the firm to the total costs necessary to transform the product. If the cost to the individual producer of operating and maintaining a physical production facility of mean capacity one unit of completed product per unit time were C_1, then the same facility is assumed to have the average capacity of two units per unit time of half-completed products. In other words, the cost of maintaining and operating a productive facility of mean capacity one unit half completed per unit of time is $\frac{C_1}{2}$. This assumes that there are no economies or diseconomies of production resulting from fewer units of product on which the production facility operates in a given time or because of variations in the number of product setups. The variable x_m is thus normalized between zero and one and is equal to $\frac{B}{C_B}$. B is the amount of actual costs incurred in physical production, and C_B are the costs necessary to transform the product from the form in which it is purchased by the m sellers to the form in which it is demanded by the n buyers, when all production is organized to be done prior to order. The variable is, of course, dimensionless and hence applicable to all products, given the assumptions on the production process.

All the assumptions made for the last model of Chapter 6 not explicitly discussed for this model are again made. Recalling the notation from the last model of Chapter 6 and the assumptions implicit in the definition of the symbols we have:

C_1 = cost of holding one unit of the physical product in inventory per unit time when it is in the completed form, when the total transformation in its form is performed in the firm's production sector. Note that the total amount of such transformation to be performed in the structure is considered a given.

C_2 = cost of running short of one unit of the physical product in its finished form.

C_3 = cost per unit time of maintaining and operating a physical production facility (the production sector) with an average output capacity of one unit of product in its finished form per unit time.

C_4 = cost of having an order in the firm's system per unit time. An order is in the system from the moment it arrives until the moment it is filled, or released unfilled but compensated for being unfilled and for the time it has spent in the system.

C_5 = cost per unit of time of maintaining and operating an order-filling facility with an average output capacity of one per unit time, when no physical production is performed by the facility. Thus, some facility of unit cost of C_5 will have an expected capacity of less than one if any physical production is performed on the product after the order's arrival.

μ_m = average capacity of the physical production facility, i.e., the mean rate of production of the firm's producing sector.

v_m = capacity of the marketing facility sector which would be expected if *no* physical production whatever is performed there.

x_m = degree of the product's completeness when it leaves the production sector and enters inventory. $0 < x_m < 1$.

$\lambda_m = \dfrac{\lambda}{m}$ average rate at which orders arrive at the firm's operation, given that the average rate at which all orders are generated by the *n* buying firms is λ.

The firm again is viewed as a system of two queuing and order-servicing operations. The first term in the total cost per unit time equation is the cost of shortage to the individual seller in the initial level of *m* firms. The assumption is made that the firm cannot fill an order if none is in inventory. Inventory of the product is carried in the form in which it leaves the producing sector. It is assumed, in effect, that the marketing sector will perform physical production operations to finish the product after an order arrives only when the product is found in inventory. No production in the marketing sector occurs on products not completed to degree x_m, as that is determined to lie somewhere *between* 0 and 1. The marketing sector has as its input for physical production only the output of the production sector. The total shortage cost is thus identical to that of the model in Chapter 6 where, of course, $x_m = 1$ by assumption. The firm's expected shortage cost per unit time is:

(1)
$$C_2(\lambda_m - \mu_m)$$

The firm's expected inventory holding costs are derived by first obtaining the average number of units of product held in inventory per unit time. The number is identical to that in the last model: $\left(1 + \dfrac{\mu_m^2}{\lambda_m(\lambda_m - \mu_m)}\right)$ units of product per unit time. The cost of holding one product one unit of time when the product is in finished form is C_1. If we now assume that the holding cost per unit is a linear function of the amount of the cost of production (in the producing sector) which is incurred before the product goes into inventory, the holding cost per unit would be $C_1 x_m$. The holding cost per unit is thus in a very simple relation to the amount of money actually invested in the production of a product. Since x_m is normalized as a ratio between 0 and 1, and since the cost of holding a unit is C_1 when $x_m = 1$, the expected cost of holding per unit time is:

$$(2) \qquad C_1 x_m \left(1 + \frac{\mu_m^2}{\lambda_m(\lambda_m - \mu_m)} \right)$$

If it costs C_3 to maintain and operate a physical production facility of expected capacity per unit time of one completed product, then it costs $C_3 x_m$ for the operation when the product is completed up to the degree x_m. Expected costs of the production sector of the firm are thus:

$$(3) \qquad C_3 x_m \mu_m$$

When the marketing facility performs no physical production whatsoever, then the expected costs of waiting are shown in the last model to be $C_4 \left(\dfrac{\lambda_m}{v_m - \lambda_m} \right)$. It is now assumed that the expected capacity of the marketing sector falls from one unit per unit time for every C_5 cost incurred to some number less than one. In fact it is assumed that the capacity per C_5 cost incurred falls linearly with the amount of production which the marketing sector has to perform. The effective expected capacity is x_m units per unit time for every C_5 cost incurred. If the firm decides on an expected unit capacity of v_m, then its effective expected capacity is $x_m v_m$. The marketing sector engages in $(1 - x_m)$ of the total product transformation activity. This assumption leads to a total cost of waiting which is of the same form as that in the model of Chapter 6. Both models make the same assumptions on the average output capacity of the marketing sector, with one main exception. This difference is that the effective capacity of the sector is $x_m v_m$ whereas earlier it was v_m, i. e., x_m was assumed to be equal to one. Total waiting costs are therefore:

$$(4) \qquad C_4 \left(\frac{\lambda_m}{x_m v_m - \lambda_m} \right)$$

The assumption on the capacity of the marketing sector leads to meaningless results for a value of $x_m = 0$, when no pre-order production is undertaken. It is used here to simplify the analysis, which becomes very complex despite the assumption. Furthermore, for $x_m = 0$ or $x_m = 1$, the solutions to the problem are to be found in Chapters 5 and 6, and this model applies only if the parameters are such as to allow x_m to take on values other than 0 or 1 at the optimum. As it stands the assumption states reasonably that a marketing facility with capacity of one unit per unit time without any physical production would have its capacity reduced to less than one unit when it has to do *some but not all* of the physical production. The smaller x_m, the greater is the reduction in this effective capacity, which is thus assumed to be $x_m v_m$.

Since v_m refers to the capacity which is to be expected from the marketing facility when $x_m = 1$, with all production pre-order and none post-order, the firm's expected cost of maintaining and operating an order-filling facility is:

$$(5) \qquad\qquad C_5 v_m$$

As in the previous chapter, the expected cost of holding the product during the time the order is being filled is ignored because it is a minor cost component that adds complication but little understanding of the phenomenon of vertical market structures.

The total expected costs for the seller among the m sellers in the absence of intermediaries is given by the sum of the terms (1) to (5), i. e.,

$$(6) \quad \begin{aligned} TEC_m &= C_2(\lambda_m - \mu_m) + C_1 x_m\left(1 + \frac{\mu_m^2}{\lambda_m(\lambda_m - \mu_m)}\right) + C_3 x_m \mu_m \\ &\quad + C_4\left(\frac{\lambda_m}{x_m v_m - \lambda_m}\right) + C_5 v_m \end{aligned}$$

The variables to be optimized are μ_m, the expected capacity of the continuously operating physical production sector; x_m, the degree to which production is to be performed prior to the arrival of the order; and v_m, the expected capacity of the firm's marketing sector, if it were to do no physical production (but in fact it does some production) which makes its effective capacity $x_m v_m$, less than v_m.[6] For $x_m = 1$, the last model of Chapter 6 is the relevant one, though the solution to this model shows that the case of $x_m = 1$ is a special example of the more general case for $1 > x_m > 0$. The case of $x_m = 0$ is not meaningfully characterized by this model. Given, therefore, that x_m is at its optimum value when it is not zero, the costs in (6) can be minimized with respect to the three decision variables. Let $\rho_1 = \frac{\mu_m}{\lambda_m}$ and $\rho_2 = \frac{\lambda_m}{v_m}$. Then the problem is to minimize:

$$(7) \quad \begin{aligned} TEC_m &= C_2\lambda_m(1 - \rho_1) + C_1 x_m\left((1 - \rho_1) + \frac{\rho_1}{(1 - \rho_1)}\right) + C_3 x_m \lambda_m \rho_1 \\ &\quad + C_4\frac{\rho_2}{(x_m - \rho_2)} + \frac{C_5\lambda_m}{\rho_2} \end{aligned}$$

To minimize its total expected costs per unit time, the firm sets

$$(8) \qquad \frac{\partial}{\partial \rho_1} TEC_m = -(C_2 - C_3 x_m)\lambda_m - C_1 x_m + \frac{C_1 x_m}{(1 - \rho_1)^2} = 0$$

$$(9) \qquad \frac{\partial}{\partial \rho_2} TEC_m = \frac{C_4 x_m}{(x_m - \rho_2)^2} - \frac{C_5\lambda_m}{\rho_2^2} = 0$$

$$(10) \quad \frac{\partial}{\partial x_m} TEC_m = C_1\left[(1 - \rho_1) + \frac{\rho_1}{(1 - \rho_1)}\right] + C_3\lambda_m\rho_1 - \frac{C_4\rho_2}{(x_m - \rho_2)^2} = 0$$

The solutions of equations (8) and (9) for the optimum ρ_1 and ρ_2, and the substitution of $\frac{\mu_m}{\lambda_m}$ and $\frac{\lambda_m}{v_m}$ for these gives the optimum values for μ_m and

v_m in terms of parameters and the variable x_m. Thus the optimal μ_m is:

$$(11) \qquad \hat{\mu}_m = \lambda_m \left[1 - \sqrt{\frac{C_1 x_m}{(C_2 - C_3 x_m)\lambda_m + C_1 x_m}} \right]$$

This equation is a special case of equation (24) of Chapter 6, i.e., one in which by postulate, x_m is not considered a variable and is set at a value of 1. Exactly the same conclusion is obtained for the optimal v_m, which is thus:

$$(12) \qquad \hat{v}_m = \lambda_m \left[\frac{1}{x_m} + \frac{\sqrt{C_4 x_m}}{x_m \sqrt{C_5 \lambda_m}} \right]$$

This equation is identical to equation (25) of Chapter 6 for $x_m = 1$

The solution for the optimal level of x_m (providing it is not zero) involves solving equation (10) for x_m in terms of ρ_1 and ρ_2 and then substituting into the solution the optimal values for μ_m and v_m. Thus equation (10) yields an implicit equation in the one variable x_m, and the solution to this equation would yield the value of the optimal x_m, or $\hat{x}_m$. Thus:

$$(13) \qquad 0 = \frac{\sqrt{C_1}\,[2C_1 x_m + (C_2 - 2C_3 x_m)\lambda_m]}{\sqrt{C_1 x_m^2 + (C_2 - C_3 x_m)x_m \lambda_m}} + C_3 \lambda_m$$
$$- C_1 + \frac{C_5 \lambda_m + \sqrt{C_4 C_5 x_m \lambda_m}}{x_m^2}$$

That x_m which satisfies this equation, given all the parameters, is the optimal $\hat{x}_m$. For numerical values of these parameters, $\hat{x}_m$ should be capable of evaluation (providing the parameters are such as to make $0 < \hat{x}_m \leq 1$, for otherwise the model is inapplicable.) For obvious reasons writing an explicit equation for x_m in terms of parameters only is no easy matter. This difficulty does not permit one to state in general terms how the entry of middlemen is likely to affect the optimum amount of pre-order production performed in the system by the m sellers.[7] It is possible nonetheless to arrive at conclusions on how entry of middlemen affects the total system's costs when after this introduction the new optimum values for μ_m, v_m, and x_m are set. In fact, it is possible to discuss system efficiency when only $\hat{\mu}_m$ and $\hat{v}_m$ become $\hat{\mu}_w$ and $\hat{v}_w$, while $\hat{x}_m$ is left unchanged for the two systems, one with and one without a single level of middlemen.

Though the notion of pre-order and post-order distinguishes simply between the operations which can and those which cannot precede an order, the distinction, in fact, is not quite so simple. It is conceivable that every single operation necessary for exchange be performed prior to the actual acceptance of the exchange transaction by a buyer. The exception in a free economy is the operation related to the receipt of funds from the buyer. It is possible that the seller goes to the length of delivering a product to the control of the would-be buyer prior to the agreement of the buyer to enter into an exchange transaction. Committing a product to a geographic area for storage prior to its sale is in essence pre-order transportation to some degree. Many of the so-called marketing operations, which in the model are by assumption limited to the firm's sector which operates only on the receipt of an order, are possible to perform in the pre-order operating sector. The assumption of the model is realistic, however, if we realize that some operations involve a very large cost if done prior to and in anticipation of an order. One can postulate with little loss of generality, therefore, that such activities must be left for performance after the receipt of an order. These are the operations which are generally termed the marketing ones for purposes of exposition.

One product form, variable extent
of completeness, and middlemen

In a structure with w middlemen, the middlemen would perform all post-order operations and the m sellers the pre-order production. That is, the cooperation of these m sellers cannot be obtained by the w middlemen unless the sellers' profits are at least unchanged, and unless they are allowed to continue to exist. They will not cooperate themselves out of existence. The individual middleman must then optimize all values of the relevant variables, namely μ_w, v_w, and x_w. He would carry inventories of the product in some form with a degree of completion x_w, and receive the product into inventory at some average rate μ_w. The m sellers would each be producing continuously at a mean rate $\frac{w\mu_w}{m}$, and the production of the product would be completed by them to degree x_w. The middleman would also have a marketing facility with effective expected capacity of $x_w v_w$, where orders would be filled, and $(1 - x_w)$ of the total transformation in the product's form would be performed after each order is received from the n buyers.

The optimal values of μ_w, v_w and x_w are obtained in the manner shown above. Thus, the optimal pre-order productive capacity is:

$$(14) \qquad \hat{\mu}_w = \lambda_w \left[1 - \sqrt{\frac{C_1 x_w}{(C_2 - C_3 x_w)\lambda_w + C_1 x_w}} \right]$$

The optimal order-filling capacity which would give an expected effective capacity of $x_w v_w$ is:

$$(15) \qquad \hat{v}_w = \lambda_w \left[\frac{1}{x_w} + \frac{\sqrt{C_4 x_w}}{x_w \sqrt{C_5 \lambda_w}} \right]$$

The optimal degree of completeness of the product when it leaves the pre-production sector is that which satisfies equation (13) with λ_w substituted for λ_m and when x_w is substituted for x_m.

Since the explicit optimal values of x_m and x_w are not available, the system's minimum total expected costs with and without middlemem are given in terms of the parameters and x_m and x_w. The system's relevant expected costs for direct exchange and exchange through intermediaries simplify respectively to $SEC_m = mTEC_m$ and $SEC_w = wTEC_w$ or to:

(16)
$$SEC_m = m\left[\frac{\lambda_m C_5}{\hat{x}_m} - C_1\hat{x}_m + \frac{2}{\sqrt{\hat{x}_m}}\sqrt{C_4\lambda_m C_5} + C_3\lambda_m\hat{x}_m\right.$$
$$\left. + 2\sqrt{(C_1\hat{x}_m)^2 + C_1\hat{x}_m(C_2 - C_3\hat{x}_m)\lambda_m}\right]$$

(17)
$$SEC_w = w\left[\frac{\lambda_m C_5}{\hat{x}_w} - C_1\hat{x}_w + \frac{2}{\sqrt{\hat{x}_w}}\sqrt{C_4\lambda_w C_5} + C_3\lambda_w\hat{x}_w\right.$$
$$\left. + 2\sqrt{(C_1\hat{x}_w)^2 + C_1\hat{x}_w(C_2 - C_3\hat{x}_w)\lambda_w}\right]$$

The two systems' total expected costs for values of w cannot be compared directly because the explicit values for $\hat{x}_m$ and $\hat{x}_w$ are not known. It still can be proven, however, that expected costs for the system with intermediaries is less than that for the system of direct exchange. This conclusion holds, providing the number of middlemen in the primary level is smaller than the number m and there are no system costs other than those shown in equations **(16)** and **(17)**. The proof is obtained simply if we assume that each of the w middlemen optimizes μ_w and v_w, but retains the same value for x_w as would have been the optimum in the system without any intermediaries. That is, let $\hat{x}_w$ in equation **(17)** be left as $\hat{x}_m$. Then in the fashion in which the comparison between equations **(27)** and **(30)** of the previous chapter is made, it can be shown that $SEC_w < SEC_m$ for all $w < m$, and that SEC_w is lowest for $w = 1$. It may be recalled that the proof depends upon the condition that $\lambda_m < \lambda_w$ for $w < m$, and $(C_2 - C_3 x_m) > 0$. If this is true when the middlemen do not necessarily pick the optimal x_w, then it must be true when they do pick an optimum x_w, which by definition can lead to an expected total cost situation equal to or less than that obtained from using the value $\hat{x}_m$.

Providing, therefore, that no new kinds of costs are added in the system when middlemen enter into a primary level, such a system is more efficient than one of direct exchange if $w < m$. If rebates are demanded by the m sellers from the w middlemen, and if the added placement of orders by the w middlemen involves a cost, then the equilibrium number of middlemen will be less than the number m. Obviously the system costs shown in equation **(17)** increase as w increases. If, furthermore, we let rebates plus order handling costs be some monotonically increasing function of w, namely $R(w)$, then the equilibrium number of middlemen w is that number for which the two systems' costs are equal. Thus w is that number which satisfies the equality

(18)
$$SEC_w + R(w) = SEC_m$$

In comparing the optimum levels of total system pre-order production capacity and post-order marketing sector capacity, it is seen that the conclusions are similar to those of Chapter 6 when x_w is left at $\hat{x}_m$. That is, the entry of middlemen leads to an increase in $m\hat{\mu}_m$ to $w\hat{\mu}_w$ of total capacity, with the increase being larger the smaller the number w is. The reverse is true for the expected capacities $\hat{v}_m$ and $\hat{v}_w$. However, if x_w is set at the optimum value it is not entirely clear how the capacities of the system will change.

Given that one level of middlemen can exist in the system and have an equilibrium number of firms in it that is smaller than m, then other levels could possibly also exist. Since there is in this system some post-order production, while the model in Chapter 6 had none, the conclusions for the two systems on multi-levels of middlemen are different. If the primary level performs the post-order production, then a firm in a level between this one and the n buyers takes over the order-filling functions, including post-order production. If this is the case on the sellers' side of the primary intermediate level, there are no possibilities for the development of added intermediary levels, unless the middleman there behaves as a pure coordinator. Since post-order production and marketing operations need not, in this model, be performed anywhere except in a single level, all intermediary levels between this one and the m sellers operate as pure coordinators providing they are not logically necessary to the existence of this order-filling level.

The primary intermediate level must be convinced to cooperate before a level w_2 between it and the n buyers is possible. If this new level fills orders, then the firms in the primary level would merely operate as handlers (not decision makers on the inventory level or on capacities) of the pre-order produced product. The w_2 firms could, however, operate as pure coordinators, directing orders to the free members of the primary intermediate level in the manner described in Chapter 5. The firms in a level between the primary intermediate level and the m sellers can only operate as pure coordinators, directing the arriving products to the middleman with no inventory (free of waiting *goods*). If the firms attempted to operate as order fillers, and take over the functions of the primary middlemen, those firms in the intermediate level selling to the n buyers could not operate as order fillers. In such a case the primary middlemen would be mere order handlers and those selling to the buyers, pure coordinators.

It is not possible to state generally which of the levels will become the order-filling level and which the pure coordinator. The answer will depend upon the relative costs of waiting (orders in system) or products in system (inventory holding). It is possible to state, however, that since only one post-order producing and order-filling level is possible, only one of the two intermediary levels will perform as such. The other operates as a coordinator of pre-order produced goods or orders, moving to firms. It is not until the next chapter's analysis that multiple levels of post-order producers become possible. At this moment no system efficiency is gained by having the marketing operations (including post-order production) performed in more than one level. The analysis on further levels beyond w_2 and w_3 proceeds in the same manner. If the introduction of the function $R(w)$ means that each new level involves an increase in some cost, then each level will have fewer firms that those on whose existence it is logically dependent. The end result is a finite number of levels in equilibrium, of firms in levels, and a set of operations by pairs in each level that is not the same for all levels.

The nature of the structure that emerges in equilibrium will depend for its details on the system's parameters. Thus, for example, how much pre-production is performed and how large x_m or x_w will be, will depend upon the expenses associated with carrying the product. If perishability of style or physical structure were viewed as a holding cost, then more perishable products will involve more post-order production. Similarly the product for which customer waiting costs are relatively higher will be produced in a larger degree of completeness prior to order than a product with a lower level of waiting costs. In general the reduction in system costs brought about by the creation of the primary intermediate level of one middleman also will depend on the system's parameters. In turn, the equilibrium number of firms in this level will depend on this total reduction. The effects of the parameters are thus carried through the structure to determine its specific equilibrium characteristics of the number of levels and the number of firms and their manner of operation in each level.

Variable product form

In a vertical market structure a single product is exchanged for money. The n buyers do not, however, demand a product which is identical in every respect. One characteristic of the product is measurable in a single dimension, and each of the orders generated by the n buyers specifies a value that this characteristic must take. Thus, an order would be for a unit of the product with a value k which this particular characteristic must have. It is assumed that there exist a maximum and a minimum value for this characteristic which any order generated could specify. Since the product demanded is identical in all but this one characteristic, we can state that each order is for a unit of the product with attribute k which lies between two finite limits.

For the individual seller the problem is a simplified form of the problem of optimal choice of assortment to carry in inventory. Though as yet the problem is not fully specified, in general the seller must make the choice of the attributes which the units of the product carried in inventory must have.

The product may be, for example, paint and the attribute specified, its color. Another possibility is to define the attribute as the length and the product as steel beams. In fact, a model developed by Sadowski[8] treats just such a problem. This model forms the basis for the analysis which follows. In general, the more attributes the inventory of products includes, the lower the costs of filling orders or the better the orders are matched. More of the various attributes in inventory would also involve greater production or inventory costs. The particular model developed identifies these specific cost relations and permits an optimal balance between them.

A model is developed to solve for the optimal attributes which the units of product carried in inventory are to have. Its aim is to investigate the effects on these optimal values, and on total system costs, of variations in the vertical market structure. In terms of the "principle of postponement" the problem again reduces to one of pre-order and post-order production. If it is possible to vary the attribute of one or more units of the product carried in inventory in order to meet the specific attribute requirement of an order, then this process of variation is post-order production. In cases where the amount of such production varies inversely with the number of different attributes which units in inventory have, the problem is one of determining how much production to postpone until the arrival of an order. The greater the pre-order production performed, the larger the number of attributes which units of inventory have, and the smaller the amount of post-order production which is to be expected. The upper limit on the amount of pre-order production would be to have units which have attributes such that every conceivable attribute demanded can be met directly from inventory. The lower limit, of course, occurs when no pre-order production is performed whatsoever. In this problem, therefore, pre-order and post-order production affect the degree to which the inventory matches the demand requirements for product units of given attributes.

If one were to compare the model of this section with the previous model, one could label the latter a model of *depth* in pre-order production, and the former one of *breadth* in pre-order production. Previously the issue was to determine to what extent to pre-order produce a product of a *given* (single) attribute. Now the issue is to determine how many sets of products, each with a given attribute, are to be produced prior to the order. It is assumed that every unit produced is complete in its production, providing that it matches exactly the attribute demanded. In effect, once the attribute which a product is to take when it is produced prior to order is determined, the product will be produced fully in this form. We return therefore to the assumption relaxed in the previous model, and relax instead the assumption on the uniqueness of the form in which the product is demanded. The term "form" now refers to the attribute of a product, and the attribute is measured along a single dimension of a given product characteristic. The choice of the depth of pre-order production of a single form is now replaced by the breadth of the number of forms which are to be completely produced prior to order.

The conclusions that emerge from the model relate to three decision variables. They involve the optimal values of the capacities of the pre-order production facility and the marketing sector (post-order production) facility. The set of attributes in which products are to be pre-order produced and thus carried in inventory must also be determined. It is shown that a vertical market structure with intermediaries in one level of fewer than m firms is more efficient than that of direct exchange between the m sellers and n buyers. It is also shown that the former structure has an optimal value for the *number* of different attributes in which products are pre-order produced that is not necessarily the same as that of the latter. In other words, the existence of a level of middlemen alters the postponement of production which occurs in the structure.

The n buyers generate orders at a mean rate λ, and it is assumed that the probability distribution of the orders generated is a Poisson. Let:

$p(k)$ = probability that the next incoming order is one for a product with attribute value k.

$S(k)$ = probability that the next incoming order is one for a product with an attribute value in *excess* of k.

k_i = the ith attribute value of pre-order produced products. In an inventory there will exist products that have specific attribute values, and k_i is the ith such value.

If an order specifies an attribute value which is not one of those which the pre-order produced units have, then the order is filled after a production process which involves a combination of units in inventory. Pre-order produced units of attributes lying on either side of that attribute which is demanded are, by a process of post-order production, combined in some manner to produce units of the product with the demanded attribute. Thus, it is assumed that for an order of size q_r specifying an attribute value k_r which lies between the classes of attributes carried in inventory, k_i and k_{i+1},

$$q_r = \alpha_{r,i} q_i + \beta_{r,i} q_{i+1}$$

where $\alpha_{r,i} + \beta_{r,i} = 1$, $0 \leqslant \alpha_{r,i} \leqslant 1$, $0 \leqslant \beta_{r,i} \leqslant 1$,

and $\alpha_{r,i} = \dfrac{k_r - k_i}{k_{i+1} - k_i}$

It is assumed that linear combinations of products of given attributes produce products of intermediate attributes. Thus, one unit with attribute of $\dfrac{1}{2}$ is obtained from a combination of one-half a unit with attribute of $\dfrac{1}{4}$ and one-half a unit with attribute $\dfrac{3}{4}$. When $q_r = q_i$ then of course $\alpha_{r,i} = 1$, and $\beta_{r,i} = 0$.

There are, of course, many possible processes which will match an attribute in inventory with an attribute demanded. It is possible, for example, to take the existing attribute and reduce it to the one required in the case of lengths of steel beams, of pipes, etc. If the required length of pipe is five feet and the ones in stock are four feet or six feet, it may be possible to shorten a six-foot pipe to make a five-foot one.[9] The particular process chosen here is in this sense purely for purposes of general analysis and not necessarily one which characterizes faithfully all such adaptation processes. Furthermore, it is assumed that the firm will only engage in post-order production processes which involve the combining of products of existing attributes. At the very minimum the firm must have in inventory units of product with the lowest value of attribute demanded and with the highest value of attribute demanded. In other words, all post-order production is limited to this "blending" process, with pre-order production, at the very minimum, limited to the production of products with the lowest and highest values for k. The value of k is normalized between zero and one, and thus $k_1 = 0$ and $k_{N+1} = 1$. The variable N refers to the number of different attribute values which the pre-order production sector produces in addition to the largest attribute value. The minimum value for N is postulated to be 1, in which case the firm pre-order produces only products with attribute values of 0 and 1.

It is assumed that the time it takes to obtain a product of attribute value r, lying between attributes carried in inventory k_i and k_{i+1}, depends upon the range between the attribute k_i and k_{i+1}. Thus $t_r = \theta(k_{i+1} - k_i) = $ average time required to complete the "blending" of one unit of product with attribute k_r, where θ is a parameter.

The expected time, therefore, which an order will take to match the attribute it specifies from the blending of products with attributes carried in inventory is:

(19) $$E(t) = \sum_{i=1}^{N} \int_{k_i}^{k_{i+1}} \theta(k_{i+1} - k_i)p(k)dk$$

Since $p(k) = -\dfrac{d}{dk}S(k)$ and $S(k) = \int_{k}^{k_{\max}} p(k)dk$, where $k_{\max} = 1$,

then $$E(t) = \sum_{i=1}^{N} \theta(k_{i+1} - k_i)\left\{\int_{k_i}^{1} p(k)dk - \int_{k_{i+1}}^{1} p(k)dk\right\},$$

which finally gives:

(19a) $$E(t) = \theta \sum_{i=1}^{N} (k_{i+1} - k_i)\{S(k_i) - S(k_{i+1})\}$$

The expression in the summation sign can be illustrated by Chart 7.1.

The first problem to be solved by the individual firm is that of determining the optimum k_i for all values of i, given a fixed N. The firm wishes to minimize $E(t)$, and to simplify the analysis, it is assumed that the distribution of $p(k)$ is rectangular. That is, the probability that the attribute takes on any given value between the two limits is constant for all values including the limits.[10] Thus in Chart 7.1 the function is assumed to be linear. The

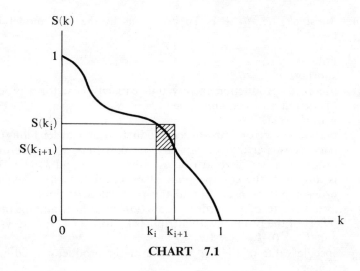

CHART 7.1

solution stated in terms of N, the number of different attributes to be carried in inventory, gives the optimum ranges $k_{i+1} - k_i$ for any given N.

Setting the partial derivative of $E(t)$ with respect to k_i when attribute demand is characterized by a rectangular distribution between the limits $k = 0$ and $k = 1$ (hence $S(k_i) = \delta + \phi k_i$), yields:

$$\frac{\partial}{\partial k_i} E(t) = 2\phi\theta[k_{i-1} - 2k_i + k_{i+1}] = 0$$

or,

(20)
$$k_i = \frac{k_{i+1} + k_{i-1}}{2}$$

This last equation holds for $i = 2, 3, \ldots, N$, and by postulate at least two attributes must be carried in inventory, $k_1 = 0$ and $k_{N+1} = 1$. The solution to this set of recursive equations gives the optimal k_i as

(21)
$$\hat{k}_i = \frac{i-1}{N}$$

which implies: $\hat{k}_{i+1} - \hat{k}_i = \frac{1}{N}$, for all values of $i = 1, 2, \ldots, N$. Thus, whatever the number of attributes which the products in inventory are to have, the range between successive attributes must be equal. This is true only because the distribution of $p(k)$ is assumed to be rectangular. For example, if $N = 2$, then $k_1 = 0$, $k_2 = \frac{1}{2}$, and $k_3 = 1$. Given the rectangular distribution of attribute demands, the least "blending" time is encountered when the attributes are set at equal distances along the characteristic's dimension, assuming that the number of attributes to be carried in inventory is $N + 1$. There is still the problem of determining the *optimum* number of attributes to stock, i.e., $N + 1$. To do so, as in the first model in this chapter,[11] let:

$C_1 =$ holding cost.

$C_2 =$ shortage cost.

$C_{3,i} =$ pre-order production facility unit capacity cost for a product of attribute k_i per unit time.

$C_4 =$ waiting cost.

$C_5 =$ marketing sector (post-order production and order filling) capacity cost per unit of capacity per unit time, when pre-order production is of two attributes only, $k_1 = 0$ and $k_2 = 1$. This is, in effect, the cost per unit of expected capacity when pre-order production is kept to the postulated minimum.

$\mu_i =$ average rate of pre-order production by a firm among the m sellers of the product with attributes k_i, for $i = 1, 2, \ldots, N+1$, and $k_1 = 0$, $k_{N+1} = 1$.

$k_i =$ specific value of the ith attribute of the product carried in inventory.

$v_m =$ expected rate of order filling of the marketing sector per unit time when $N = 1$ and $k_1 = 0$ and $k_2 = 1$. This is the rate that would be expected per C_5 cost incurred. Post-order production is kept at its postulated maximum when only two attributes of the product are carried in inventory.

$\lambda_{m,i} =$ order rate for product of attribute k_i from the firm in the m seller group.

In the absence of intermediaries the individual seller operates a firm which can be divided conceptually into two sectors. The pre-order production sector operates continuously, producing $N + 1$ different attribute products. The products then enter into inventory. The marketing sector of the firm operates only upon existing orders. The sector fills orders by performing necessary functions, one of which involves post-order physical production. This production operates to "blend" only products found in inventory in order to match exactly the requirements of the order for a product attribute. The firm's expected total cost equation is made up of holding costs, shortage costs, two capacity cost elements, and a waiting cost element.

The first two terms derived in the total expected cost expression are those related to inventory. Assume that the pre-order production process *concurrently* produces output at an average rate of μ_i units of each of the attribute types. Assume also that the output time distribution is exponential. The inventory is depleted at an aggregate average rate $\lambda_m = \dfrac{\lambda}{m}$. The average demand rate for the k_i attribute product ($i \neq 1$ and $i \neq (N + 1)$) is $\lambda_{m,i}$ and this is equal to $\dfrac{\lambda_m}{N}$ since $p(k)$ is a constant. The average demand rate for products of attributes k_1 and k_{N+1} is $\dfrac{\lambda_m}{2N}$, since neither is used in blending to produce products with attributes *beyond* these two limits. For all other attributes, the product with that attribute having a value on either side of it is used for blending to fill the demand. The expected time a unit of product of attribute k_i ($i \neq 1$, $i \neq (N+1)$) will spend in inventory when such products arrive at rate $\mu_{m,i}$ and depart at a rate $\lambda_{m,i}$ is

$$E(t_i) = \frac{\mu_i}{\dfrac{\lambda_m}{N}\left(\dfrac{\lambda_m}{N} - \mu_i\right)}; \quad i = 2, 3, \ldots, N.$$

For products of attribute k_1 or k_{N+1} the expected time each spends in inventory is

$$E(t_1) = \frac{\mu_1}{\dfrac{\lambda_m}{2N}\left(\dfrac{\lambda_m}{2N} - \mu_1\right)}$$

and

$$E(t_{N+1}) = \frac{\mu_{N+1}}{\dfrac{\lambda_m}{2N}\left(\dfrac{\lambda_m}{2N} - \mu_{N+1}\right)}$$

In addition each unit spends a period of time equal to $\dfrac{1}{\mu_i}$, in the pre-order production process ($i = 1, 2, 3, \ldots, N+1$). The total expected holding cost for all units of all attributes is:

$$C_1 \sum_{i=2}^{N} \mu_i \left(\frac{\mu_i}{\dfrac{\lambda_m}{N}\left(\dfrac{\lambda_m}{N} - \mu_i\right)} + \frac{1}{\mu_i} \right) + C_1 \mu_1 \left(\frac{\mu_1}{\dfrac{\lambda_m}{2N}\left(\dfrac{\lambda_m}{2N} - \mu_1\right)} + \frac{1}{\mu_1} \right)$$

$$+ \; C_1 \mu_{N+1} \left(\frac{\mu_{N+1}}{\dfrac{\lambda_m}{2N}\left(\dfrac{\lambda_m}{2N} - \mu_{N+1}\right)} + \frac{1}{\mu_{N+1}} \right)$$

This expression reduces to:

$$\text{(22)} \quad C_1 \sum_{i=2}^{N} \left(1 - \frac{N\mu_i}{\lambda_m} + \frac{\mu_i}{\left(\dfrac{\lambda_m}{N} - \mu_i\right)} \right) + C_1 \left(1 - \frac{2N\mu_1}{\lambda_m} + \frac{2N\mu_1}{\lambda_m - 2N\mu_1} \right)$$

$$+ \; C_1 \left(1 - \frac{2N\mu_{N+1}}{\lambda_m} + \frac{2N\mu_{N+1}}{\lambda_m - 2N\mu_{N+1}} \right)$$

The shortage costs stem from depleted inventories, or, in terms of queues, from the time when the system is empty of the arriving units of the product. For purposes of simplicity it is assumed that a product with attribute k_r can only be obtained from the combination of units with attributes k_i and k_{i+1}, where k_r lies between these two values. Thus, if inventory is empty of products of either attribute k_i or k_{i+1}, it is assumed that a product of attribute k_r will not be available to fill demand. This permits a fairly simple derivation of the shortages in the system, which would be extremely involved otherwise. There are, in effect, inventories of products with $N+1$ different attributes. If we now consider only one such inventory I_i, then it, as a system of waiting lines, is empty with probability P_0. This is equal to $1 - \dfrac{N\mu_i}{\lambda_m}$ for

$i = 2, 3, \ldots, N$ only. The total number of units of product of the ith attribute which the firm can expect as a shortage per unit time is

$$\frac{\lambda_m}{N} P_0 = \frac{\lambda_m}{N} - \mu_i$$

For products of attribute k_1 and k_{N+1} the numbers of units short to be expected are:

$$\frac{\lambda_m}{2N} - \mu_1, \text{ and } \frac{\lambda_m}{2N} - \mu_{N+1}, \text{ respectively.}$$

The total expected shortage cost term is thus[12]:

$$\sum_{i=2}^{N} C_2 \frac{(\lambda_m - N\mu_i)}{N} + C_2 \left(\left(\frac{\lambda_m}{2N} - \mu_1 \right) + \left(\frac{\lambda_m}{2N} - \mu_{N+1} \right) \right)$$

The expected shortage costs reduce to:

$$(23) \qquad C_2 \left(\lambda_m - \sum_{i=1}^{N+1} \mu_i \right)$$

It is to be noted that this shortage cost is applicable only if a firm cannot substitute one attribute for another in "blending" to meet the order specification. Once the attributes carried in inventory are set, by postulate, each is "blended" only with either of the two attributes which lie on either side and only if these are in inventory. The limiting attributes are, of course, combined with just one such contiguous attribute.

The expected capacity cost of the pre-order production sector of the firm is the sum of the expected capacity costs of all the facilities within the sector. Each of these facilities produces an average of μ_i units of product with attribute k_i. Total expected capacity costs are therefore:

$$(24) \qquad \sum_{i=1}^{N+1} C_{3,i} \mu_i$$

In equation (21) the optimal range $\hat{k}_{i+1} - \hat{k}_i$ is found to be $\frac{1}{N}$. When this value is substituted into expression (19), the minimum expected time spent by an order in service is

$$\hat{E}(t) = \theta \sum_{i=1}^{N} (\hat{k}_{i+1} - \hat{k}_i)[S(\hat{k}_i) - S(\hat{k}_{i+1})], \text{ which reduces to:}$$

$$\hat{E}(t) = \theta \sum_{i=1}^{N} \frac{1}{N} \cdot \frac{1}{N}, \text{ or:}$$

$$\hat{E}(t) = \frac{\theta}{N}$$

If we let $\theta = 1$ (for simplicity) then the expected time an order spends in service is an inverse function of the number of intermediate product attributes stocked plus one. The intermediate attributes are those which do not, by postulate, have to be carried, namely, k_i for $i = 2, 3, \ldots, N$. If the capacity of a given marketing sector is v_m when N takes its minimum value of one (i.e., only the two limiting attributes are carried, k_1 and k_{N+1}), then its capacity increases at the rate N as N increases. Thus effective expected service capacity is N per C_5 cost incurred in the marketing sector. A facility's effective capacity is thus Nv_m. The average time an order spends in the system is thus $\dfrac{1}{Nv_m - \lambda_m}$, and the expected waiting costs incurred are:

(25)
$$\frac{C_4 \lambda_m}{Nv_m - \lambda_m}$$

The expected cost of operating and maintaining a marketing (post-order production) facility is:

(26)
$$C_5 v_m$$

where the effective capacity of that facility is Nv_m.

The total expected costs for the firm per unit time are made up of the sum of the terms given in expressions (22) to (26). In order to optimize, the individual seller in a vertical market structure must minimize total expected costs with respect to μ_i, $(i = 1, 2, \ldots, N+1)$, v_m, and N.

(27)
$$
\begin{aligned}
TEC_m = {} & C_1 \sum_{i=2}^{N} \left(1 - \frac{N\mu_i}{\lambda_m} + \frac{N\mu_i}{\lambda_m - N\mu_i}\right) + C_1\left(2 - \frac{2N}{\lambda_m}(\mu_1 + \mu_{N+1})\right. \\
& + \frac{2N\mu_1}{\lambda_m - 2N\mu_1} + \left.\frac{2N\mu_{N+1}}{\lambda_m - 2N\mu_{N+1}}\right) + C_2\left(\lambda_m - \sum_{i=1}^{N+1}\mu_i\right) \\
& + \sum_{i=1}^{N+1} C_{3,i}\mu_i + \frac{C_4\lambda_m}{Nv_m - \lambda_m} + C_5 v_m
\end{aligned}
$$

Assume, for the moment, that N is a given, then minimize the cost equation with respect to capacities only. Then:

$$\frac{\partial}{\partial \mu_i}TEC_m = -(C_2 - C_{3,i}) - \frac{NC_1}{\lambda_m} + \frac{N\lambda_m C_1}{(\lambda_m - N\mu_i)^2} = 0, \quad \text{for } i = 2, 3, \ldots, N.$$

$$\frac{\partial}{\partial \mu_1}TEC_m = -(C_2 - C_{3,1}) - \frac{2NC_1}{\lambda_m} + \frac{2N\lambda_m C_1}{(\lambda_m - 2N\mu_1)^2} = 0$$

$$\frac{\partial}{\partial \mu_{N+1}}TEC_m = -(C_2 - C_{3,N+1}) - \frac{2NC_{N+1}}{\lambda_m} + \frac{2N\lambda_m C_1}{(\lambda_m - 2N\mu_{N+1})^2} = 0$$

$$\frac{\partial}{\partial v_m}TEC_m = C_5 - \frac{N\lambda_m C_4}{(Nv_m - \lambda_m)^2} = 0$$

The solutions to these four equations give the optimal values of the capacity variables in terms of N and parameters. Thus:

(28a)
$$\hat{\mu}_i = \frac{\lambda_m}{N}\left(1 - \sqrt{\frac{NC_1}{\lambda_m(C_2 - C_{3,i}) + NC_1}}\right); \quad i = 2, 3, \ldots, N$$

(28b)
$$\hat{\mu}_1 = \frac{\lambda_m}{2N}\left(1 - \sqrt{\frac{2NC_1}{\lambda_m(C_2 - C_{3,1}) + 2NC_1}}\right)$$

(28c)
$$\hat{\mu}_{N+1} = \frac{\lambda_m}{2N}\left(1 - \sqrt{\frac{2NC_1}{\lambda_m(C_2 - C_{3,N+1}) + 2NC_1}}\right)$$

$$\text{(28d)} \qquad \hat{v}_m = \frac{\lambda_m}{N}\left(1 + \sqrt{\frac{NC_4}{\lambda_m C_5}}\right)$$

Since N is actually a variable, the optimum value of which is also desired, we can substitute equations (28a), (28b), (28c), and (28d) into equation (27) and have an expected total cost equation with N the only variable. Performing this substitution, assuming that $C_{3,i} = C_3$ (for $i = 1, 2, 3, \ldots, N + 1$), and manipulating the terms extensively yields the following total cost expression in the one decision variable N:

$$
\begin{aligned}
\text{(29)} \qquad TEC_m^* = {} & 2(N-1)\sqrt{C_1^2 + C_1(C_2 - C_3)\frac{\lambda_m}{N}} \\
& + 4\sqrt{C_1^2 + C_1(C_2 - C_3)\frac{\lambda_m}{2N}} + C_3\lambda_m \\
& - (N+1)C_1 + 2\sqrt{\frac{C_4 C_5 \lambda_m}{N}} + \frac{C_5 \lambda_m}{N}.
\end{aligned}
$$

To obtain the optimal N, one can now "difference" equation (29) with respect to N. The number N is of course an integer, since it refers to the number of specific attribute values which may be carried in inventory; also, if N tends to be small finite differencing of TEC_m^* may be required.

Middlemen and pre-order production

In a vertical market structure with one level of middlemen of w firms, all pre-order production remains with the m initial selling firms. All post-order operations are performed by the middlemen. The reason for this split is that the middlemen's existence is predicated upon the cooperation of the m sellers and n buyers. The cooperation of the m sellers is forthcoming only if the middlemen do not remove the m sellers from existence. If the middlemen are to operate as more than pure coordinators, as postulated here, they will perform only some of the functions which the m sellers would perform in their absence. The middlemen, however, still remain at the point where the decisions on all the system's decision variables are best made. For the individual middleman in such a level, the decisions to be made are the optimum choice of the average rate at which he receives the products from the m sellers, the number of products of different attributes he will so receive and carry in inventory, and the number of orders which his post-order operation may be expected to handle.

The optimum solution of the middleman's problem is of the general form of that of the individual seller as shown in the previous model. In effect, for the middleman equations (28a) to (28d) and (29) hold, with the simple substitution of the middleman's order arrival rate for λ_m. The new arrival rate of orders is $\lambda_w = \frac{\lambda}{w}$. For the initial seller, the rate at which it produces a product of given attribute will, of course, now be an average of $\frac{w}{m}\hat{\mu}_i$. It is also necessary, for this analysis to hold, that we assume that the m sellers produce continuously at this mean rate and allocate their output randomly among the w middlemen.

It can be shown that the structure with middlemen involves lower expected costs, given the optimum values for all decision variables, providing that $w < m$. It can also be shown that the number of different attributes of products carried in inventory $(N + 1)$ has a larger optimal value in the case of the structure with one level of middlemen than in that of direct exchange, again providing $w < m$. In Chart 7.2, these conclusions are illustrated. The chart shows the total cost functions $m(TEC^*_m) = SEC^*_m$ and $SEC^*_w = w(TEC^*_w)$, and that SEC^*_m lies above SEC^*_w for all values of N.

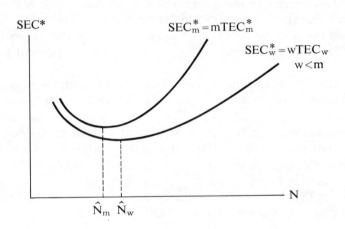

CHART 7.2

To prove that the structure with one level of middlemen is more efficient than that of direct exchange, given $w < m$, it must be shown that $m(TEC^*_m) > w(TEC^*_w)$ for any given value of N. Thus:

$$SEC^*_m = 2(N - 1)\sqrt{m^2 C_1^2 + C_1(C_2 - C_3)\frac{m\lambda}{N}}$$

$$(30) \qquad + 4\sqrt{m^2 C_1^2 + C_1(C_2 - C_3)\frac{m\lambda}{2N}} - (N + 1)mC_1$$

$$+ C_3\lambda + 2\sqrt{\frac{C_4 C_5 m\lambda}{N}} + \frac{C_5\lambda}{N}$$

since $m\lambda_m = \lambda = w\lambda_w$.

For the case of the structure with middlemen in one level, the system's expected costs are:

$$
\begin{aligned}
SEC^*_w = {} & 2(N-1)\sqrt{w^2 C_1^2 + C_1(C_2 - C_3)\frac{w\lambda}{N}} \\
& + 4\sqrt{w^2 C_1^2 + C_1(C_2 - C_3)\frac{w\lambda}{2N}} - (N+1)wC_1 \\
& + C_3\lambda + 2\sqrt{\frac{C_4 C_5 w\lambda}{N}} + \frac{C_5\lambda}{N}
\end{aligned}
$$

(31)

Since $C_2 > C_3$ it follows that $SEC^*_m > SEC^*_w$. Note that the first terms under the radicals increase monotonically with m and w respectively, and their sums exceed $(N+1)\,mC_1$ and $(N+1)\,wC_1$, respectively.

It the system's costs when middlemen exist are lower than those for the system with no middlemen when the N is the same in both cases, then the conclusion must hold when the N is optimized in both systems. Thus, the entry of middlemen into the system would lower costs (given $w < m$) even if the only changes they introduce are in the capacity variables (μ_i and v_m). They hold the N to the value it has as an optimum in the system without them. When N is also optimized, the system's expected cost must fall even further.

In discussing the operations of middlemen in a unique intermediary level, no mention was made of the possibility that their existence may permit each of the m sellers to specialize in the production of particular attributes. Such specialization, which could exist with or without middlemen in the structure, requires an analysis which studies the conditions under which the pre-order costs of production vary with N. For this reason no attempt is made to detemine how the optimal N varies with the introduction of middlemen. Finally, the analysis of equilibrium structures for the conditions given by the last model parallels very closely that made for the other model of this chapter and hence is not repeated.

1   Alderson, Wroe, *Marketing Behavior and Executive Action* (Homewood, Illinois: Richard D. Irwin, Inc., 1957).

2   Bucklin, Louis P., "Postponement, Speculation and the Structure of Distribution Channels," *Journal of Marketing Research* (February, 1965) pp. 26–32.

3   Alderson, *op. cit.*, pp. 423–427.

4   *Ibid.*, p. 425.

5   Bucklin, *op. cit.*

6   To achieve steady state, the system requires that $x_m v_m > \lambda_m$, or that $x_m > \frac{\lambda_m}{v_m}$.

7   The next model does permit a general statement on how structural variations change the optimal amount of post-order production which for most order-filling middlemen, means the production done at the level selling directly to the n buying firms.

8   Sadowski, Wieslaw, "A Few Remarks on the Assortment Problem," *Management Science* VI (October, 1959), and Frank, Charles R., Jr., "A Model on the Assortment Problem," *Management Science: Series A* XI (May, 1965).

9   Sadowski, *op. cit.*, has another kind of cost of matching the order's specifications from the available units in stock.

10   Sadowski, *op. cit.*, and Frank, *op. cit.* These two authors develop methods of solutions where the assumption that $p(k)$ is rectangular does not hold.

11   A detailed explanation of these cost parameters is found on pages 166 and 167.

12   This ignores the case where two or more adjacent inventories are empty simultaneously. Such an assumption is partially justified by the fact that shortages tend to reduce the depletion rate of adjacent inventories.

8

Specialization and Scale of Production

Some production considerations

The models developed to this point characterize vertical market structures in which the locations of production activities are distributed among levels on the basis of pre- and post-order production considerations. The result is that in no structure are production activities optimally located in more than two levels. The product exchanged is limited to two forms, one of which is the given final form. It is obvious that such models are limited to the characterization of particular structures, but in any economy there can be observed structures in which the product is exchanged in several forms as it goes from one level to the next. That is, throughout a structure the product is transformed at several levels; and the models so far developed essentially characterize only a segment of such a structure. The connection of such segments into more complex vertical market structures requires the development of models which permit production activities to exist at more than two levels. Hence they must allow the product's form as it is bought and sold by every level to be a variable. These variables determine the efficiency of the structure. Such models would permit the study of more general forms of vertical market structures.

In order to characterize the problem in this fashion, the specific aspects of pre- and post-order production are ignored and the entire concept of production developed anew. Thus, although the models are in some senses more general than those preceding them, they are less so in others. At the end of the analysis, points at which the two kinds of models might be meshed and the conditions that such incorporation requires are briefly discussed. The complexity of each model does not seem to make it worthwhile to combine them into one.

Different products are the results of production activities which vary tremendously from one another along a large number of dimensions. Physical and economic requirements for different products are often greatly dissimilar. The concept of production used for the analysis of this chapter is thus, of necessity, a general and simple one. It is based upon the idea of characterizing the transformations wrought in a product by a project graph which would characterize the sequence of activities that have to be performed in the production of a product. Whatever the definition of activities employed, the graph would be in essence an ordered set, the members of which would constitute the units of activity. A detailed graph would include not only the identification of these set members but also their sequence, or the location within the set that each member must occupy, if any such constraints are involved. The simplest project graph is that in which the members of the set are all constrained to a unique sequence which excludes the possibility of a simultaneous performance of any two members or their transposition within the sequence. It is this last project graph which defines for purposes of this analysis the production process.

Given any set of production activities $A = \{A_1, \cdots, A_r\}$, with a unique location for each A_i within the set, the question arises as to whether or not any given A_i is itself a set. That is, in characterizing the production process the choice of what constitutes an activity is open. The member A_i of the set A could very well be defined as the set $\{a_1, \cdots, a_s\}$ for all i, with every a_j again uniquely located within the set. One could, in effect, continue in this fashion so that the set A would continue to have a larger number of members each of which would be a set of a smaller number of members. If this were continued indefinitely with the unit activities defined in terms of extremely small variations, then one might justifiably view the set A as a *continuum* of activity. The production process would be considered as a continuous process rather than a set of finite activities. Accordingly, one could identify the degree to which the production process was completed by reference to the relative size of the segment along the continuum which defines it. The single dimension so created for defining the set A would obviously have meaning only between the values zero and some positive finite number. This is necessary if the production process is at any point to be considered complete in a finite period of time. This dimension, identified as being represented by any value x_i, is normalized between the limits of zero and one for purposes of analysis. That is, x_i is defined to be the relative degree of completeness of the product at the beginning of the ith production stage. It measures the proportion of the production activities completed by the end of the $(i-1)$th stage. We further define y_i as the relative amount of the production activities engaged in at the ith stage, defined as $y_i = x_{i+1} - x_i$, which is uniquely identified along the continuum of production activities as the ratio of activities completed by the ith stage to those necessary for the full completion of the product. It is assumed that the incremental cost and the revenue associated with the production activities in the segment y_i are independent of the exact location of y_i within the total production segment. It is also assumed that over the range $0 \leq y_i \leq 1$, dy_i exists, requiring that x_i be continuous over the range $0 \leq x_i \leq 1$. These assumptions permit an algebraic solution to the model, but the essential nature of the analysis is not changed with their removal. The analysis assumes that the time it takes to complete any given segment (series of activities) of the production process is the same for all i providing y_i is constant for all i. The time it takes to complete a segment of the process is independent of the location of that segment in the production process.

The form in which the product is bought and sold by a firm in the vertical market structure can be uniquely identified by the single demension of degree of completeness. With the strict constraint on the sequence of activities, two units of the product must be in identical form if they are of equal degrees of completeness. The analysis, then, which permits the firm to choose the amount of production in which it is to engage, is that which permits it to choose the form of the product bought or sold. Within the given limits of the form in which the product is bought by the m and n firms, the firm, in the analysis, is permitted to choose the values of x_{i+1} which the product it produces and sells has and, hence, the exact segment of the process it is to undertake to perform. Unlike the previous model, the problem involves more than the choice of the simple pre-order production value of x_{i+1}.

The segment y_i is defined as that proportion of the production process in which all resources operate upon one unit of the product at any time. Whereas between segments y_i and y_{i+1}, inventories of product in the form identified by the value x_{i+1} may be carried, there are no inventories within any production process segment other than the unit being processed. It is possible that more than two levels in the structure engage in the production process and that more than one form of the product is carried in inventory. The basic concepts on which this analysis rests are the relationships which the specialization, scale, and coordination of production activities have to output and costs. Their introduction into the discussion generalizes the production analysis of the previous model.

Specialization and scale economies

We consider that the resource inputs which perform the activities in the segment y_i perform no other activities in any other segment. Every unit of resource input limited to the segment y_i also performs all the activities in this segment. Thus, in a segment all resource inputs operate continuously on the unit of product to complete the segment of the production process for it; and all are used to perform all the activities in the segment.

If such an organization of the production process and any segment of it is a physical and engineering possibility, then within any segment there is no economic reason to have any resource input be idle while another is busy. In the concept of production outlined above, resource inputs could be idle while others are operating only if the two groups are in different segments of the production process. Within the segment *all* resource inputs are either busy or idle, while all resource inputs in segment y_i could be busy when all resource inputs in segment y_{i+1} are idle for lack of a product on which to operate. Once a resource input is allocated to operating in a segment y_i, then it is *specialized* in the activities making up that segment. This means that it is assumed that this resource input cannot, at less than infinite costs, be employed in any other segment in the short run. ,

If $y_i = 1$ then all resource inputs allocated to the ith production stage would be totally *unspecialized*. All would perform all the activities in the entire production process, and none would be idle when any other is busy. Performing the entire production process in more than one segment makes the probability that some resource inputs are idle while others are operating on a unit of the product greater than zero. Segmentation of the production process would thus be economically feasible if the specialization of resource inputs increases their output capacity more than proportionately to the reduction in their operating range within the process. For example, a reduction of one-half in the activities which a resource must perform must more than double its output capacity on the activities allocated to it if segmentation is to be economically feasible. The cost of idleness which segmentation produces must be counterbalanced by increased resource input capacity. The determination of the optimum number of segments and the relative size of each segment is the aim of the model.

To specialize a resource input is to decrease its flexibility, to lower the number of activities which it is capable of performing in the entire production process. Within certain ranges, it is obviously true that the human resource input has outputs that vary with its flexibility. The larger the number of kinds of skills expected from the human being, the lower the skill level of any one kind one can expect—all other things being equal. The nature of physical and engineering relationships is often such as to make the flexibility of machines rise less than proportionately to the costs of building and operating the machines. In short, the model rests on the contention that specialization of production resource inputs increases their output by more than the proportion of the reduction in their flexibility over some range of activities. Lower flexibility also implies that a resource input which could be employed in some activities of the production process must remain idle while a unit of the product is being processed by some other set of resource inputs and, hence, is a temporary excess capacity source. The relationship between the output capacity of a resource input and the range y_i, i.e., its specialization within the production process, is exemplified in Chart 8.1.

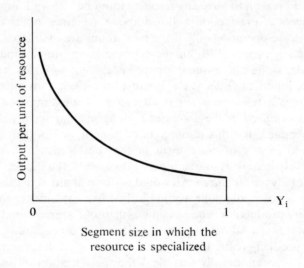

Segment size in which the
resource is specialized

CHART 8.1

The other concept in this analysis of vertical market structures is that of economies of scale. It is postulated that in many production processes the output increases more than proportionately to the increases in all resource inputs, given that the degree of specialization of each is held constant. Though such economies are not essential to the model developed, we are interested in their effects. If y_i is held constant, then increases in inputs in relation to output changes determine economies of *scale*. If the inputs are held constant and y_i is varied, then output changes determine economies of *specialization*. Chart 8.2 shows the relationship between scale (in terms of the number of units of resource inputs employed) and output for given levels of specialization when there are economies of scale.

Once the production process is segmented and resources are specialized, a new dimension of coordination is created. The increase in output that

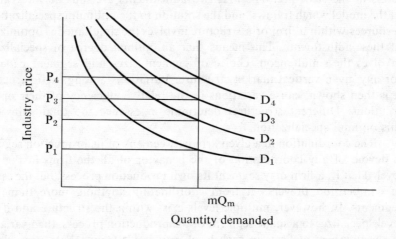

Quantity demanded

CHART 8.2

specialization actually brings also depends on the coordination of the specialized segments. The increase in capacity of a resource unit which results from its specialization is a potential increase which the decision maker may tap through the coordination of these inputs. Market mechanisms which produce coordination would also permit defferent levels in the structure to take advantage of specialization if any exists. In the case at hand, the segmentation decision must, of necessity, create sub-systems (segments) in the production process, Any segmentation scheme would produce potential increases in output, but actual increases would depend upon the relationships among decision variables on the segments' characteristics. Thus, both the relative sizes of the segments and their capacities are problem variables for which a simulataneous solution brings coordination of the sub-systems created and determines the actual output and costs of specialization.

The coordination of a vertical market structure in which levels specialize within the overall production process involves three sets of adjustments. The first is the adjustment between the segment sizes y_i, for $i = 1, 2, \cdots, N$ (where N is the number of producing levels in the vertical market structure); the second is that between all segment capacities; and the third is that between the unit arrivals at each firm within a specialized level. For any value of N total efficiency depends upon these adjustments and thus the optimal segmentation is a function of these variables, and their adjustment. For an individual firm with single stations for each segment, the first two adjustments remain, whereas the third disappears in this characterization of the problem. This last type is, of course, the subject matter of the chapter on the pure coordinator who, in this case, coordinates the specialized production levels in the structure. The first two adjustments are thus an integral part of the model which follows, and the solution to the optimum specialization of resources within a firm or a structure involves the simultaneous optimization of these adjustments. This means that an optimal degree of specialization involves the simultaneous choice of segment sizes and segment capacities for any given vertical market structure. Variations among these structures, it is then shown, cause variations in the relative efficiency of their optimal solutions. Different structures determine in essence the total gains from this optimal specialization.

The coordination in a given firm between any of its production segments is devoid of any coordination of the behavior of all the firms in the same level. That is, a firm may segment its own production process, but the essence of competition prevents it from coordinating anything more than these segments. If, however, multiple levels exist within the structure and if each level specializes in a single segment of the production process, then variations in the numbers of firms in each level may result from rebate strategies. In effect, the existence of such levels may permit the coordination of the behavior of firms in other levels by evening out to some extent the allocation of units of product to the production segments of firms in other levels. The coordination of production segments may be achieved within the firm or between levels, but the coordination of firms which compete within a level and specialize in the same segment can only come from collusion or from the allocation of a single segment to each level in a multi-level structure.

The nature of the market partially determines the coordination which the system has without collusion. The existence of such specialized levels permits a greater degree of coordination between production segments by permitting a pure coordinating middleman to operate between levels. His presence minimizes the occurrence of situations where some resources are idle in one unit while other resources in another unit of the same segment have inventory of product units waiting for processing. The allocation of production segments to levels frees the entire system from the restrictions which come from limiting the single station in one segment to a single source of the product on which it is to operate.

If the firm segments its entire production process, then each segment is fed only from within the preceding segment. Each set of resource inputs making up a competing unit not only competes with other similar units in what would be the same level in a structure, but it is prevented from cooperating with units in preceding and following segments outside a single group which makes up a sequence of the production process. That is indeed the essence of the vertical integration of segments of a production process. If, however, the segments are freed from this restriction or integration, the possibilities for cooperation and, hence, coordination emerge. Each combination of resource inputs making up a competing production segment may be larger or smaller than it would be in the locked combination of segments which characterizes the vertically integrated firm, depending upon the number of firms in the level. The smaller this number, the greater the system's coordination, as shown generally in Chapter 6. Furthermore, between levels a pure coordinator may exist whereas it could not if all firms were vertically integrated; at least it would not coordinate production segments specifically. As the model shows, the allocation of productive segments to levels in a structure permits one to make all these assertions. It also permits the extension of the limits of the starting and ending point of the vertical market structures discussed in all previous models.

Abstractions of the analysis

Because of the highly simplified concept of production which is used, it may be difficult to identify actual examples of the vertical market structure characterized by the model. However, a little imagination and the ability to see the similarity between finite and easily identifiable segments of production and a continuous process would certainly identify such an example. Thus, consider the production of a tool such as a wrench. The iron ore is the main source of the raw material for its manufacture. If we ignore other raw materials, the process of the production of the finished tool can be clearly identified in terms of sets of activities. These sets could be identified as mining the ore, smelting, forging, and forming. All these broadly defined activities are performed by resource inputs, which could or could not be specialized each within a segment. The vertical market structure which involves the exchange of the tool in its various forms of ore, iron, steel, etc., is an example of the general form of the structure characterized by the model. It is possible that all resource inputs are unspecialized and used in all activities. It is also possible that the organization of the process is such that all resource inputs are engaged in the production of a single unit of the product at any instant in time. In effect, resources could also be specialized to various degrees and organized into multiple units or service stations, each operating on one unit of the product within a segment of production and simultaneously with some other unit in the same segment. Large numbers of structures are also possible, with the limiting case being that which decrees that any service station receive its product from only a partial set of all possible stations in the previous segment. Obvious variations on these decisions exist.

It is to resolve these problems that the model is developed. However, rather than solve as many problems as there are peculiarities of production requirements, the most general form of the problem is dealt with. There may be no single product whose requirements are characterized by the model;

hence, any specific use of the analysis for a particular structure must adapt the model. Furthermore, the relevant decision variables are not necessarily found for every product in the model. The basic costs may be many more than the two included in the model. Finally, the model abstracts from the issue of overlapping vertical market structures and from other problems—for example, the relationship between the product's structure and that which is relevant to the resource inputs used in its production, such as the vertical market structure for labor.

The time which a unit spends in the vertical market structure is a source of costs for two basic reasons. If the production process of the unit starts only upon receipt of an order from one of the n buyers, then this time is the time when the buyer is in the system and the costs are buyer waiting costs. If, on the other hand, the n buyers are serviced from an inventory of the product in its final form, then the reason for the "time" cost is somewhat more involved. The time a unit of product spends in the system, in this case, is that which constitutes the lead time for the replenishment of the inventory of the product in final form. If the cost of carrying this inventory at an optimal level is a function of this lead time, and if this cost increases with increases in lead time, then the cost of *lead time* is the added cost. On the other hand, the cost can also be veiwed as the cost of holding inventories of the product in its beginning form, in process, and various intermediate forms. The time a product spends in the production process of a vertical market structure involves costs of holding. The longer the holding time, the higher the costs. Though some specific assumptions are made about the behavior of these "time" costs, the source can be viewed as a combination of holding and lead time costs, or of customer waiting.

Specialization within vertical market structures

If it is possible to distinguish between marketing and production functions, then earlier models allow mostly for specialization in the marketing functions of a vertical market structure, while this analysis allows for specialization in production functions. With the proper adaptation the models could be combined, but the result would be extremely complex. As a partial combination one could define the production process as including all functions and activities previously distinguishable in the production and marketing groups. However, even such a partial combination requires careful integration of the assumptions, concepts, and analyses involved in each separate model.

Given then a production process with known starting and ending points we define:

μ_0 = average level of the usage of the resource input which is contract-
ed for per unit of time per production segment.

β = a pure number.

k = units of output per (unit of input) β per unit time where output
is in terms of capacity of units of product per unit time.

μ_i = average output of the resources specialized in the segment y_i of
the production process, in terms of units of product per unit time.

To introduce the concepts of economies and diseconomies of scale, we
must set some values for the ranges of β in the equation

(1) $$\mu_i = k\mu_0^\beta$$

which relates outputs to inputs *when there is no specialization whatsoever of
the resource inputs*, i.e., where $y_i = 1$. If $\beta > 1$, then there are economies
of scale; when $\beta < 1$, there are diseconomies of scale; and when $\beta = 1$,
there are constant returns to scale. For purposes of analysis, we *assume*
that $\beta > 1$.

Note also that:

$y_i = x_{i+1} - x_i$, a segment of the production process in which resources
are specialized, for $i = 1, 2, \cdots, N$.

N = number of specialized segments of the production process, such
that if $N = 1$, then $y_i = 1$ and there is no specialization. In
general[1] $y_i = \dfrac{1}{N}$.

α = a pure number.

Equation **(1)** is the production function when no specialization exists.
To allow for the possibility of specialization and of economies from such
specialization, the general equation relating output to input is

(1a) $$\mu_i = k\frac{\mu_0^\beta}{y_i^\alpha}$$

If $\alpha > 1$, then there are economies of specialization; if $\alpha < 1$, there are
diseconomies of specialization; and if $\alpha = 1$, there are constant returns to
specialization of the resource inputs. It will be recalled that μ_i is the expected
capacity measured in terms of units of products which the resource inputs
are capable of completing per unit time.

Finally, define as parameters:

C_1 = cost per unit of resource input per unit of time.

C_2 = cost per unit of time of having the product in the structure.

λ = mean total number of orders generated by the n buyers per
unit time, and $\dfrac{\lambda}{m}$ is the number of orders expected by a firm
in any level in which there are m competing firms per unit of time.

To the individual firm among the m sellers, the problem is formed by the
nature of the vertical market structure. In the case where there are no levels
whatsoever between the m firms and n buyers, each selling firm performs

the entire production process. If it should segment this process into a number of specialized stations operating in sequence on the product, then every station cannot receive a unit of product from a preceding segment in any other firm. It can be easily shown, given our assumptions, that the optimal segment size for the firm is the same in all segments, and the optimal number of stations in any segment is one. These conclusions stem essentially from the nature of queuing models and the assumptions made earlier, and are clearly demonstrated in earlier chapters. The optimum pattern is, then, to have an optimum number of segments each of optimum capacity, with one station in each segment and all segments of equal size. A station, it may be recalled, is defined as a set of resource inputs which operate continuously on a single unit before they all start on the next unit, if available. Suppose, therefore, that there were multiple segments within the firm. Any segment receives orders at rate $\frac{\lambda}{m}$ and releases them at the same rate. The next station, performing the next segment, has as its source of arrival the departures from the preceding segment. Thus, its arrivals are at rate $\frac{\lambda}{m}$ and limited to the single source of the station in the firm which performs the previous segment.[2]

There are, therefore, two basic cost terms for the firm. The first term is that of total capacity costs. In every station there are μ_0 resource inputs employed, each costing C_1 dollars, and there are N segments and, therefore, N stations. Total capacity costs are therefore

(2) $$C_1\mu_0 N$$

In every station the unit arrives at the rate λ/m. If the mean capacity of each station is u_i and is distributed in a Poisson fashion about this mean, the unit will remain in each segment $\frac{1}{(\mu_i - \lambda/m)}$ units of time from arrival to completion of the segment activities. Since on the average $\frac{\lambda}{m}$ units are handled per unit time, the expected cost of holding time in the system per unit in one segment is $\frac{C_2\lambda/m}{(\mu_i - \lambda/m)}$. The moment a unit leaves one segment it can be assumed that it has arrived at the next segment. If at each segment the total costs are as stated and μ_i is the same for all stations, expected holding cost for N segments will be equal to $\frac{C_2 N\lambda/m}{(\mu_i - \lambda/m)}$. Assume that $k = 1$. Since μ_i is a function of μ_0, we substitute from equation (1a) for μ_i, $\frac{1}{N}$ for y_i, and manipulate to obtain the expected costs per unit time of having the products in the system of the firm which performs all the given production processes:

(3) $$\frac{C_2\lambda N}{m\mu_0^\beta N^\alpha - \lambda}$$

The selling firm's total expected costs are:

(4)
$$TEC_m = C_1\mu_0 N + \frac{C_2\lambda N}{m\mu_0^\beta N^\alpha - \lambda}$$

Though N is a discrete variable, and there is no meaning to the concept of part of a segment in our notions and assumptions, nontheless, for simplicity we will differentiate with respect to N. The general nature of the conclusions is not affected by this simplification, but the algebra is made considerably easier and, hence, solvable for a general solution explicitly stated in terms of the parameters C_1, C_2, α, β, m, and λ. Thus, we differentiate equation (4) partially with respect to μ_0 and N and set each partial equal to zero:

(5)
$$\frac{\partial}{\partial\mu_0}TEC_m = C_1 N - \frac{\beta C_2 m\lambda N^{(1+\alpha)}\mu_0^{(\beta-1)}}{(m\mu_0^\beta N^\alpha - \lambda)^2} = 0$$

and

(6)
$$\frac{\partial}{\partial N}TEC_m = C_1\mu_0 - \frac{\alpha C_2 m\lambda N^\alpha\mu_0^\beta}{(m\mu_0^\beta N^\alpha - \lambda)^2} + \frac{C_2\lambda(m\mu_0^\beta N^\alpha - \lambda)}{(m\mu_0^\beta N^\alpha - \lambda)^2} = 0$$

From equation (5) we have

(5a)
$$(m\mu_0^\beta N^\alpha - \lambda)^2 = \frac{\beta C_2 m\lambda N^\alpha\mu_0^{(\beta-1)}}{C_1}$$

and from equation (6) we have

(6a)
$$(m\mu_0^\beta N^\alpha - \lambda)^2 = \frac{C_2\lambda[(\alpha - 1)m\mu_0^\beta N^\alpha + \lambda]}{C_1\mu_0}$$

Equating (5a) and (6a) and simplifying gives

(7a)
$$(1 + \beta - \alpha)m\mu_0^\beta N^\alpha = \lambda$$

and

(7b)
$$[(\alpha - \beta)m\mu_0^\beta N^\alpha]^2 = [m\mu_0^\beta N^\alpha - \lambda]^2$$

Equation (5a) and (7b) have identical terms, which leads to

(8)
$$(\alpha - \beta)^2(m\mu_0^\beta N^\alpha)^2 = \frac{\beta C_2\lambda m\mu_0^{(\beta-1)}N^\alpha}{C_1}$$

which reduces to

(8a)
$$\mu_0 = \left(\frac{\beta C_2\lambda}{C_1(\alpha - \beta)^2}\right)\left(\frac{1}{m\mu_0^\beta N^\alpha}\right), \text{ for } \alpha \neq \beta.$$

But from (7a)

(7c)
$$m\mu_0^\beta N^\alpha = \frac{\lambda}{1 + \beta - \alpha}$$

which is true if and only if $(1 + \beta - \alpha) \neq 0$. Thus the solution from this point is predicated upon the condition that α does not equal β or $1 + \beta$. From equations (7c) and (8a),

(9)
$$\hat{\mu}_0 = \frac{\beta C_2(1 + \beta - \alpha)}{C_1(\alpha - \beta)^2}$$

There are thus two conditions on the nature of the economies of scale and specialization which permit a "non-corner" point solution.

In order to obtain the optimum value for the number of segments N, we have from (7c)

$$N = \left[\frac{\lambda}{m(1 + \beta - \alpha)} \right]^{\frac{1}{\alpha}} \mu_0^{-\frac{\beta}{\alpha}}$$

or by substituting for μ_0 the value of $\hat{\mu}_0$ and simplyfing, the optimal value of N is:

(10)
$$\hat{N} = \left[\frac{\lambda(\alpha - \beta)^{2\beta} C_1^{\beta}}{m\beta^{\beta}(1 + \beta - \alpha)^{(\beta+1)} C_2^{\beta}} \right]^{\frac{1}{\alpha}}$$

The substitution of the optimal values of $\hat{\mu}_0$ and $\hat{N}$ into the total expected cost expression for the firm would give the minimum total cost of operation under the stated vertical market structure conditions. Thus

$$T\hat{E}C_m = C_1\hat{\mu}_0\hat{N} + \frac{C_2\lambda\hat{N}}{m\hat{\mu}_0^{\beta}\hat{N}^{\alpha} - \lambda}$$

Substituting for $\hat{\mu}_0$ and $\hat{N}$ we have:

(11)
$$T\hat{E}C_m = \alpha \left[\frac{C_2^{(\alpha-\beta)} C_1^{\beta} \beta^{-\beta}}{(\alpha - \beta)^{2(\alpha-\beta)}(1 + \beta - \alpha)^{(1+\beta-\alpha)}} \right]^{\frac{1}{\alpha}} \left(\frac{\lambda}{m} \right)^{\frac{1}{\alpha}}$$

If we now let A stand for the first term of this product, the optimal cost for the firm is

(11a)
$$T\hat{E}C_m = A \left(\frac{\lambda}{m} \right)^{\frac{1}{\alpha}}$$

The total expected costs for the system when all firms optimize and there are no intermediate levels between the m sellers and n buyers is merely $mTEC_m$. Since the term A is totally independent of m, this total cost figure is

(12)
$$SEC_m = A \lambda^{\frac{1}{\alpha}} m^{\frac{\alpha-1}{\alpha}}$$

It is this figure which must be compared to the optimal costs of totally processing an average of λ units of products or orders per unit of time for different configurations of structures.[3]

Specialized levels in multileveled structures

The first structure to be analyzed is that in which there are a number of levels of firms, and the firms limit their activities to the performance of one or more segments of the production process. A firm would, therefore, obtain units of the product from the preceding level in some form and sell to the next level units of the product in some more complete form. Two issues arise; the first is the identification of the equilibrium structure under these restrictive conditions and the second is to find the optimal structure—whatever form it may take. We shall discuss the second issue first.

We first consider equation (12). If it is true, as assumed, that the only relevant costs are those included in the model, then the minimum cost for a structure with a single level of producers can be easily identified by considering the rate of change of SEC_m from (12) with respect to m. Thus

$$\frac{\partial}{\partial m}SEC_m = \left(\frac{\alpha-1}{\alpha}\right)A\left(\frac{\lambda}{m}\right)^{\frac{1}{\alpha}} \quad \text{(since the term } A \text{ is independent of } m\text{)}$$

which gives

(13) $$\frac{\partial}{\partial m}SEC_m = \left(\frac{\alpha-1}{\alpha}\right)T\hat{E}C_m$$

If the economy of specialization factor were not greater than one, only the issue of scale would matter. Segmentation obviously increases the time an order spends in the system, unless the specialization of resources and the economies of scale increase the system's capacity and counterbalance this effect. It is contended that the aim is to characterize structures in which specialization produces some economies. If, therefore, $\alpha > 1$, it follows that $\left(\frac{\alpha-1}{\alpha}\right)T\hat{E}C_m$ is positive, and the minimum cost structure which would handle the same output is that with $m = 1$ and the optimal μ_0 and N for that value. If $\alpha < 1$, there would be diseconomies of specialization and the conclusions would be reversed. If it is true that the ownership of the stations in each segment does not affect total costs, then equally as good is the structure with $\hat{N}$ levels, each with one firm specializing in $\frac{1}{\hat{N}}$ of the production process. That is, if it costs no more to transfer a unit from one station of a firm to a station in another firm than it would to transfer it between stations in the same firm, then the two structures are equally efficient.

If the minimum cost structure with no intermediaries is that given in equation (12), then no structure with intermediaries could have a higher minimum cost. Assuming no rebates and no added cost of product transfer resulting from the entry of firms, levels of intermediaries could develop between the m firms and the n buyers. These are intermediaries in the sense that their operations, if limited to a segment, are conditional upon the cooperation of other levels whose output is the intermediaries' input, and vice versa. The group of m sellers and the group of n buyers are by postulate the limiting levels in the structure and not intermediaries in this sense. If any of these intermediaries should perform the entire segment, then it would in essence be an added firm in the initial selling level which is again by postulate not permitted in the analysis.

We assume that such intermediaries would perform less than all segments of the production process and that the m firms would never cooperate with any intermediary unless they, the m firms, remained in the structure. This means that in any structure the minimum operation for the m group is the first segment of the production process. When all intermediaries who can profitably operate (the limit being zero profits) are in the structure, then an equilibrium structure is attained. The conditions of entry for an intermediary are the non-reduction in the profits of any firm with which it cooperates in order to exist, and a non-negative profit for the entering firm.

In the structure where each of the m firms performs the entire production process, the expected cost for each production segment for all firms is $\frac{1}{\hat{N}}$ of the total cost of all production segments. This conclusion is merely a direct result of the fact that the assumptions of the analysis render all segment sizes and station capacities equal. The expected cost, then, of a single segment in such a structure is

(14) $$\left(\frac{1}{\hat{N}}\right) A\lambda^{\left(\frac{1}{\alpha}\right)} m^{\left(\frac{\alpha-1}{\alpha}\right)}$$

An entering firm could, for example, take over the portion of the production process which constitutes the last segment. If we assume that only one such firm exists and that there are no rebates, the firm would optimize by solving its specialization problem for that portion. What may have been a single segment may now be some larger number. If the firm had the entire production process, the optimal number of segments would be different from what it would have been if there were m competing firms. If the single entering firm optimizes for the entire production process, its costs would be $A\lambda^{\frac{1}{\alpha}}$. Since it is operating with only $\frac{1}{\hat{N}}$th of the total number of segments it would have had if it had performed the entire process, and since the total cost per segment is equal for all segments, its minimum costs are merely $\hat{N}^{-1}A\lambda^{\frac{1}{\alpha}}$. Thus, in what would have been the last segment of the production process, there may be more than one segment when there is only one firm. This firm's revenues are the costs of the segment that would have been incurred in its absence, namely, $A\hat{N}^{-1}\lambda^{\left(\frac{1}{\alpha}\right)} m^{\left(\frac{\alpha-1}{\alpha}\right)}$. Total expected profits for the firm in this unique intermediate role are

(15) $$ETP = \left(\frac{1}{\hat{N}}\right) A\lambda^{\left(\frac{1}{\alpha}\right)} m^{\left(\frac{\alpha-1}{\alpha}\right)} - \left(\frac{1}{\hat{N}}\right) A\lambda^{\left(\frac{1}{\alpha}\right)}$$

This is a positive number and, therefore, is an inducement to the entry of other firms. The limit to the number of firms which can enter is that for which their total revenues equal their total costs, namely:

$$\left(\frac{1}{\hat{N}}\right) A\lambda^{\left(\frac{1}{\alpha}\right)} m^{\left(\frac{\alpha-1}{\alpha}\right)} = \frac{1}{\hat{N}} A\lambda^{\left(\frac{1}{\alpha}\right)} w^{\left(\frac{\alpha-1}{\alpha}\right)}$$

where $w = m$. This is the equilibrium number in this one level of inter-mediaries. At this number of intermediaries, each firm will find that the optimal number of producing segments *it* should have in the $\frac{1}{\hat{N}}$th share of the total production process is just one. In fact, as the number of firms competing in any segment of the production process approaches the number m, the number of segments into which each organizes its $\frac{1}{\hat{N}}$th share will fall. When the number of firms reaches m, each will have a single segment. The total number of segments in the structure when there is one level of intermediaries operating in the last segment of size $\frac{1}{\hat{N}}$th of the total is greater than $\hat{N}$ when w is less than m. It would have $(\hat{N} - 1)$ segments of equal size, and also more than one segment operated by each intermediary.

The first entering firm, of course, to maximize its profits, would have taken over as many segments as it could have. It would have left only $\frac{1}{\hat{N}}$ of the total production process to the m firms, which would insist on keeping at least that. The firm's total number of optimum segments in the $\left(\frac{\hat{N}-1}{\hat{N}}\right)$th portion of the process would be greater than the $(\hat{N} - 1)$ segments when m firms operated in competition. The single firm, having optimized the value of its segment sizes, would have expected total profits of:

$$(16) \qquad ETP = \left(\frac{\hat{N}-1}{\hat{N}}\right)A\lambda^{\left(\frac{1}{\alpha}\right)}\left[m^{\left(\frac{\alpha-1}{\alpha}\right)} - 1\right]$$

which, of course, are larger than the profits given in expression **(15)**. In both cases the derivations of the revenue term and the cost term are the same. The entry of firms to compete with this intermediary reduces its profits and the optimum number of segments it should have in the $\left(\frac{\hat{N}-1}{\hat{N}}\right)$th portion of the production process in which they both operate. Both the optimum number of segments and profits would continue to fall until the former would reach $(\hat{N} - 1)$ and the latter would reach zero when the number of intermediaries competing in the level reaches the equilibrium number m. The equilibrium number is reached when equality holds:

$$\left(\frac{\hat{N}-1}{\hat{N}}\right)A\lambda^{\left(\frac{1}{\alpha}\right)}m^{\left(\frac{\alpha-1}{\alpha}\right)} = \left(\frac{\hat{N}-1}{\hat{N}}\right)A\lambda^{\left(\frac{1}{\alpha}\right)}w^{\left(\frac{\alpha-1}{\alpha}\right)}$$

which is again, $w = m$.

In obtaining the equilibrium number in this one level, the cost of the portion of the production process performed is taken to be:

$$\left(\frac{\hat{N}-1}{\hat{N}}\right)A\lambda^{\left(\frac{1}{\alpha}\right)}w^{\left(\frac{\alpha-1}{\alpha}\right)}$$

when it is at its minimum. That is, the minimum cost is identical in form regardless of whether the station at any given segment is free to receive its inputs from any station in the preceding segment. The cost is uniquely related to the number of stations in the level and independent of the constraints on the transfers of units of the product from one segment to the next. At one extreme, every station receives its input from a single station in the preceding level. At the other there is complete freedom, and the inputs are allocated randomly. In all cases the arrival rate at every station is distributed in a Poison fashion with a mean rate $\frac{\lambda}{w}$. If $w < m$, then the arrival rate is greater than $\frac{\lambda}{m}$. The distribution is still a Poison, and at equilibrium the rate is equal in both cases to $\frac{\lambda}{m}$. The total cost for the segment varies with the number of firms, and the expected total cost term merely requires the substitution of w for m. In effect, for every station in a segment, the time a unit spends in its system is always $\frac{\lambda/w}{\mu_i - \lambda/w}$, regardless of the limitation on the source of its product input.

Just as such a level developed, so there could develop another level, which would take over all but one segment from the first intermediary level. Since the group of m sellers operates in segment one, the first intermediary level with its equilibrium number $w = m$ will operate in segment two, and the third would operate in the remaining $(\hat{N} - 2)$ segments. Again, the analysis is repeated until at equilibrium there are $(\hat{N} - 1)$ levels of intermediaries with m firms in each level. Two conditions are necessary for this equilibrium. If every firm cooperates with others only on the condition that it remains an active member of the structure and a producer in at least one segment, then this equilibrium may result. It also requires that the optimum value for N be independent of the degree to which any station is free to obtain its inputs from any station in the previous segment. Thus, no firm would find it more profitable at equilibrium to buy and sell the product in any but the forms in which it would have been transferred from segment to segment in the firm's absence. The most efficient size of a given segment for a firm is independent of the number of segments in which it actually operates.

In the absence of costs of entry, rebates, added costs of separate station ownership, and coordinators between the production segments, it would be impossible to identify the equilibrium without the two conditions cited above. To make a segment station available to a firm, and to avoid the exit of a firm from the structure with less than $(\hat{N} - 1)m$ intermediaries when the first intermediary enters, it must be assumed that no firm cooperates if it is to leave the structure, and no firm refuses cooperation providing it operates at least a single station in one segment. Obviously any firm may refuse to cooperate, but it cannot prevent, in this analysis, another firm from competing in the same level. These conclusions could be derived directly by optimizing the structure for each of the m firms, and then maximizing the number of firms in the structure subject to the constraint that the total cost of the structure not exceed the minimum total cost of the original (given) m firms.

The introduction of the concepts of rebates, cost of entry, pure coordinating firms between segments, and added costs of separating the ownership of stations within segments, make possible some conclusions on the equilibrium structure without recourse to these two conditions. It permits a discussion of vertical integration, namely, the limitation of the stations in the previous segment from which a given station is to receive its units of product for processing. Since the m firms and the n buyers are givens in the analysis, this refers to all remaining $(\hat{N} - 1)m$ stations or firms at equilibrium.

It should be noted that the derivation of the equilibrium of the structure is not conditional upon the capacity of a single firm to integrate a number of levels without increasing the costs over the case where each segment identifies a single firm. If there exists a cost to such vertical integration, then the analysis of equilibrium would still arrive at the same conclusion. The exposition of the process by which such equilibrium is reached must differ, however, from that used here. In the case where firms encounter positive costs of integration through, for example, loss of entrepreneurial specialization resulting from integration, their search for maximum profits would give the same equilibrium results derived earlier. Each firm in attempting to maximize its profits, would find it optimal to operate a single segment, and *to cooperate* with others specializing in the preceding and following segments. When all firms attempt to maximize profits, specialization and cooperation will result, and the equilibrium state is that already shown. The analysis which shows this situation clearly is to be found in Chapter 9. The concept of cost-free vertical integration is used in the above analysis only for simplicity of exposition.

The coordination of segments

The vertical market structure with multiple levels of intermediaries is that structure in which a station in any level may be free to receive its inputs from any of the stations in the preceding level. The fewer the levels, the fewer the number of stations in levels with such freedom. When two stations are "locked in" (integrated vertically with stations in the preceding segment), one receives its product inputs only from that single station in the prior production segment or level, and to this one station no such freedom exists. The efficiency of the structure in which fewer stations are "locked in" is higher, providing the number of stations in some segments is less than the number of initial sellers, m. Since the total output rate of the structure is a constant, it can be stated alternatively that larger station sizes with larger input rates lead to efficiencies. In the limiting case of one station per segment of intermediary operations, the first station in the sequence is free to receive its inputs from all the m sellers. Fewer stations in each segment thus entails more freedom in the structure since the m stations of the first segment are given in the analysis.

A certain amount of coordination is introduced into the structure with the reduction in the number of stations in each level of intermediaries. At the limit of one station in each of these levels, the structure is at its most efficient state, given that the m firms must remain as producers. As the number increases in each level, there is greater competition at each intermediary level, which means a larger number of sub-systems into which the entire system is divided. Each sub-system treated independently means less total system coordination. If the number of firms in the initial level of sellers is given by postulate, increases in the system's coordination can come only by the creation of intermediary levels in which the number of stations is less than m, and by the introduction of more freedom to each station in terms of its source of input. If, however, the number of firms in each of the intermediary levels is at its equilibrium number m, no more coordination exists in the system, despite the freedom that each station has, than existed in the total absence of freedom and intermediary levels.

For simplicity, we can look at the two limiting structures. The first is that of m firms, each with a single station in N segments. Every station receives its inputs from *only* the single station in the preceding segment. The other is the equilibrium structure with N levels of stations, m stations in each level, and a completely *random* movement of the output of all stations in one level to stations in the next. These two structures are equally efficient, but the second has the possibility for coordinating this random movement of the outputs of a level. The first structure, through its vertical integration, for that is exactly what is meant by the "locking in" process that defines competition in this case, has no possibility for such coordination. The coordination of the N levels may result from creating a single pure-coordinator middleman between every two producing levels. Every pair of such levels would, in effect, be analogous to the two starting levels of the analyses of Chapters 5 and 6.

Between any two levels, the m stations in one segment send their outputs randomly to the m stations in the next segment. The emission of units of product from the entire level is at a mean rate λ and is distributed in a Poisson fashion. The average arrival rate at each independent station in the next level is at rate $\frac{\lambda}{m}$, and the costs for this level are those of capacity and the time the product is in their productive system. The first level is thus analogous to the level which emits the random orders in Chapters 5 and 6, and the second is analogous to the order-filling level. A single pure coordinator between the two levels would operate by holding the units of product in a single queue and feeding them to the m units in the next processing segment as they become free. It would, in fact, make each level a single system of m stations rather than m sub-systems.

This case of a vertical market structure is a multiple extension of the structure analyzed in these two previous chapters. Locking in any two segments would prevent the application of this analysis since it means that the m stations may not be treated as a single system, for if they were, no locking-in would exist, by definition. However, combining the analysis of this chapter with that of the "pure coordinator" in order to identify the equilibrium total structure involves more than treating each two levels independently. If the introduction of a pure coordinator alters the optimal capacities of each of the m firms, then the equilibrium number of producing levels may differ from the number $\hat{N}$ obtained from the partial analysis ignoring the pure coordinator. The simultaneous solution requires that one solve the problem of segmentation with multi-service stations in each segment. There is, however, clearly a vertical market structure with multiple levels of producers and multiple levels of pure coordinators that is in equilibrium. Algebraic solutions for this equilibrium are complicated because of the complex terms in the two partial analyses to be combined, and no attempt at such combination is made here.

Rebates and strategy

If the entry of firms into the vertical market structure is predicated upon the payment of rebates to those units whose cooperation it seeks, then the equilibrium structural configuration will differ from that just described. If the transfer of the product between independent firms involves a cost—for example, a transaction cost—not present in the transfer of a unit of product between stations within a firm, then again the equilibrium structure will be different. Considering the required rebates and this cost as some total rebate, then each equilibrium number of intermediaries in each level will be smaller than m if this rebate is positive. With fewer firms in each level, the equilibrium number of pure coordinators will be smaller, and the equilibrium structure involving both kinds of levels will thus be different. Finally, if the rebates paid by intermediaries are a function of the size of the segment of the production process, as well as a function of the number of intermediaries and units of product handled, then the equilibrium number of levels (segments) may well differ from the $\hat{N}$ obtained in the absence of rebates. In general, the effects of rebates in this analysis are similar to their effects in the preceding analysis, although interesting variations do exist and should be investigated briefly.

The specialization of any intermediary in any segment of the production process is predicated upon the availability of inputs, that is, firms whose output is the product in the form sought by this intermediary. With just m firms in a single level, each with $\hat{N}$ stations or segments as the starting point, what is the nature of the logical sequence for intermediary development? If the m firms insist on performing the first segment, then the intermediary whose logical existence is possible is that one who starts his production process with the input from this segment. Given rebates by firms who are willing to take over the $\hat{N} - 1$ segments starting with the second, there is created a level of such middlemen. It is now logically possible for an intermediary to specialize in the production process which it is to perform starting with either the beginning of what was the third segment or beginning with what was the second and excluding the $\hat{N}$. In effect, this can be continued with each level in the sequence being a necessary one for the existence of the level in the next sequence. It is not possible for a firm to specialize in the sixth segment if there are no firms with an output in the form of the completed fifth segment. It is also logical for firms to attempt to obtain from the initial structure as many segments as possible. In other words, the logical sequence is for some firms to take over $(\hat{N} - 1)$ segments from the given m firms, offering them rebates, and then to give up in sequence $(\hat{N} - 2)$ segments in return for rebates and so on until every firm specializes in a single segment. The first logical level is, therefore, that in the second segment. Assuming for the moment that the number of segments is to remain at $\hat{N}$, the number of firms in this level w_1 will be less than m. A next logical level is that with firms specialized in the third segment and giving rebates to the w_1 firms. The number of firms in this level at equilibrium, w_2, will in turn be smaller than the number w_1. This continues for all segments, the simple reason being that for the firm in segment i, total revenues are what the costs of that segment would be in the firm's absence, excluding the rebates given by firms operating segments i and $(i - 1)$ in its absence. Because this number for $(i - 1)$ is $w_1 < m$, the revenues will be only $\frac{1}{\hat{N}} A \lambda^{\left(\frac{1}{\alpha}\right)} w_1^{\left(\frac{\alpha-1}{\alpha}\right)}$. Since the w_2 would be expected to give rebates, R_2, to the w_1 firms, the equilibrium number is

$$(17) \qquad \frac{A \lambda^{\left(\frac{1}{\alpha}\right)} w_1^{\left(\frac{\alpha-1}{\alpha}\right)}}{\hat{N}} - R_2 = \frac{A \lambda^{\left(\frac{1}{\alpha}\right)} w_2^{\left(\frac{\alpha-1}{\alpha}\right)}}{\hat{N}}$$

which is true for some value of $w_2 < w_1$. The equilibrium structure with such rebates is thus not symmetric, and the possibilities for pure coordinators to exist between levels become smaller as the levels approach that of the n buyers.

The analysis of equilibrium structures with and without rebates never considers the issue of stability. As with all previous analyses, the conditions that would identify the firms existing at equilibrium are not possible to obtain. The constant tendencies for firms to by-pass the equilibrium structure may suggest that the equilibrium is unstable. However, the by-passing merely brings new competitive forces which, by the entry and competition of firms, return the structure to its equilibrium form, though possibly with different players in the set positions. In this case a firm in level w_{i+1} would probably perform more efficiently if it (in the absence of pure coordinators) were to perform segment $(i + 1)$ and segments i, $i - 1$, etc., providing that the number of firms with which it competes and who are attempting to do the same is $w_{i+1} < w_i < w_{i-1}$, etc. But if that should occur and the w_{i+1} firms now performing a series of segments are making profits, more firms will enter and profits will disappear. This again would lead to the creation of firms who would take over from this newly attained equilibrium number all but one segment, and the cycle toward the same equilibrium structural configuration is started.

The discussion of strategy formulation by would-be or actual intermediaries in such a structure with pure coordinators deals, of course, with cooperation among the firms in order to minimize the cost of coordination. The manner in which competing coordinators operate requires the cooperation of all producing levels in the structure and is hence part of their decision problem. The new strategy possibility for competing producing intermediaries is that by which a firm would offer a rebate to the m firms to exclude the possibility of any other firm's existing in the structure.

In the manner of the discussion of Chapter 2 we must determine that level of rebates which a middleman knows will permit only one intemediary to exist. The conditions are thus those in which would-be intermediaries bid for a single spot by offering rebates to the m firms for their cooperation. The winner (offering the highest rebate) would take over $\left(\dfrac{\hat{N} - 1}{\hat{N}}\right)$ of the entire production process. Given the intensity of the bidding, and the organized bargaining strength of the m firms, the rebate which is expected to "win" will be determined. Its highest limit is, of course, $R_{\max}$ and is equal to

$$\left[\left(\frac{\hat{N} - 1}{\hat{N}}\right)A\lambda^{\left(\frac{1}{\alpha}\right)}m^{\left(\frac{\alpha-1}{\alpha}\right)}\right] - \left[\left(\frac{\hat{N} - 1}{\hat{N}}\right)A\lambda^{\left(\frac{1}{\alpha}\right)}\right]$$

giving the winner zero profits. The lower limit is that which would exlcude the next firm from belonging to the structure along with the first, i.e., that level which would guarantee that two firms could not profitably exist.

If the m firms are then to keep the first segment as their area of operation, total profits, from which the rebate would be granted, for the single intermediary would be

$$(18) \qquad TP_1 = \left(\frac{\hat{N} - 1}{\hat{N}}\right)A\lambda^{\left(\frac{1}{\alpha}\right)}\left(m^{\left(\frac{\alpha-1}{\alpha}\right)} - 1\right)$$

The firm pays for this total amount the lower limit of rebate R_1, so that the second firm's profits would be zero. The second firm's profits are merely

$$(19) \qquad TP_2 = \frac{1}{2}\left[\left(\frac{\hat{N} - 1}{\hat{N}}\right)A\lambda^{\left(\frac{1}{\alpha}\right)}\left(m^{\left(\frac{\alpha-1}{\alpha}\right)} - 2^{\left(\frac{\alpha-1}{\alpha}\right)}\right) - R_1\right]$$

Thus, it sets:

(20)
$$R_1 = \left(\frac{\hat{N}-1}{\hat{N}}\right) A\lambda^{\left(\frac{1}{\alpha}\right)} \left[m^{\left(\frac{\alpha-1}{\alpha}\right)} - 2^{\left(\frac{\alpha-1}{\alpha}\right)}\right]$$

and the firm's profits with this total rebate to the m firms would be

$$\left(\frac{\hat{N}-1}{\hat{N}}\right) A\lambda^{\left(\frac{1}{\alpha}\right)} \left[2^{\left(\frac{\alpha-1}{\alpha}\right)} - 1\right]$$

Any rebate greater than the R_1 given by expression (20) implies that only a single intermediary would exist between the m sellers (producing a product in some form) and the n buyers (purchasing the product in the required form from the intermediary). That intermediary would not only minimize the cost of performing the $\left(\frac{\hat{N}-1}{\hat{N}}\right)$ portion of the production process but would also optimally coordinate the structure in terms of all the cost-incurring functions to be performed in effecting exchange. In every case considered, the structure with the single intermediary is the optimal one under the conditions assumed. Optimal structures are not necessarily equilibrium structures. Though optimality is obtained here without any consideration of the issues of monopoly power and its effects on society's welfare, it is clear that the competition which leads to equilibrium structures involves society in some costs. In part to elucidate this point and in part to integrate the analysis of the previous chapters, the subject of prices is taken up in Chapter 9.

1   All segments are of equal size. The assumptions on the nature of the process of production lead directly to this conclusion.

2   Note that if a station has Poisson arrivals with mean rate λ and an exponential service time distribution, then the departure of completed units from the station is a Poisson distribution with the same mean rate λ.

3   An interesting sidelight on the conclusions of the model is that the firm's optimal size is at a point where it is experiencing increasing returns to scale, even under conditions of pure competition. This results because of the external diseconomies of coordination, but in essence the firm's real costs involve more than those of physical production. Thus it might be noted that the assumed increasing returns to specialization and scale merely imply that optimizing firms operate in such ranges if these ranges *exist*. This does not mean that decreasing returns to specialization and scale do not exist in some ranges.

9

PRICES

A mechanism of cooperation

Economic structures exhibit sufficient similarities so that the analysis which applies to one kind of organization is easily adaptable to another. This is but a direct conclusion of the more general concepts which attempt to characterize the essence of what constitutes a system without ever needing to refer to the particular form (e.g., economic or electric) of the system. Thus some organization theorists have analyzed successfully the organization that is a firm in terms of the concepts developed in the analysis of the organization that is an economy. A complex firm may be viewed as an economy in which the element of the firm is replaced by that of the segment or department. The issue of the centralization of a firm is cast into the general framework for the discussion of planned (centralized) and free (decentralized) economies. The discussion of the use of shadow prices in planned economies and transfer prices in firms shows further that the basic issues of cooperation, coordination, and competition within an economy and a firm are similar and thus permit interchangeable analytic treatments.

In the theoretic analysis to this point, the vertical market structure is discussed without any reference whatsoever to the mechanisms which create the conditions of cooperation, coordination, and competition which define it. Clearly, in a planned and controlled economy the entire structure would have a single objective function, the maximization of which would be the aim of the design of the structure with or without the use of the price mechanism. The economy and the firm are in this case similar and the discussion of the price mechanism is not essential in either. In a free economy, price is the main mechanism of transmitting market information, and hence of creating the relationships which define the vertical market structure. Each element in the free economy must be permitted to work to its own advantage, and no objective function for the entire structure is available to determine its design. If such firms operate through the price mechanism, then the previous analysis is applicable to free economies only after prices are incorporated into the analysis.

By offering to buy and sell a product in different forms, at different prices, and in different quantities, the firms in the system attempt to maximize their profits. This behavior by many firms yields a vertical market structure in which various forms of cooperation, competition, and coordination are evident. The structure is one of firms buying and selling products to one another and competing among sub-sets of all firms in the structure. When prices are ignored, the nature of these relationships may or may not be different from what they would be when price is the mechanism which characterizes them. The analysis of this chapter therefore provides some answers to a number of questions dealing specifically with this issue.

Price, form, and output

The three main variables which are now of concern are the price, form, and quantity which prevail when a product is bought and sold within a vertical market structure. If there exists a single equilibrium value for each of these variables, then the structure consists of only two levels—the buyers and sellers—making up a single market. If more than two levels exist, then at equilibrium there would be more than one value for the price, form, and quantity variables. For three levels there would be one intermediate market with its equilibrium value for price, form, and output, and one final market with its own such values. Within any given market the three equilibrium values are obviously related, as they also are among the markets in the structure. One added variable, therefore, for which the analysis must be capable of producing an equilibrium value, is that of the number of intermediate markets for the product. Finally, the number of buyers and sellers in any given market within the vertical market structure can, in the long run, be considered a variable (through the entry and exit of firms into the structure) for which an equilibrium must be found.

A vertical market structure is defined as a set of firms and consumers. The elements of this set are there by virture of cooperative relationships. The existence of competitive relationships creates sub-sets of the elements in the total set, and each sub-set is defined as a level in the structure. If the competition among the members of such sub-sets is assumed to be perfect, then an equilibrium single price, single form, and single output would exist between every two cooperating levels. For the entire vertical market structure, there must be determined simultaneously the equilibrium set of prices, set of forms, and set of quantities. This, it may be noted, is for a single vertical market structure with only one final consumer market. In the Walrasian analysis the last element in the set of equilibrium values for the variables is obtained in both the partial and general solutions. The general equilibrium of Walrasian analysis is for multiple vertical market structures each with two levels, whereas this analysis stresses multi-market vertical structures and solves for a single such structure. In this one way the models of this chapter are a variation on the partial equilibrium analysis of traditional economic theory, but they also differ from it in other ways involving the concept of product form.

The concepts of price and quantity involved in the sale of products in all markets making up the vertical market structure need little discussion. The concept of form, though used earlier in the analysis of production relationships, requires some attention. We *postulate* that the consumer's purchasing decision problem involves both the products he purchases *and* the form in which he purchases these products. The postulate means that the consumer is not indifferent to different forms of what is normally understood to be the same product at a given price. The need for the postulate is based upon the concept that the distinction between what differentiates products and what differentiates form is an important difference which serves to explain, among other things, the fact that households engage in what is generally understood to be production. The consumer purchases inputs which he employs to alter the physical form of the product, carries inventory, incurs marketing costs, and so on. He is thus involved in deciding just what form of product he is to purchase, given the form in which he is actually to derive the utility from its use.

More important, the distinction which permits us to identify different products is not sufficient for the analysis of vertical market structures, where it is quite obvious that the very same physical product is sold at different prices at different levels. Something about the product must be different if such price differences are to be logically explained. The thing that is different is the product's form. A concept of form is both reasonable and useful in permitting the concepts of price and quantity of economic theory to be incorporated into the analysis of vertical market structure with its central concepts of *cooperation* and *competition*.

Whatever it is about a product that determines its form must be closely related to some of the inputs involved in its production and marketing. In order to identify the form of the product one must recognize all those aspects associated with its sale to which the buyer is not indifferent. Such relevant aspects are those which are under the control of the seller and hence are related to his decision on the inputs employed and the manner of their employment. Therefore, for a given unit of product, the form it takes is defined by some set $\{x_1, x_2, \ldots, x_R\}$, where x_s is a function of the amount of one or more inputs included in the production and marketing of the product. Some such aspects may be physical, others may involve temporal and spatial dimensions. All aspects of the unit of product are important to the buyer because they determine in all dimensions what it is he receives when he pays the money price.

When a buyer purchases a product he either derives a utility from his purchase or uses it to make profits. Consider the case of a person who pays some price P for a product of a particular physical form delivered to his doorstep. If that person no longer incurs any costs in gaining utility from its consumption, the product's cost to him is P per unit. The same person's paying the same price for the identical physical product 100 miles from his doorstep must incur further costs in order to obtain the same utility as before from the product's consumption. If this transportation cost was T per unit, the net price paid for the same gross level of utility derived from consuming the principal product is now $(P + T)$. Meanwhile the seller in both cases receives a net price for the physically identical product that is dependent upon its location delivery requirements. The basic concept of product form is introduced to permit easier comparison by stating that in this case, the price paid and received was identically P in both cases, but it has a different value to the buyer, and involves a different cost to the seller in that the form of the product exchanged was different. In the one case each unit when received by the buyer has a characteristic, the transportation input; in the other it does not.

From the seller's point of view, the production function relates the cost-incuring inputs to a *quantity* of physical units of the product and the *form* of a unit of product. What is sold is a unit of product that is a package of input combinations of various kinds and not merely a physical unit. From the buyer's side the conditions of sale, including the product's physical form, determine the value of the unit of product purchased either in terms of utility or in terms of costs. In the case of the firm, for his decision problem, the price paid by the buyer in the market thus meaningfully defines the cost per unit he incurs only if the product's form is identified. The form outcome of a package of inputs in a unit of product is what the buyer receives for the payment of the money price, and this latter is his cost for that product in that form.

It is the central thesis of this work that the nature of the allocation of all the production and marketing operations in a vertical market structure is an important determinant of the structure and efficiency of an economy. The market price which holds between any two levels is closely related to this allocation. Meanwhile the allocation which emerges is the result of the behavior of profit-maximizing firms in response to prices. The relationship of this allocation to prices is in essence the relationship of product form to prices. If there were no issue of allocation, then the product's form would be frozen and firms would only have to make the decision on output in response to price. Since cooperation involves the determination of this allocation, firms must make decisions on it and on output in response to prices. Allowing the product form to be defined in terms of relevant aspects permits the analysis to have both buyer and seller use the same market price as a parameter in their decision problems. In turn, the equilibrium market price has meaning to buyer and seller only if to it are added the other variables which determine the profits or utility from buying or selling.

The decision problems of both buyer and seller are not only related through price in terms of the "market price," but also through the manner in which the operations of each are determined and allocated between them. This is the essence of the concept of cooperation. If the concept of a single market price to which both buyer and seller respond in their decision making is to be meaningful, some consideration must be given to the relationships of the two decisions that stem from the allocation of operations. One way would be to identify the net selling price and the gross buying price, and to allow the market price to be determined by some mechanism which would reflect the allocation of the difference between the two. This would not, however, allow the individual firm to respond as a cooperator to *the market price*. In every market there must be determined the three prices, two to be used as relevant decision parameters by the buyer and two by the seller. The market price is that which emerges by this complex response problem. However, if one defines the form of the product exchanged in terms of aspects related to the inputs incorporated in it, received by the buyer, and involving the seller in costs, both buyer and seller can respond to the single market price and include as a profit variable the product's form for which any market price is relevant. The concept of form thus links the individual firm's decision problems in the relevant manner without modifying the relationships that come directly through the concept of market price.

The firm in its role as a seller is faced with a production function that is logically the same as that commonly employed in the economic theory of the firm.[1] Varying the combination of inputs may vary the number of units produced and/or the cost, but now it may also vary the form of each unit. This variation is unlike that related to the multiple product form of production functions. The difference is that in this latter there exists a finite number of different products, and the problem is to determine the amounts of each which the firm is to produce. The question is, however, what products? Why the particular finite combination of aspects which determine variations in form or, in this case, identify different products? Furthermore, it may not be possible to vary the combination of some inputs without identifying a new product or new form. Thus the concept of form for the same product is introduced. A product may be defined in terms of the particular kinds of inputs that are embodied in it while its form is defined in terms of values which are functions of the amounts of some or all of these inputs. For a given product, therefore, the firm's problem is to determine its output and the form each unit of output has. In addition, it may also have these problems for a series of products.

To the buyer, it is postulated, not all input combinations involved in the production and marketing of a product are equally preferable. The consumer may not be indifferent to the amount of labor involved in the production of the unit of product. The product form may include an aspect related in some fashion to the amounts of this input (hand-made vs. machine-made). The demand function the consumer presents relates price, quantity, and form. The derivation of this demand function of a buyer who is not the consumer may be based upon the nature of his production function vis-a-vis some ultimate consumer demand surface, perhaps through the demand functions of other buying firms in the vertical market structure. The firm is not indifferent to the product's form, at a given price, since its costs and revenues are related to that form.

The distinction between form and product in the case of the consumer requires much theoretic work on utility functions. For our purposes it is sufficient to indicate that the distinction is both useful in the analysis of vertical market structures, and reasonable. Its source is the assumption that the consumer does not respond in identical fashion to the changes in the inputs embodied in a product from which he derives utility. A variation in the input combination entails no relevant change in form or product if there exists indifference to the change, given a unit price. An input change entails a change in form if at all market price combinations, one single value for that input in combination with fixed values for some others is always to be preferred. That is, at all price combinations the buyer will purchase only a single form. A variation in an input entails a change in product if, at all market price combinations, the buyers always prefer to purchase a positive number of units of the combination of all inputs with and without the variation in the one input. Products must be in combination to maximize utility, and forms of products are things for which maximum utility occurs with the purchase of a single form, given the price relationship between forms.

The concept of a product form is thus a useful analytic addition since it weds price and quantity theory to the theory of intermediate price and quantity relationships. Without it, the concept of a vertical market structure and the analysis of single level price and quantity relationships could not be combined. What changes are there if a product is exchanged at two different prices in two markets in a vertical market structure? Is it an entirely different product, so that by using the traditional utility concepts, the consumer would maximize utility by buying in two market levels? The answer must surely be negative, and no issue as to the logical existence of such a vertical market structure can be raised, in view of both the theory in the last seven chapters and elsewhere and the empirical evidence. The same unit at the same quantity commands a different price because the form is different. It may be the same physical quantity but its condition of sale is different, and what the buyer sees in the two markets in the vertical market structure at different prices is a different product form. Concepts of a market price and of sequences of cooperating firms and hence, a vertical structure of prices, are incorporated into one analysis by the concept of product form. The simultaneous determination of the price, form, and quantity relationships which characterize a vertical market structure is the subject of the remainder of this chapter.

The firm's decision problem

There are two main differences between this discussion of the firm's decision problem and those developed earlier. The firm is now viewed in its most general form as an operator on a series of inputs to produce an output of some form. No specific cost functions are identified. Secondly, the firm's cooperative and competitive relationships are now identified specifically through the price mechanism.

Generally speaking the firms considered are, by assumption, engaged in the purchase, sale, and production of one single product. The firm's optimum decision constitutes the basis for deriving the number of levels that will exist, under varying conditions, in the vertical market structure for this product. Simultaneous with the determination of the equilibrium structure, the equilibrium price and quantity in all intermediate markets in the structure must be derived. The result is the determination of vertical structures of market prices.

The relationship between the vertical market structure and the firm's problem lies in the firm's choice in both its competitive and its *cooperative* relationships. Quite obviously, therefore, the following model involves the crucial determination of how the cooperative relationship is to be stated in terms of price, quantity, and form relationships. Since cooperation is not in this discussion the equivalent of collusion, its introduction suggests that a given set of firms limited in operations on a single product may compete, or they may create sub-sets in which the elements compete and also cooperate with elements in other sub-sets. The element of cooperation suggests the possibility that firms may optimally specialize in one section of the total production and marketing requirements of any given product. Thus, firms may have the choice of the other firms with which they compete and those with which they cooperate. The choice in both cases is in this model characterized uniquely in terms of the optimal response to price relationships.

To develop the firm's decision model let:

$\pi_{r,i}$ = selling price of the rth firm in the ith level; $r = 1, 2, \ldots, w_i$ and $i = 1, 2, \ldots, N$.

$p_{r,i}$ = purchase price of the rth firm in the ith level; $r = 1, 2, \ldots, w_i$ and $i = 1, 2, \ldots, N$.

$q_{r,i}$ = quantity sold by the rth firm in the ith level; $r = 1, 2, \ldots, w_i$ and $i = 1, 2, \ldots, N$.

$h_{r,i}$ = quantity purchased by the rth firm in the ith level; $r = 1, 2, \ldots,$ w_i and $i = 1, 2, \ldots, N$.

$x_{r,j,i}$ = value of the jth dimension of the product's form sold by the rth firm in the ith level; $j = 1, 2, \ldots, R$, $r = 1, 2, \ldots, w_i$, and $i = 1, 2, \ldots, N$.

$TP_{r,i}$ = total profits of the rth firm in the ith level, $r = 1, 2, \ldots, w_i$, and $i = 1, 2, \ldots, N$.

N = number of levels of firms (and households) in the vertical market structure.

w_i = number of firms in the ith level of the vertical market structure; $i = 1, 2, \ldots, N$.

$y_{r,j,i}$ = value of the jth dimension of the product's form purchased by the rth firm in the ith level; $j = 1, 2, \ldots, R$, $r = 1, 2, \ldots, w_i$, and $i = 1, 2, \ldots, N$.

Also let:

$F_{r,i}$ denote the function,

$F_{r,i}(x_{r,1,i}, x_{r,2,i}, \ldots, x_{r,R,i}, y_{r,1,i}, y_{r,2,i} \ldots, y_{r,R,i}, q_{r,i}, h_{r,i})$,

which is the *unit cost* of the rth firm's output net of purchase costs, i.e., net of $p_{r,i}$. The specific discussion of the derivation of this cost function from the relationships between inputs, outputs, and form is made in the next section.

The rth firm in the ith level has the problem of maximizing its total profits by determining the R values of the product form dimensions which it sells, the R values of the product form dimensions which it buys, the quantity of output sold, the quantity of output bought, the selling price, and the buying price. It has, therefore, the following variables to determine:

$x_{r,j,i}$ for $j = 1, 2, \ldots, R$
$y_{r,j,i}$ for $j = 1, 2, \ldots, R$
$q_{r,i}$
$h_{r,i}$
$\pi_{r,i}$
$p_{r,i}$

The firm has a total of $2(R + 2)$ decision variables to be optimized in order to maximize profits. The function to be maximized by the rth firm in the ith level is:

(1a) $$TP_{r,i} = q_{r,i}(\pi_{r,i} - F_{r,i}) - h_{r,i}p_{r,i}$$

The number of decision variables for the rth firm can be reduced as a result of a number of market conditions and the fact that all w_i firms in all $N - 1$ levels and the consumers making up the Nth level also have related decision problems which are to be optimally solved. Thus, since this analysis is one of comparative statics, no inventory is carried by any firm, and we can assume that the optimal value for $h_{r,i}$ is equal to the optimal value of $q_{r,i}$. Units purchased are thus equal to units sold or:

(2) $$h_{r,i} = q_{r,i}, \text{ for all } r \text{ and } i.$$

For the last level, the Nth in the structure (the equivalent of the level of n buyers), two possibilities exist. If the level is one of firms then,

$$h_{r,N} = q_{r,N}$$

If the level is one of households (consumers), then $q_{r,N}$ is the level of consumption, and

$$h_{r,N} = q_{r,N}$$

For this level of consumers, the decision problem would be to maximize utility, and equation **(1a)** would be replaced by the appropriate utility function. In any case, for all N levels equation **(2)** holds.

Substituting for $h_{r,i}$ in equation **(1a)** gives the objective function for the firm as:

(1) $$TP_{r,i} = q_{r,i}(\pi_{r,i} - p_{r,i} - F_{r,i}) \text{ for all } r \text{ and } i$$

It is *assumed* that pure competition exists in all buying and selling markets, which entails the conclusions that:

$$\frac{\partial p_{r,i}}{\partial h_{r,i}} = 0 \text{ and } \frac{\partial \pi_{r,i}}{\partial q_{r,i}} = 0$$

for all r and i. It is also assumed that there exists a particular basic behavioral relationship among cooperating firms. The relationship is one in which the selling firm may gain the cooperation of a buying firm so long as the selling firm does not reduce the profits of the buying firm with respect to the *form* of the product sold by the selling firm. A firm is thus willing to buy a product in some form only under this minimum necessary condition. Of course, changing the form in which the product is purchased may alter the firm's type and scale of operations. All changes in form are thus as a minimum condition uniquely related to the unit price acceptable to the buyer. We will have occasion to assume that this necessary condition is also sufficient for cooperation, but for the moment the necessary condition as it stands states that the kth firm in the $(i + 1)$th level will cooperate with the rth firm in the ith level only if

(3) $$\frac{\partial TP_{k,i+1}}{\partial x_{r,j,i}} \geqslant 0, \text{ for all } k, r, j, \text{ and } i.$$

Examination of equation (**1**) shows that $x_{r,j,i}$ is not contained in the expression of $TP_{k,i+1}$ unless $x_{r,j,i} = y_{k,j,i}$, i.e., unless the form in which the product sold by the rth firm in the ith level is identical to the form of the product purchased by the kth firm in the $(i+1)$th level. For any two specific firms, of course, the product sold to and bought from one another has the identical form; indeed, it may be recalled, that is the reason for the creation of the concept of form. However, in order to conclude that the product sold by one set of firms is identical to that bought by another set, we will assume identical firms in each set. We thus assume that all firms in any level deal with the same product forms, or that:

(**4**) $$x_{r,j,i} = x_{j,i} \text{ for all } j \text{ and } i,$$

and

(**5**) $$y_{r,j,i} = y_{j,i} \text{ for all } j \text{ and } i.$$

These two equalities and the equality of the form of the product bought and sold by two specific firms to one another permit us to state

(**6**) $$y_{j,i} = x_{j,i-1} \text{ for all } j \text{ and } i,$$

and, therefore, for the rth firm in level i, that:

(**7**) $$y_{r,j,i} = x_{j,i-1}.$$

Finally, because the form in which the product is bought and sold in the perfect markets is the same, it can be concluded that:

(**8**) $$p_{r,i} = p_i \text{ for all } r \text{ and } i, \text{ and}$$

(**9**) $$\pi_{r,i} = \pi_i \text{ for all } r \text{ and } i.$$

The perfect markets are cleared at a price at some level such that the purchase price of the ith level is equal to the selling price of the $(i-1)$th level.

(**10**) $$p_{r,i} = \pi_{i-1} \text{ for all } r \text{ and } i.$$

From equations (**2**), (**7**), and (**10**) the firm's problem can be reduced to the maximization of profits (**1**) subject to equation (**3**). In other words, the problem is to maximize profits subject to the condition that the profits of the firms in the buying level are not reduced with respect to the selling firm's choice of:

$x_{r,j,i}$ for all i and j,
$q_{r,i}$ for all i and r
$\pi_{r,i}$ for all i.

The condition of cooperation which the selling firm must meet is given in equation (**3**) as:

(**3**) $$\frac{\partial TP_{k,i+1}}{\partial x_{r,j,i}} \geqslant 0,$$

where, as a result of the analysis of the relations between variables in consecutive structure levels,

$$TP_{k,i+1} = q_{k,i+1}(\pi_{i+1} - \pi_i - F_{k,i+1})$$

This condition can now be seen to require that:

(3a) $$0 \geqslant \frac{\partial \pi_i}{\partial x_{r,j,i}} + \frac{\partial F_{k,i+1}}{\partial x_{r,j,i}}, \text{ for all } j, r, k, \text{ and } i$$

In general, therefore, one can state that there exists a relationship of the form:

(11) $$\pi_{r,i} \leqslant g_i(x_{r,1,i}, x_{r,2,i}, \ldots, x_{r,R,i}; \sum_{r=1}^{w_i} q_{r,i})$$

which satisfies condition **(3a)**. This functional relationship may in fact be considered to be the demand function in the ith output market. It identifies the requirement which the selling firm must meet in order to gain the cooperation of the firms in the $(i+1)$th level. If it is not met these firms would "make" instead of "buy".

Because of the assumption of perfect competition, the firm is a price taker and $\pi_{r,i} = \pi_i$, since no firm will reasonably sell below the market price and no firm can sell at above the market price. Furthermore, for simplicity we will assume that *the sufficient condition for cooperation is actually the minimum necessary one*. This assumption can be interpreted to mean that the cooperating relationship is in and of itself non-competitive. In terms of the preceding chapters no rebate is demanded by the buyer as a condition of cooperation with the seller. The advantages which such cooperation brings to the buyer will be dependent, as is shown below, on the adjustment in output which cooperation brings as a result of the optimizing behavior of the sellers, and on the extent of competition among the firms in the buying and selling levels. Expression **(11)** is thus now the *equality*

(11a) $$\pi_i = g_i\left(x_{r,1,i}, x_{r,2,i}, \ldots, x_{r,R,i}; \sum_{r=1}^{w_i} q_{r,i}\right)$$

The firm's problem can now be identified as the maximization of:

(12) $$TP_{r,i} = q_{r,i}\left[g_i\left(x_{r,1,i}, x_{r,2,i}, \ldots, x_{r,R,i}; \sum_{r=1}^{w_i} q_{r,i}\right) - \pi_{i-1} - F_{r,i}\right]$$

The first-order conditions for maximum profits with respect to the variables $x_{r,j,i}$ (for all j) and $q_{r,i}$ are that

(13) $$\frac{\partial TP_{r,i}}{\partial x_{r,j,i}} = q_{r,i}\left(\frac{\partial \pi_i}{\partial x_{r,j,i}} - \frac{\partial F_{r,i}}{\partial x_{r,j,i}}\right) = 0$$

or

(13a) $$\frac{\partial \pi_i}{\partial x_{r,j,i}} = \frac{\partial F_{r,i}}{\partial x_{r,j,i}},$$

and

(14) $$\frac{\partial TP_{r,i}}{\partial q_{r,i}} = q_{r,i}\left(\frac{\partial \pi_i}{\partial q_{r,i}} - \frac{\partial \pi_{i-1}}{\partial q_{r,i}} - \frac{\partial F_{r,i}}{\partial q_{r,i}}\right) + (\pi_i - \pi_{i-1} - F_{r,i}) = 0.$$

Since perfect markets in all levels are assumed to exist, this reduces to

(14a)
$$\pi_i = \pi_{i-1} + \frac{\partial}{\partial q_{ri}}(q_{r,i}F_{r,i})$$

This condition is illustrated in Chart 9.1 and states that the marginal revenue π_i must be equated to the marginal cost, $\frac{\partial}{\partial q_{r,i}}(q_{r,i}F_{r,i}) + \pi_{i-1}$. Condition **(13a)** states that the rate of change of selling price with respect to the aspect j must be equated to the rate of change in unit cost with respect to the same aspect, for all R aspects of the product's form. Both conditions are not sufficient for the existence of intermediate markets, with the number of levels in a vertical market structure being greater than two. In fact, they are not even sufficient for the existence of a final market. What is required is the analysis of the basic elements that underlie the firm's cost functions, and the second-order conditions for a maximum profit to exist.

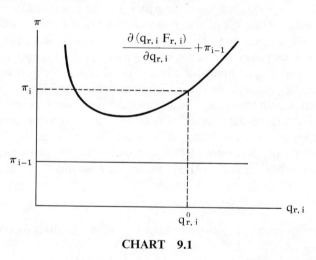

CHART 9.1

The firm's production process

For condition **(13a)** to be nontrivial, $F_{r,i}$ must be some nonlinear function of $x_{r,j,i}$ (for all j). Extreme point solutions will result when $F_{r,i}$ is *not* a strictly convex function of the decision variables $x_{r,j,i}$ (for all j). In traditional microeconomic theory where the j dimensions of $x_{r,j,i}$ would be treated as inputs with prices ϕ_j, and where one assumes perfect input markets, $F_{r,i}$ would be represented as:

$$F_{r,i} = \frac{1}{q_{r,i}}\left[\sum_{j=1}^{R}\phi_j(x_{r,j,i} - x_{j,i-1})\right], \text{ where } x_{r,j,i} - x_{j,i-1}$$

would represent the usage level of the ith "input" by the rth firm. Hence:

$$\frac{\partial F_{r,i}}{\partial x_{r,j,i}} = \frac{\phi_j}{q_{r,i}}$$

which means that $F_{r,i}$ is a *linear* function of $x_{r,j,i}$.

In the analysis of vertical market structures, however, $x_{r,j,i}$ is not an input, but is postulated to be the value taken by an aspect or dimension of the unit of output of the rth firm in the ith level. A particular value of $x_{r,j,i}$ is achieved by the application of a set of H inputs which might be denoted by $z_{r,a,i}$ (for $a = 1, 2, \ldots, H$). The following inplicit function in $q_{r,i}, x_{r,j,i}$ (for all j), and $z_{r,a,i}$ (for all a) may be used to characterize the transformation process of the H inputs into a quantity of output from one of form given by $x_{j,i-1}$ to one of form $x_{r,j,i}$ (for all j):

(15) $\qquad 0 = f_i([x_{r,j,i} - x_{j,i-1}], z_{r,a,i}, q_{r,i})$, for all j and a,

which will be denoted by f_i from here on.

If the ath input price is denoted by θ_a, then the firm's costs are:

(16) $\qquad TC_{r,i} = q_{r,i}(\pi_{i-1} + F_{r,i})$ where

(17) $\qquad q_{r,i}F_{r,i} = \sum_{a=1}^{H} \theta_a z_{r,a,i}$

The firm's problem is thus to maximize:

(18) $\qquad TP_{r,i} = (\pi_i - \pi_{i-1})q_{r,i} - \sum_{a=1}^{H} \theta_a z_{r,a,i} + \lambda_i f_i$

where $\pi_i = g_i\left(x_{r,1,i}, x_{r,2,i}, \ldots, x_{r,R,i}; \sum_{r=1}^{w_i} q_{r,i}\right)$, and is the same cooperation condition function discussed in the previous section. For a maximum the first-order conditions are:

(19) $\qquad \dfrac{\partial TP_{r,i}}{\partial z_{r,a,i}} = -\theta_a + \lambda_i \dfrac{\partial f_i}{\partial z_{r,a,i}} = 0$, for all a;

(20) $\qquad \dfrac{\partial TP_{r,i}}{\partial x_{r,j,i}} = q_{r,i}\dfrac{\partial \pi_i}{\partial x_{r,j,i}} + \lambda_i \dfrac{\partial f_i}{\partial x_{r,j,i}} = 0$, for all j;

(21) $\qquad \dfrac{\partial TP_{r,i}}{\partial q_{r,i}} = \pi_i - \pi_{i-1} + \lambda_i \dfrac{\partial f_i}{\partial q_{r,i}} = 0 \left(\text{since } \dfrac{\partial \pi_i}{\partial q_{r,i}} = 0\right)$;

and

(22) $\qquad \dfrac{\partial TP_{r,i}}{\partial \lambda_i} = f_i = 0.$

From the set of equations the general form of which is represented in expression **(19)**, we obtain the well known decision rules on prices and the rate of input substitution:

$$\frac{\theta_a}{\theta_b} = \frac{\dfrac{\partial f_i}{\partial z_{r,a,i}}}{\dfrac{\partial f_i}{\partial z_{r,b,i}}} = -\frac{\partial z_{r,b,i}}{\partial z_{r,a,i}}$$

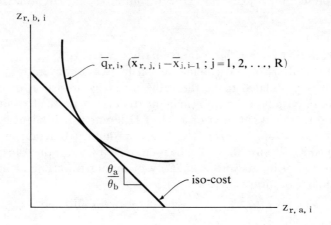

Here $\dfrac{\partial f_i}{\partial z_{r,a,i}}$ involves more than the rate of change of output quantity with respect to the input, and includes the effects on product form as well. From the set of equations represented by expression (20), we get the decision rules that:

$$-\frac{\partial \pi_i}{\partial x_{r,j,i}} = \frac{\lambda_i}{q_{r,i}}\frac{\partial f_i}{\partial x_{r,j,i}}, \text{ for all } j.$$

From equation (13a) we know, however, that

$$\frac{\partial \pi_i}{\partial x_{r,j,i}} = \frac{\partial F_{r,i}}{\partial x_{r,j,i}}$$

and hence,

$$-\frac{\lambda_i}{q_{r,i}}\frac{\partial f_i}{\partial x_{r,j,i}} = \frac{\partial F_{r,i}}{\partial x_{r,j,i}},$$

and,

$$-\frac{\partial x_{r,k,i}}{\partial x_{r,j,i}} = \frac{\dfrac{\partial \pi_i}{\partial x_{r,j,i}}}{\dfrac{\partial \pi_i}{\partial x_{r,k,i}}} = \frac{\dfrac{\partial F_{r,i}}{\partial x_{r,j,i}}}{\dfrac{\partial F_{r,i}}{\partial x_{r,k,i}}} = -\frac{\partial x_{r,k,i}}{\partial x_{r,j,i}}.$$

The first two terms are derived from the revenue relationship and the second two from the cost relationship. The decision rule is illustrated in Chart 9.3 and states that rate of *revenue transformation* between any two aspects of form must be equated to the rate of cost transformation between the same two aspects of form for all R aspects.

Finally, from equation (21) we obtain the decision rule:

$$\pi_i - \pi_{i-1} = -\lambda_i \frac{\partial f_i}{\partial q_{r,i}}$$

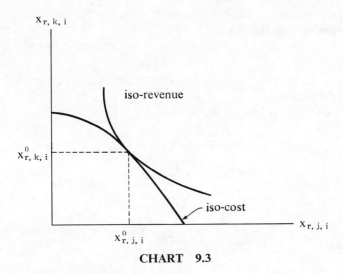

CHART 9.3

Using expression (**14a**) we obtain,

$$\pi_i - \pi_{i-1} = \frac{\partial (q_{r,i} F_{r,i})}{\partial q_{r,i}} = -\lambda_i \frac{\partial f_i}{\partial q_{r,i}}$$

Chart 9.4 illustrates this rule.

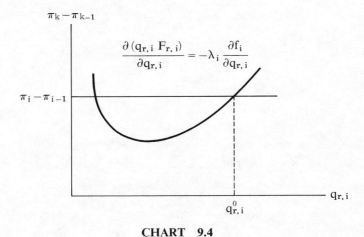

CHART 9.4

If we view f_i to be, for example, of the form $f_i = q_{r,i} - h(z_{r,a,i}, x_{r,j,i}^{-1})$ for all a and j, then the decision rule states that the optimal output is that for which the marginal revenue net of product purchase cost is equal to the marginal cost $(-\lambda_i)$.

Second-order conditions

In order to state the second-order conditions we first define the following second-order partials:

$$Q_h^{(x)} = \frac{\partial^2 TP_{r,i}}{\partial q_{r,i} \partial x_{r,h,i}}$$

$$Q_a^{(z)} = \frac{\partial^2 TP_{r,i}}{\partial q_{r,i} \partial z_{r,a,i}}$$

$$Q = \frac{\partial^2 TP_{r,i}}{\partial q_{r,i}^2}$$

$$X_{k,h} = \frac{\partial^2 TP_{r,i}}{\partial x_{r,k,i} \partial x_{r,h,i}}$$

$$X_{k,a}^{(z)} = \frac{\partial^2 TP_{r,i}}{\partial x_{r,k,i} \partial z_{r,a,i}}$$

$$X_k^{(q)} = \frac{\partial^2 TP_{r,i}}{\partial x_{r,k,i} \partial q_{r,i}}$$

$$X_k = \frac{\partial^2 TP_{r,i}}{\partial x_{r,k,i} \partial \lambda} = \frac{\partial f_i}{\partial x_{r,k,i}} = F_k^{(x)}$$

$$Z_{a,b} = \frac{\partial^2 TP_{r,i}}{\partial z_{r,a,i} \partial z_{r,b,i}}$$

$$Z_a^{(q)} = \frac{\partial^2 TP_{r,i}}{\partial z_{r,a,i} \partial q_{r,i}}$$

$$Z_a = \frac{\partial^2 TP_{r,i}}{\partial z_{r,a,i} \partial \lambda}$$

$$F_k^{(x)} = \frac{\partial^2 TP_{r,i}}{\partial \lambda \partial x_{r,k,i}} = \frac{\partial f_i}{\partial x_{r,k,i}}$$

$$F_a^{(z)} = \frac{\partial^2 TP_{r,i}}{\partial \lambda \partial z_{r,a,i}} = \frac{\partial f_i}{\partial z_{r,a,i}}$$

$$F_q = \frac{\partial^2 TP_{r,i}}{\partial \lambda \partial q_{r,i}} = \frac{\partial f_i}{\partial q_{r,i}}$$

$$F = \frac{\partial^2 TP_{r,i}}{\partial \lambda^2} = 0$$

To have a maximum $TP_{r,i}$ the bordered principal minors of the relevant bordered Hessian determinant must alternate in sign beginning with a minus. The relevant bordered Hessian determinant is

$$\begin{vmatrix} X_{1,1} & X_{1,2} & \cdots & X_{1,R} & X_{1,1}^{(z)} & X_{1,2}^{(z)} & \cdots & X_{1,II}^{(z)} & X_1^{(q)} & F_1^{(x)} \\ X_{2,1} & X_{2,2} & \cdots & X_{2,R} & X_{2,1}^{(z)} & X_{2,2}^{(z)} & \cdots & X_{2,II}^{(z)} & X_2^{(q)} & F_2^{(x)} \\ \cdot & \cdot & & \cdot & \cdot & \cdot & & \cdot & \cdot & \cdot \\ \cdot & \cdot & & \cdot & \cdot & \cdot & & \cdot & \cdot & \cdot \\ \cdot & \cdot & & \cdot & \cdot & \cdot & & \cdot & \cdot & \cdot \\ X_{R,1} & X_{R,2} & \cdots & X_{R,R} & X_{R,1}^{(z)} & X_{R,2}^{(z)} & \cdots & X_{R,II}^{(z)} & X_R^{(q)} & F_R^{(x)} \\ Z_{1,1}^{(x)} & Z_{1,2}^{(x)} & \cdots & Z_{1,R}^{(x)} & Z_{1,1} & Z_{1,2} & \cdots & Z_{1,II} & Z_1^{(q)} & F_1^{(z)} \\ Z_{2,1}^{(x)} & Z_{2,2}^{(x)} & \cdots & Z_{2,R}^{(x)} & Z_{2,1} & Z_{2,2} & \cdots & Z_{2,II} & Z_2^{(q)} & F_2^{(z)} \\ \cdot & \cdot & & \cdot & \cdot & \cdot & & \cdot & \cdot & \cdot \\ \cdot & \cdot & & \cdot & \cdot & \cdot & & \cdot & \cdot & \cdot \\ \cdot & \cdot & & \cdot & \cdot & \cdot & & \cdot & \cdot & \cdot \\ Z_{II,1}^{(x)} & Z_{II,2}^{(x)} & \cdots & Z_{II,R}^{(x)} & Z_{II,1} & Z_{II,2} & \cdots & Z_{II,II} & Z_{II}^{(q)} & F_{II}^{(z)} \\ Q_1^{(x)} & Q_2^{(x)} & \cdots & Q_R^{(x)} & Q_1^{(z)} & Q_2^{(z)} & \cdots & Q_{II}^{(z)} & Q & F_q \\ F_1^{(x)} & F_2^{(x)} & \cdots & F_R^{(x)} & F_1^{(z)} & F_2^{(z)} & \cdots & F_{II}^{(z)} & F_q & 0 \end{vmatrix}$$

The second-order conditions require that:

$$\begin{vmatrix} X_{1,1} & F_1^{(x)} \\ F_1^{(x)} & 0 \end{vmatrix} < 0, \quad \begin{vmatrix} X_{1,1} & X_{1,2} & F_1^{(x)} \\ X_{2,1} & X_{2,2} & F_2^{(x)} \\ F_1^{(x)} & F_2^{(x)} & 0 \end{vmatrix} > 0, \cdots,$$

$$(-1)^R \begin{vmatrix} X_{1,1} & X_{1,2} & \cdots & X_{1,R} & F_1^{(x)} \\ X_{2,1} & X_{2,2} & \cdots & X_{2,R} & F_2^{(x)} \\ \cdot & \cdot & & \cdot & \cdot \\ \cdot & \cdot & & \cdot & \cdot \\ \cdot & \cdot & & \cdot & \cdot \\ X_{R,1} & X_{R,2} & \cdots & X_{R,R} & F_R^{(x)} \\ F_1^{(x)} & F_2^{(x)} & \cdots & F_R^{(x)} & 0 \end{vmatrix} > 0, \cdots$$

Careful examination of the conditions shows that it is sufficient to satisfy them that (a) each input $z_{r,a,i}$ (for all a) exhibit a diminishing marginal product in $x_{r,j,i}$ (for all j), and in $q_{r,i}$; (b) each aspect $x_{r,j,i}$ (for all j) and $q_{r,i}$ exhibit decreasing returns to scale in the optimum combination of inputs $z_{r,a,i}$ (for all a). These conditions mean that at some point the firm encounters increasing marginal costs of producing greater output levels in the optimum form. Under these conditions, the firm in level i as a condition of cooperation would present the firm in level $(i - 1)$ with the particular relationship between price and form shown in equation (**11a**). Since the second-order conditions state that the marginal cost to the firm in level i is rising at the optimal level and form of its operation, it is willing to offer a price to the firm in level $(i + 1)$ which decreases with decreases in the values of the aspects of form of the selling firm's output. In addition, the more unbalanced the form of the product bought by the firm in level i in relation to the form in which it sells it, the higher its total cost for a given output. That is, the more the firm concentrates on some aspects to the exclusion of others, the higher its total cost for the some level of output. Both these situations guarantee that the firm, when it transfers its marginal cost into a marginal revenue for its would-be supplier, offers this supplier a marginal revenue surface which is falling monotonically after some point with respect to the form it produces (at all given output levels). The conditions also guarantee a minimum point to $F_{r,i}$ with respect to $x_{r,j,i}$ (for all j), i.e., a minimum cost condition for the $x_{r,j,i}$ (for all j) at any given output. If we also assume that marginal costs of the firm in level i first fall and then increase with increases in the values of $x_{r,j,i-1}$, then the marginal revenue for the firm in level $(i-1)$ with respect to form will be at first increasing and then decreasing at all output levels. A finite number of points at which cooperation with intermediaries may exist will occur if and only if the marginal cost function first falls, then rises, for all firms in all levels. A unique optimum form for the product at the point of cooperation will exist when the condition on the transformation rate between all pairs of $x_{r,j,i}$ (for all pairs of values of j) for all given cost levels gives an iso-cost curve like that in Chart 9.3. Such a form gives a iso-revenue curve as in Chart 9.3 to the firm in level $(i-1)$, and so on between all levels.

Equilibrium states of the structure

The analysis of the equilibrium of a vertical market structure includes as an integral part the issue of cooperation. Such cooperation finds its way into the equilibrium states through the specific variables of form and the number of levels. Both these variables are parameterized in the usual partial equilibrium analysis of the two-level, fixed-form structure of economic theory. Their inclusion as variables in our analysis expands the dimensions of equilibrium and of the different equilibrium states which might be considered.

When the analysis is limited to the three variables of price, quantity, and the number of sellers in a single level, there exist two main equilibrium states—the short and long run states. In our analysis there are more variables to be held fixed or to be solved for at equilibrium, and therefore there are, in effect, three equilibrium states which are of interest: the short run, the intermediate run, and the long run. In the first state we consider the form and the number of levels in the structure, the total number of firms in the structure, and the total number of firms in each level to be fixed. In the second state we consider the total number of firms in the structure to be the only fixed variable, all others being dimensions of the equilibrium state of the structure. In the third state this number is not held constant. The addition of the intermediate run suggests that firms already in the structure adjust by choosing and creating levels in their search for profits, even though the entire structure does not have any entering or exiting firms. It is of interest to consider the adjustments *within* a structure independently of adjustments *between* structures. Ignoring product form and multiple (more than two) level structures excludes the possibility for the discusison of this intermediate equilibrium state.

The three states of static equilibrium for a vertical market structure may be summarized as follows:

a.   Short run equilibrium with $w_i, W, (N > 2)$ as parameters and π_i, $x_{r,j,i}$ and $q_{r,i}$ as solution variables.

b.   Intermediate run equilibrium with W as a parameter and π_i, $x_{r,j,i}, q_{r,i}, w_i$, and N as solution variables.

c.   Long run equilibrium with $\pi_i, x_{r,j,i}, q_{r,i}, w_i, W$, and N as solution variables.

The symbol W refers to the total number of firms in the vertical market structure, and $\bar{W}$ refers to a given value for this number. Similarly $\bar{w}_i$ and $\bar{N}$ refer to specific values of w_i and N respectively.

In the analysis of all three equilibrium states a number of conditions are necessary to have sufficient cooperation to allow pure competition to exist in any and all levels. In the first place, $y_{r,j,i} = x_{j,i-1}$ and $x_{r,j,i} = x_{j,i}$, which are the conditions for common output form. Secondly, the number w_i must be sufficiently large to produce pure competition in the ith level (for all i). Thirdly, the initial conditions of the $\pi_0, \pi_N, x_{j,0}$, and $x_{j,N}$ relations are such as to allow the existence of pure competition in these two markets which lie half in and half out of the vertical market structure analyzed. These two markets are the markets in which level 1 buys and the last level N sells. If this last level is that of consumers, then the conditions on π_N and $x_{j,N}$ are meaningless and are to be replaced by the demand condition derived from the postulated utility function, and the analysis of equilibruim is to be suitably modified for the special case.

Short run equilibrium

There exists the set of parameters $\bar{w}_i, \bar{W}, \bar{N} > 2$, which define the short run nature of the cooperating or vertical market structure. This structure is thus one in which $x_{r,j,i} = x_{j,i} = y_{j,i+1} = y_{k,j,i+1}$, and $q_{r,i} = h_{r,i}$, and the set of parameters is such that the firms in any level in the structure can be said

PRICES

to be in pure competition with all others in that level. Under these conditions we wish to determine the equilibrium values of prices π_i (for all i), forms $x_{r,j,i}$ (for all j and i), and quantities $q_{r,i}$ (for all i). In this structure the number of levels is given at $\bar{N}$ and $i = 1, 2, \cdots, \bar{N}$, and the total unit costs for the structure (Z) is:

(23)
$$Z' = \sum_{i=1}^{N} F_{r,i}$$

To minimize Z' (given $\bar{N}$) with respect to output form we set[2]

(24)
$$\frac{\partial Z'}{\partial x_{r,j,i}} = \frac{\partial F_{r,i}}{\partial x_{r,j,i}} + \frac{\partial F_{k,i+1}}{\partial x_{r,j,i}} = 0$$

and, hence, at short run equilibrium for all firms

(24a)
$$\frac{\partial F_{r,i}}{\partial x_{r,j,i}} = -\frac{\partial F_{k,i+1}}{\partial x_{r,j,i}}.$$

If this were not the case, then a firm in, say, the ith level could operate in a manner to gain higher profits. That is, the optimizing firm in a cooperating structure as given by conditions **(3a)** and **(13a)** must set, to gain cooperation,

(3b)
$$\frac{\partial \pi_{r,i}}{\partial x_{r,j,i}} = -\frac{\partial F_{k,i+1}}{\partial x_{r,j,i}}.$$

By substituting **(3b)** for an optimizing firm into **(24a)** we get

$$\frac{\partial F_{r,i}}{\partial x_{r,j,i}} = \frac{\partial \pi_{r,i}}{\partial x_{r,j,i}},$$

which is condition **(13a)** for the optimal product form. In consequence one may conclude that the short run equilibrium structure is one which, for a given number of levels of firms, produces output in its most efficient set of forms. *That is, the particular form of the output of the short run equilibrium structure is the one which minimizes the cost of the production of a unit in the structure given $\bar{N}$ operating levels of firms.*

It may be recalled that condition **(14a)** is the condition which gives the optimum quantity. The condition yields a relationship between output quantity and the form and price of this output. Together with **(24a)** and the parameter $\bar{w}_i$, this condition **(14a)** can be used to form a short run supply function for each of the $\bar{N}$ levels in the structure. The application of the given demand relationship at the $\bar{N}$th level will then allow for the simultaneous determination of the equilibrium price, form, and quantity variables at every level. In other words, the use of expression **(3b)** along with the given demand equation yields the family of form-price-quantity demand relationships for the $\bar{N}$ levels. The application of **(13a)**, the form determining conditions, to the family of demand equations will yield *the set* of $\bar{N}$ demand equations which *correspond to the form of output produced by each level* in the structure.

For each level we now have the intersection of the supply and demand equations which identifies, for the form which characterizes that level's output, an equilibrium price π_i^0 and quantity Q_i^0 where,

$$Q_i^0 = \bar{w}_i q_{r.i}^0.$$

Obviously the firms which form any level i, and which optimize their behavior given the environmental parameters, will not purchase more units of the product than they will sell. They also may not sell more units of the product in some form $x_{r,j,i}$ (for all j) than they buy in some form $x_{r,j,i-1}$ (for all j) from the $(i-1)$ level. Since furthermore each firm is both a buyer and a seller, the firm specifies its cooperating condition in its role as a buyer, such that the price and product form purchases so specified result in

$$Q_i^0 = Q_{i+1}^0; \quad \text{for } i = 0, 1, \ldots, \bar{N} - 1$$

The short run equilibrium state of the vertical market structure is thus obtained from the parameters and equations so derived from firm-optimizing behavior. The variables and equations for the determination of this equilibrium state are given in Table 9.1.

TABLE 9.1 **Short Run Equilibrium Variables and Equations**

	Variable	No.	Equation	No.
Firm	$q_{r,i}$	$\bar{W}$	$\dfrac{\partial TP_{r,i}}{\partial q_{r,i}} = 0$ (**14b**)	$\bar{W}$
	$x_{r,j,i}$	$R\bar{W}$	$\dfrac{\partial TP_{r,i}}{\partial x_{r,j,i}} = 0$ (**13a**)	$R\bar{W}$
	$\pi_{r,i}$	$\bar{W}$	$\pi_{r,i} = \pi_i$	$\bar{W}$
Level	π_i	$\bar{N}$	$\pi_i = g[x_{j,i} \text{ (for all } j), Q_i]$	$\bar{N}$
	Q_i	$\bar{N}$	$Q_i = \sum\limits_{r=1}^{w_i} q_{r,i}$	$\bar{N}$
	w_i	$\bar{N}$	$w_i = \bar{w}_i = \text{parameter}$	$\bar{N}$
Structure	W	1	$W = \sum\limits_{i=1}^{\bar{R}} \bar{w}_i = \bar{W}$	1
	N	1	$\bar{N} = \text{parameter}$	1

Total: $\bar{W}(R+2) + 3\bar{N} + 2$ Total: $\bar{W}(R+2) + 3\bar{N} + 2$

Intermediate run equilibrium

A cooperating structure[3] with a fixed number of profit-maximizing firms ($\bar{W}$—a number sufficiently large to allow for pure competition at each *level* in the system), each of which is free to enter any level in the structure, is defined to be a structure capable of attaining an intermediate equilibrium. That is, equilibrium values exist for each firm of price ($\pi_{r,i}$), quantity ($q_{r,i}$), and form of output $x_{r,j,i}$ (for all j), as well as the equilibrium levels of prices (π_i), quantities (Q_i), form transactions ($x_{j,i}$), and numbers of competing firms (w_i). Such a structure results in an equilibrium number of levels (N) which, in economic analysis, is its unique characteristic and is, given the number $W = \bar{W}$, the reason for the title "intermediate equilibrium".

As in the case of short run equilibrium, the total unit system costs are:

$$(25) \qquad Z_N = \sum_{i=1}^{N} F_{r,i}$$

For any given N, to minimize Z_N we must satisfy the first-order conditions: for all j, r, and i:

$$(26) \qquad \frac{\partial Z_N}{\partial x_{r,j,i}} = \frac{\partial F_{r,i}}{\partial x_{r,j,i}} + \frac{\partial F_{k,i+1}}{\partial x_{r,j,i}} = 0$$

From (24) we can derive for each value of N a set of "optimal" $x_{r,j,i}$'s (for all j), which, when substituted into $F_{r,i}$ yield

$$Z_N^0 = \sum_{i=1}^{N} F_{r,i}^0$$

One may also follow a similar procedure for ($N - 1$) and ($N + 1$) levels—yielding Z_{N-1}^0 and Z_{N+1}^0. Then N is the number of levels which minimizes the total unit cost for the vertical market structure if:

$$(27) \qquad Z_{N-1}^0 \geq Z_N^0 \leq Z_{N+1}^0$$

This expression assumes, of course, that the set of minimum unit cost points with respect to $x_{r,j,i}$ (for all j) and N(i.e., Z_N^0) is ordered in a manner equivalent to a continuous function which is monotonically increasing on either side of a single minimum point. The existence of a unique minimum cost value for the number of levels is required by the second-order conditions discussed earlier.

As in the case of short run equilibrium, expression (26) is that condition which must be satisfied by any profit-maximizing cooperating firm in the structure. The application of this expression will then result[4] in the statement of the optimal values of $x_{r,j,i}$, (for all j) for every level in the structure, as a function of price π_i and quantity $q_{r,i}$. This functional relationship and expression (14a) together allow for the derivation of a supply function for each level. In effect R of the ($R + 1$) equations can be used to eliminate R of the ($R + 3$) unknowns, leaving for each level one equation in the two unknowns ($\pi_i - \pi_{i-1}$) and Q_i. The demand equations for each level are derived in a manner identical to that described for the case of short run equilibrium. The intersections of the demand and supply equations for every pair of cooperating levels result in the equilibrium values of π_i and Q_i for all i.

The *determination* of both the supply and demand equations (with the exception of the exogenously determined demand of the level beyond the structure being analyzed) is dependent upon the simultaneous determination of the equilibrium value for w_i—the number of firms in each level. In effect, each firm's application of expressions (**13a**) and (**14a**), the profit-maximizing conditions, determines its profit potential in each level. A firm performs such an analysis for each level and locates itself in the level giving the highest level of profits $TP_{r,i}$. Since all firms are engaged in an identical process and have identical operating structures, a specific equilibrium result will emerge. This result is that where each firm will make profits of $TP_{r,i} = k$, for all r and i. The value for k is a parameter which is dependent upon the nature of the cost functions and the number of firms $\bar{W}$.

The determination of the value of N is *independent* of the determination of the specific final location of firms in levels or the process by which this location is determined by the individual firm. The only requirement necessary for the determination of the equilibrium and optimal N is that firms attempt to maximize profits by selecting among other things the level in which they are to operate. The equilibrium value for the number of levels N emerges when the firms seek to optimize their behavior by choosing $x_{r,j,i}$ (for all j), i.e., create particular levels and specific cooperating agrreements. The same value emerges when the structure is optimized directly as in expression (**27**). This equality is clear because both cases satisfy the conditions given in (**24**), *and* the optimum form-(level-) seeking firms. If not restricted, as in the short run to a given N, firms will continue to change levels until no further form changes are profitable. The heart of the analysis is, of course, the concept of cooperation as it is expressed through the decision on form and its relation to price, and the possibility for profitable exchange. The creation of levels is the outcome of the concept that a firm is both a buyer and a seller, and in its search for profits is willing to adjust its operations through the price mechanism with other firms from whom it may buy or to whom it may sell. The end result is a vertical market structure of possibly more than two levels.

The structure in which the Nth level is that of consumers involves a variation in the discussion of equilibrium. Profit is not a sufficient inducement to urge consumers to turn themselves into firms. This means that the number of buyers in the Nth level cannot be determined by the profit equation as the other $(N-1)$ values of w_i. In its place there must be substituted the consumer's utility-maximizing behavioral equation. In the case where all N levels are of firms, the intermediate equilibrium analysis results in the replacement of the statement in Table 9.1 that w_i is a parameter. In its place is substituted the expression $TP_{r,i} = TP_{k,i+1}$ for all r, k, and i. In addition the parameter value for $N = \bar{N}$ is removed from the set of equations and in its place is substituted the expression $Z_{N-1}^0 \geq Z_N^0 \leq Z_{N+1}^0$.

Long run equilibrium

The analysis of the long run equilibrium of a single product vertical market structure is identical to that of the intermediate run with one exception. The value for W at equilibrium must be determined since the entry and exit of firms into and from the structure is permitted in the long run. The equilibrium value for w_i is thus that which emerges from the added condition that in the long run $TP_{r,i} = 0$. In Table 9.1, in addition to the changes made for the intermediate run, the statement that $W = \bar{W} = a$ parameter must be replaced by the condition that $\sum_{i=1}^{N} \sum_{r=1}^{w_i} TP_{r,i} = 0$. In short, firms continue to enter the vertical market structure and to optimize the relevant decision variables until the profit from these optimal values for all firms is driven to zero.

Some general conclusions and comparisons

A vertical market structure in which firms are allowed to cooperate as buyers and sellers and to create levels in the structure in their search for profits must be expected to be of a different efficiency from that in which this freedom is totally restricted to the creation of two given levels. The former is more efficient than the latter at comparable equilibrium states. This can be shown for the case of the long run equilibrium when we consider the long run condition that $TP_{r,i} = 0$. This requirement states, in effect, that

$$TP_{r,i} = q_{r,i}(\pi_i - \pi_{i-1} - F_{r,i}) = 0$$

which implies

$$\pi_i = \pi_{i-1} + F_{r,i}$$

or

$$\pi_N = \pi_0 + \sum_{i=1}^{N} F_{r,i}$$

The optimizing behavior of all firms has already been shown to produce a minimum value for $\sum_{i=0}^{N} F_{r,i}$ or Z_N^0. In consequence it can be stated that in the long run

$$\pi_N = \pi_0 + Z_N^0$$

In the analysis of traditional economic theory where the vertical market structure is limited to two levels, the long run equilibrium price would be

$$\pi_N = \pi_0 + Z_2^0$$

In the case of a given final form and a given initial price π_0, Z_2^0 would be the optimal only if the optimal number of levels N *happened* to be two. In all other cases the supply function in the final market when $N \neq 2$ is optimum and must lie below the supply function for $N = 2$. One would expect then the two cases to be as in Chart 9.5.

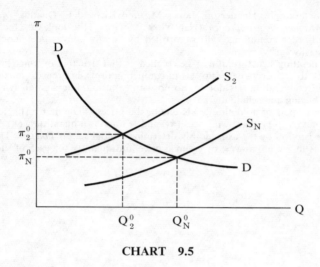

CHART 9.5

If the form is given but the initial price π_0 is not, one must expect exactly the same situation—a final market price that is lower and a final quantity that is larger when firms are allowed to optimize by choosing and creating cooperating levels than when they are restricted to structures with only two levels. There is, furthermore, no reason to expect the final product form to be identical in the two configurations of vertical market structures. In fact, there would be a change in form since the firms *reduce* the cost of the total production and marketing activities of the product in question by optimizing their cooperating (but non-collusive) behavior. If, however, the final product form changes, the comparative efficiency analysis cannot rely solely on price and quantity. The net effects of such form changes on consumer total utility would have to be favorable, but the detailed discussion of the matter is an entirely new subject.

The analysis of this chapter differs from that of the preceding seven mainly in its generality. There is a large inductive leap between the discussion of specific production and marketing costs and the general function $F_{r,i}$. The gain in generality has come at the cost of the exclusion of the relationship between the cost of a firm's operations and, among other things, the number of firms in its two cooperating levels. The function $F_{r,i}$ does not incorporate, for example, the unique aspects of coordinating these two levels' behavior under conditions somewhat less rigid than those of pure competition. The development of the more complex analysis that would treat such involved relationships, as well as other facets of vertical market structures, is outlined in the next chapter.

1   See, for example, Henderson, James M., and Richard E. Quandt, *Microeconomic Theory: A Mathematical Approach*, (New York: McGraw-Hill Book Co., Inc., 1958.)

2   Second-order conditions will be satisfied by strictly convex cost functions, as the reader can easily verify.

3   A cooperating structure, it may be recalled, is that structure in which firms compete, but also seek to cooperate with sub-sets of competing firms, in order to maximize profits. This form of cooperation has nothing to do with collusion, but is uniquely related to the creation of buying and selling markets.

4   For every pair of adjoining levels one of the prices is common. This leaves for the system in total $(N + 1)$ unknown prices (π_i) and N unknown quantities (Q_i). The price π_0 as a variable is offset by the exogenously determined initial supply *function*. There are now $2N$ equations in $2N$ unknowns, or a single price and quantity for each of the N levels in the system.

I O

Possible Directions of
Advanced Analysis

" Reculer pour mieux sauter "

Perhaps the entire work to this point might be viewed as a retreat to the basic essentials of the analysis of vertical market structures, and an attempt to explain why these are indeed the basic essentials. A more charitable view would consider the analysis as the withdrawal that permits a better jump forward in our understanding of the phenomenon. The achievements of the analysis might be characterized as more than just such a withdrawal, and as the establishment of a strategic position from which assaults upon the problem might be mounted, with high expected returns. By some, the analysis may be considered to have included the start of the move to sound understanding of this aspect of economic systems. But whatever the judgment, two points seem fairly obvious. The first is that the analysis is of the type that is necessary in understanding the nature and value of vertical market structures. The second, and more obvious, is that the analysis that remains to be done is much more than that which forms this work.

If, therefore, one had the choice between summarizing the analysis and outlining the nature and direction of future analysis, one must choose the latter. The value and achievements of the analysis in this work have already been touched upon and are either apparent within it or not. The second point has not been discussed, yet is of great importance, since vertical market structures are an integral determinant of the efficiency of an economy and the individual firm. However, further analysis must proceed by removing the limitations of the present work. In this chapter, therefore, the starting points of further analysis are identified in the discussion of the limitations of the analysis to this point. Only then is an attempt made to set up the guidelines and to identify the general nature of what remains to be done.

Points of departure

The starting points for future analysis are those aspects of the present analysis which limit its generality—the points at which it may be considered partial. There are, in effect, many such points which remain, despite the fact that every model developed above succeeds in removing some degree of partiality. The single most important aspect of the models which restricts their generality is their failure to treat combinations of overlapping vertical market structures simultaneously. The multiple product form analysis is the furthest any of the models goes in the treatment of this issue. But that is nowhere sufficient, and there is a need for more complex and less partial analyses of the whole area of assortments and multiproduct vertical market structures.

A number of exchange costs have not been considered. Among these are some costs related to functions of physical distribution and the closely related problems of spatial economics. There is no analysis made of the relationships between the spatial location of the m sellers and n buyers and the efficiencies of various configurations of vertical market structures. Furthermore, the concepts of equilibrium vertical market structures deal essentially with the number of intermediary levels, the number of firms in these, and the nature of the cooperative relationships, but do not involve as an integral dependent variable the equilibrium geographic location of such middlemen. Other exchange costs (besides transportation) that are not treated in the models are those which are closely related to market imperfections, such as promotional costs. In brief, a number of functions related to exchange are not considered in the models, and their inclusion would increase the generality of the analysis.

It would be desirable if the analysis were somewhat less relative. In all models in which actual solutions in terms of parameters are obtained, the numbers of sellers (m) and buyers (n) are treated as parameters. The equilibrium of the structure does not include these values as dependent variables in most cases. The effects of intermediary behavior on these two levels or horizontal structures is thus ignored in these detailed cost models. The system is conceptually closed at points that are not sufficiently removed from the critical variables. Thus, it would be far better if the vertical market structure had been conceptualized with parameters that included fewer economic elements. However, such a conceptual enlargement of the system at this stage would not proceed much further without a tremendous loss of analytic clarity.

At so early a stage, one does not hope to capture the system in all its complexity and still offer a balanced judgment on the relative importance of its variables in determining its efficiency. It could be argued that such costs as those of waiting, for example, are themselves functions of the existing vertical market structures and not parameters. One could continue in this fashion at great lengths, constantly adding variables and functional relationships to the analysis without ever stopping and without ever truly understanding anything about the system. What is suggested is not this increase in complexity for its own sake, but rather that the next step in the analysis be the introduction, on the basis of the existing models, of the relationships of vertical market structures to the equilibrium conditions of the horizontal structures of initial buyers and sellers. The very first step in this direction is taken in Chapter 9 of this work. But, for example, the discussion of rebate strategies might be expanded to include in more detail the aspects of monopoly power, bargaining, threat capacities, and the relationship of horizontal market structures to these—in other words, the general concepts of game theory.

Vertical market structures are dymanic, goal-directed, self-adaptive, goal-changing, and learning systems. They are, in effect, of the highest order of development in terms of general system complexity and capacity. The analysis of this work conceptualizes this phenomenon as a static system and constitutes the first order of complexity of system analysis. The next step must be to develop dynamic models of the system on the basis of what the static models have contributed to our understanding. The latter models found in this work can be considered static ones despite the fact that they treat some variables which are related in some way to time. The time an order spends in the system is a variable that might suggest that the analysis which includes it is dynamic. It is not, and the models which include such variables are static models, for they are characterizations of dynamic phenomena in their *steady state*. Since the steady state of a system is that wherein its variables are independent of time for their values, the model of such a system *can* be considered static. The obvious limitation of static models of systems that are much more complex needs no further elaboration here. What might be pointed out, however, is that the efficiency of research and the accumulation of knowledge are probably best served by the development of models which successively approach the full complexity of the system, and build one upon the other.

Market imperfections are treated rather briefly in this analysis, principally in Chapter 2. The discussions of various kinds of imperfections and of voluntary chains are intended as examples of what might be done in relating such imperfections to vertical market structures. The discussion of the middleman strategy intended to keep out other intermediaries also could be expanded to the simultaneous discussion of rebates and any other market mechanism which produces imperfect markets. As already pointed out, the competition between levels under varying conditions of imperfect competition within the structure requires more detailed discussion. The analysis of this work attempts to lay out the basic considerations of what determines vertical market structure equilibrium and efficiency, and does so mainly under the assumptions of fairly limited market conditions. Obviously, variations in its conclusions can be expected as these competitive market conditions are changed to include the large numbers of possible imperfections.

Something also needs to be said about the relationships of the mathematical models in the analysis to the generality of the concepts underlying the development of the models. Perhaps at first glance this work might seem less general than it really is. The mathematical models of Chapters 2 to 8 are less general than the concepts which underlie them, as evidenced by the generality of the model of Chapter 9. Nonetheless, it remains true that the rigorously derived conclusions are less general than those which might be derivable from the basic theory behind the models.

It is not difficult to elaborate on this point. One basic theory is that the nature of vertical market structures determines the costs of implementing a given output of exchange transactions, given that such implementation involves the two costs of servicing exchange agreements and the time that such service takes. This basic theory is rigorously proved, and specific solutions regarding equilibrium and optimal vertical market structures are derived in the particular case of the mathematical model. This model makes certain assumptions regarding the nature of the arrival of orders and the relationships between order service times and expenditures on the inputs which fill such orders. These assumptions permit the specific conclusions on system costs, illustrate the concept of coordination clearly, and point up the problems of attaining various levels of coordination under varying competitive market conditions. But the theory behind the model is not necessarily limited to situations in which the model's assumptions hold. In specific cases of order arrivals' being distributed in a form other than the Poisson distribution, the theory may not hold. In others the conclusions may be similar, but not identical, to those of the mathematical model. The latter point is not hard to accept, and what is required, essentially, is a leap of the imagination from the mathematical model to the general theory.

The very limitation of the mathematical models has its advantages at this stage of the analysis. The mathematical model's assumptions, being explicitly stated, point out clearly the conditions under which the general theory is shown to hold, and hence the critical areas in which the general theory may *not* hold. The model identifies clearly the directions in which, at present, leaps of the imagination to the applicability of the general theory are to be made, and areas in which further work leading to rigorous conclusions is required. In addition, it may be argued that the very limitation of the mathematical model now makes it possible to decide whether any more generality is even necessary, that is, whether the actual applications of the theory in its general form are so similar to each other, that all that is needed at this stage is a general theory and one specific rigorously derived form of the theory. In any specific application the actual conditions encountered will determine the requirements of actual solution. One might need first a general theory and one case, rather than a very large number of slightly different rigorously derived forms any one of which may never be actually applicable. The costs of rigorously derived solutions must be balanced against the expected value from the actual use once the basic form of the theory is developed.

In general, though, it may be more important to give the theoretical concepts on which the specific mathematical models are developed than the existing forms of rigorous proofs. In such a case, investigations into the effects on the conclusions of the mathematical models of this work of the variations in their assumptions might be conducted. In many cases such sensitivity analysis is presented along with the models in order to support the generality of the underlying theory. More along this line may be required. In many cases such analysis might find it advantageous to rely on simulation procedures rather than the more rigorous analytic techniques. Of course, the simulation would be more useful because of the availability of the basic theoretical concepts of vertical market structures and the specific rigorously and analytically developed forms of this theory.

Finally, it may be noted that the analysis is partial also because it does not consider simultaneously the full range of the firm's decision problems when it discusses its membership in a vertical market structure. In part, those problems that are not fully treated stem from market imperfections which are only briefly incorporated into the analysis. Such is not entirely the case, however, and the problem remains one of expanding the set of the firm's decisions that are simultaneously involved in the concept of the system beyond that done above. Thus though production and marketing decisions are treated simultaneously in the analysis, the issues of various forms of organizations of the production activities are not fully treated. The problem of specialization is the first step in this direction, but more is required. Issues of locations of inventories and decisions on the possibilities of employing various inputs (such as advertising) to alter shortage costs, are not considered. There are problems of sequencing production and marketing activities, of service and guarantee policies, of assortment and credit. Many of these issues would be in part resolved by the consideration of overlapping vertical market structures, others by considering more complex multi-function operations, and yet others by the simple removal of such assumptions as those on the form of the project graph that defines the production process. In any case, the concept of what constitutes a set of decisions for a firm might be made more general. The continued integration of this analysis with the many disciplines relating to all aspects of economic and business phenomena represents a vast area for theoretical research work.

Clearly the list of limitations of this work is a large one. Certainly the removal of the analysis' limitations would have vastly expanded the generality and the value it might have. It would have also retarded, possibly indefinitely, the derivation of any value it might have in helping our present understanding of vertical market structures. Hence, in place of the removal of these limitations at this instant, one can but offer the acknowledgement of their existence and an outline of the form and content that future work for their removal might take.

Overlapping vertical market structures

In describing those aspects of the analysis in which its partiality is evident, the least amount is said regarding the issue of overlapping structures. Yet this is probably the aspect where improvement is likely to have the largest returns in terms of our understanding of these cooperative and coordinating aspects of economic organization.

Overlapping structures may be viewed in one of two ways, depending upon one's definition of what constitutes their basic requirements. The distinction is made for purposes of simplifying the analysis rather than to distinguish between what are essentially different elements. They may also be combined to give a simple concept of overlapping structures. Thus, the basic element leading to overlapping structural forms may be viewed as that of multiple products, or on the other hand, as the result of the need for products and services by the members of a single structure. In either view the essence of one's analysis would be the determination of the effects of such overlaps on the conclusions of the theories relating to single structures. The basic question is whether overlapping structures involve conclusions on equilibrium and optimal structures that may not be logically obtainable from combining the theories of single structures. If they may not, then the theoretical concepts of this work are of little use. If, on the other hand, the theory of overlapping vertical market structures may be constructed logically by the modification of the theory of single structures, then this work can be the foundation of such advanced analysis. There seems to be no apparent reason why this latter should not be the case in both concepts of what constitutes an overlapping structure and in the combination of both of these concepts.

In the discussion of inventories, it is pointed out that the financial source of inventories may be some set of firms or people other than those who make the decision on the level of inventory. To carry inventories, some group should be willing to supply the funds through which waiting disutility may be transferred by carrying inventories. There is thus a possibility for the existence of a vertical market structure in which the carriers of inventory in the first structure form the group which requires such funds, and another group supplies them. Again, in the discussion of the implementation of exchange transactions and of production, the members of the vertical market structures analyzed may be the members of another vertical market structure which supplies the first structure with the resources for implementation and production. Any given structure analyzed contains members who are also members of structures through which the requirements for the functioning of the first structure are met.

It is necessary to investigate just how variations in either of these two overlapping structures will affect the efficiency and equilibrium of the other. The specific structures analyzed are interwoven with others in which the members of the first set of structures are also members of other sets of structures but in a different level. Isolating the former from the variables related to the latter ignores this relationship and makes the analysis a partial one. In order, therefore, to treat this larger system of overlapping structures, one must proceed by identifying all the requirements in terms of exchangeable goods and services that various structural configurations have, and then identify those related structures through which these requirements may be supplied. If we consider only funds, then one issue that must be settled is that of the simultaneous treatment of configurations of both structures. How, for example, is the structure through which funds are exchanged affected by the creation of middlemen in the first structure who are now the buyers of such funds, whereas before their creation, the m sellers were the buyers? Variations in the number of these buyers of funds changes the number in what would be the group of n buyers in the structure for funds. This, by changing the costs of transferring funds, introduces a new variable in the analysis of the comparative efficiencies and equilibrium states of the structure in which members use such funds.

One effect of simultaneous treatment would be to make variables of the input cost parameters of the analysis in this work. The cost of inputs may be a function of the level and number of firms in a level of the structure analyzed. The exact form of the function will in turn depend upon the manner in which the input (funds) vertical market structures respond to variations in their form which are entailed by changes in the first structure. This response in turn will be some function, in this somewhat limited system, of the costs of, and the ways in which these vary with, different configurations of the second vertical market structure. There are many different ways in which to increase rigorously the generality of the analysis that might be made.

The relation of competition to the efficiency of a vertical market structure in terms of the performance of a number of functions is considered at some length above. It is, however, a relationship between *one* vertical market structure and the competitive conditions in this structure. What might form the area for further study in some detail is the spread of the effects of competitive variations in one structure to other structures which overlap with it. What effect does the entry of a middleman have on the structure in which it is a middleman, and on all the other structures in which it is a final or intermediate buyer of the inputs which permit it to operate as a middleman in the first? The number of inputs that can be identified from the model is large, and includes funds, labor, productive resources, and so on.

The second concept of overlapping vertical market structures is already broached once one talks of a firm's being a buyer of a number of inputs. We consider the second dimension of the overlap as the case where two vertical market structures have members in common for whatever reason. We need not restrict ourselves to the overlap which stems from the requirements of firms which permit them to operate in a single structure as middlemen, sellers, etc. If for any reason multiple structure memberships for firms exist, then the analysis should develop the conditions leading to such membership, derive the nature of the relationships between firms and the manner in which these create an overlap, identify the varying characteristics of the overlap in terms of these relationships, and then develop the appropriate theory of simultaneous optimality and equilibrium for these overlapping structures. This concept of an overlap is thus more general than the first and also includes the overlap which occurs from the fact that economies are invariably systems in which more than one product is demanded by any one buyer. Hence, more than one product is possibly produced and marketed by any one firm in whatever position it lies in the vertical market structure.

How does one characterize such overlapping structures from the concepts of the vertical market structure in this work? The model on multiple product forms of Chapter 7 is a first minor step in the analysis of overlapping structures and offers a starting point for the answer to the question. The section of Chapter 2 on segmented markets is also such a starting point. In this discussion the n buyers are divided into a number of sets such that each set forms a vertical market structure with only one segment of the m selling firms. From this point of view we could say that there were as many vertical market structures as there were sets of buyers. From the point of view of the m sellers, there was only one set of m firms, all of whom were willing to cooperate with all n buyers. In the case where some of the m sellers were members in more than one vertical market structure viewed from the n buyers' willingness to cooperate, then an overlap between these structures exists. The basic explanations of this segmentation in terms of areas could easily be extended to include products. That is, various groups of n buyers might require just some of the products supplied by the m sellers, who in turn produce non-identical sets of such products. For every set of n buyers with homogeneous requirements, a group of m sellers would constitute the other members in the vertical market structure. But any seller may of course be capable of meeting the requirements of more than one group of the n buyers, and, therefore, an overlap of structures exists. The combination of unique sets of requirements and unique sets of supplied products creates a complex overlap of vertical market structures.

The model of multiple product forms could easily suggest that the distribution of demand for a specific product stems from a probabilistic order pattern and a given range of demand for any one buyer. In these circumstances sellers may specialize within a range of forms, which means they specialize in some segment of the market. If these segments, defined now in terms of the specific buyers, are not mutually exclusive, then again an overlapping set of vertical market structures, one for each segment and its potential suppliers, exists. No apparent reason is given in the analysis for the specialization of sellers within a range of the product's demanded forms, but it is not difficult to introduce. Specialization economies easily can be introduced into that analysis so that it characterizes a simple form of overlapping structures. Though the conclusions of that analysis must now be modified somewhat, the theory as it stands requires no logical transformation to be made to characterize such a phenomenon. The theory and the models require the introduction of variables and the reformulation of appropriate relation patterns.

What is referred to as a vertical market structure is really a special case of the phenomenon described most generally in Chapter 1. Since almost all the theoretical concepts were of the special case, it has acquired the epithet of vertical market structure, and the most general case now may be referred to as an overlap of such special forms. But setting aside the minor issue of definition, there is a need to develop a general method for characterizing overlapping vertical market structures in a manner that would permit the development of theory. It is not really sufficient merely to extend the characterization of this work as it may seem relevant in any particular case. The basic elements for such a characterization must indeed remain the elements of cooperation to permit exchange. The concept of the nature of cooperative relationships must be expanded to allow for variations that are based upon the different sets of products which such cooperation covers.

If this is done, then one must develop the theory which characterizes the relationships that exist between the expanded dimensions of cooperative relationships. In other words, simultaneous product inventories must be considered under various vertical market structures and under conditions of given or variable sets of required and offered products. The complex interrelationships between products—for example, a product that is used in the production of another and also used by itself—is likely to introduce levels of non-homogeneous members into the theory. The concept of a level must, in effect, be designed to include varying degrees of competition and even cooperation between firms in the level.

The theory of overlapping vertical market structures requires the reformulation of some of the concepts of this work in order that the complex interactions and cooperative sets of relationships may be capable of analysis. Much work remains to be done, and it should start with the identification of all those dimensions of the nature of the overlap. The differences in requirements and conditions of all actual and would-be members of a structure must be isolated and the source identified. Differences in product requirement, buyer utility surfaces, geographic locations, all aspects of constraints on any member, and some general institutional factors are possible sources for overlaps. Perhaps the initial characterization in the form of the products supplied by would-be sellers, the requirements of would-be buyers, each in a two-dimensional matrix, might be a useful starting point. The increases in the sources of overlap considered would then increase the dimensions of each such characterization to numbers of two-dimensional matrices. On the basis of such a description the basic concepts of the theory might then be developed and the concepts of this work expanded.

One specific aspect of overlapping vertical market structures that has received much attention in the literature is that of "assorting." Our analysis barely enters this area with the discussion on multiple product forms. There remains to be done some rigorous analysis to identify the exact nature of this cost-incurring function, which does not exist in simple vertical market structures. There is a need to identify the dimensions of the individual firm's assortment problem before any discussion of the efficiencies of overlapping vertical market structures in the performance of this function is analyzed. Just what are the basic inputs which determine for a firm the costs and revenues of its assortment decision? How do such decisions relate to production and demand considerations, to inventory and implementation of exchange transactions, to information problems, and to competitive and cooperative relationships? It seems quite clear that the efficiency of exchange in a multiproduct economy is closely related to these issues, and that overlapping vertical market structure configurations are determinants of the nature of the relationship. These are indeed vast areas for theorizing, which involve the addition of new concepts and the modification and expansion of the concepts of this work, rather than the development of an entirely new theory. Identical forms of cooperation between firms in different levels, coordination of levels, and competition among firms in the same levels may now become nonidentical. The concept of a level may require more detailed definition in terms of a larger number of dimensions. But the relationships essentially remain those of competition, cooperation, and coordination.

Dynamic analysis

The development of a dynamic analysis of vertical market structures would introduce control as an integral relationship among those that define the system. The problems of optimum response to continuing variations in the firm's environment and of optimum information patterns within the structure must now be considered. There exist in the literature[1] discussions of the behavior of certain forms of vertical market structures in dynamic situations. These discussions, however, are limited to explorations of possible efficiency outcomes of specific response patterns of firms in some general forms of structures. Therefore, more work is required which, by analyzing the various aspects of exchange requirements, would identify the general effects of structures on efficiency. It would have to start by identifying the relations of optimal response patterns of firms to the dynamic variations in the behavior of others and in the nature of the vertical market structure.

For such an analysis one must first develop concepts of dynamic structures. Again the concepts of cooperation, competition, and coordination must be expanded to deal with the new element of control and to permit the treatment of the new variables which dynamic systems introduce. Thus the model on implementing exchange transactions now must include non-steady state conditions, the determination of the design of response mechanisms in terms of time of response to environmental changes, the nature of the information on the environment that is required, and in general, all aspects of devising an optimal control system for the firms. It must do so for varying vertical market structure configurations, and then derive dynamic equilibrium conditions and optimum conditions for such structures. One element that must be added is that of the relationship of structural form to lags in responses and the consequent effects on efficiency.

In dynamic analysis one should investigate the relationship of equilibrium states to the set of historical circumstances which determine the structure's initial state. One interesting facet of this kind of analysis would be the determination of non-equilibrium states of the structure at varying points in time, and the determinants of relationships between these states. Thus vertical market structures in underdeveloped economies may or may not develop along the same lines as have those of the present-day developed economies. The nature of the effects of public policy on the development of vertical market structures, and the efficiencies of intermediate as well as equilibrium states under different circumstances, may be identified.

Understanding the highly complex economic phenomenon of vertical market structures involves more than the development of theories that abstract from its dynamic nature. There is no shortage of problems in this area to occupy many minds for many years to come. If one considers Boulding's[2] scheme of the complexity and abstraction levels of conceptual schemes, the static analysis is but the first step in many. The broad outlines of the dynamic analysis that remains to be done could be vastly expanded to show, for example, the various abstraction levels of dynamic analysis suggested by Boulding[3] in terms of the specific issues of vertical market structures. However, little is gained by the enumeration of possible relationships unless some theory is added. This, one must confess, is not as yet available in anything but the loosest outlines. From this vague outline of what forms dynamic analysis might take, it is clear its foundations lie in some large measure in the static analysis.

Stability of equilibrium

There is a need to develop a theory of vertical market structures that would determine in rigorous and detailed form the conditions necessary for the stability of the structure. Are vertical market structures inherently stable or unstable in both the static and the dynamic concepts of equilibrium? What are the kinds of variables that determine such stability? The answers to such questions seem likely to become available only after a higher degree of integration between the analysis of vertical and of horizontal market structures is attained. At the root of this integration must lie some basic concepts which identify clearly any differences between competitive and cooperative relationships which might make the conditions for the stability of each different.

In very general terms one might wish to investigate whether cooperative relations which permit exchange are more complex and varied than competitive relationships. The conditions which establish the stability of horizontal market structures in the absence of any consideration of vertical relationships are not likely to remain unchanged when these are made variables in the analysis. Not only is there a decision on what industry a firm may enter, but there is the issue of what level or combination of levels and industries it is to join. In complex overlapping vertical market structures the concepts of competition and of cooperation become blurred and multidimensional. It is the development of concepts in these areas that will permit the discussion of stability relationships.

The introduction of vertical market structures into the analysis of the general equilibrium of economic systems can be expected to develop changes in the conditions for the stability of such systems. There is also a need for this form of integration, perhaps after more is understood of the vertical structures than is available from this work. The exploration of the effects of increases in social efficiency on the general equilibrium must form an integral part of such a discussion of stability. If varying the vertical market structures involves real social cost reductions, will these reductions ever actually be attained when the vertical market structure is no longer viewed as a closed system but as part of an entire and complex economy? It is extremely difficult even to suggest the general form that such analysis might take, let alone any of its possible conclusions. If social welfare problems are to be of interest in public policy, it is hard to conceive of analyses of the problem that do not at some future time include in some detail an integrated discussion of competition *and* cooperation to permit exchange.

Epilogue and prologue

The contributions of the theory presented in this work grow increasingly smaller as the discussion of what might be yet available proceeds. But the value of these contributions may well lie in what the analysis might reveal in such future work. One must in any case dwell upon what is to come and not on what is. The last words of this work must attempt to be an indication of what the first words in the next stage might be.

Few students of economic systems would deny that an integral part of such systems is the configuration of vertical market structures. That is one aspect of the economic system. But what is needed in the analysis of this aspect is the introduction of order and the development of basic concepts, the combination of these into an integrated theory, and the continued expansion of the generality of the theory. This work has made attempts at all three requirements. It falls shortest in its generality, and furthest in its creation of rigorous and integrated theory. The final discussion on price strives hardest for the generality that is needed, and is an apt intermediate conclusion in that it builds upon the basic concepts and forms the start of what is probably the most important analysis that must emerge in the future.

1   Forrester, Jay W., *Industrial Dynamics*, (Cambridge, Mass: Massachusetts Institute of Technology, 1961), and Kuehn, Alfred A., and R. S. Day, "The Acceleration Effect in Forecasting Industrial Shipments," *Journal of Marketing* XXVII (January, 1963) pp. 25–29.

2   Boulding, Kenneth E., "General Systems Theory: The Skeleton of Science," *Management Science* II (April 1956) pp. 197–208.

3   *Ibid.* pp. 197–208.

Appendix

The purpose of this appendix is to determine the probability that in a system of m order filling sellers and n order placing buyers a given number of unfilled or incomplete orders reside in a particular selling firm's system at any point in time. It is assumed that each of the n buyers places orders randomly in time. Further, its order placement pattern is independent of the order placing or filling of any other firm in the system as well as independent of its last order placement. The average number of orders placed by each buyer per unit of time is α. Thus the order generation process of any buyer can be characterized by a Poisson distribution with parameter α. That is, the probability that a buyer places k orders in the next τ units of time is equal to:

$$p(k;\tau) = \frac{(\alpha\tau)^k e^{-\alpha\tau}}{k!}$$

If we restrict ourselves to a small interval of time, say $\tau = dt$, where dt is a sufficiently small interval so that higher orders of dt can be neglected, then

$$p(0; dt) = \frac{(\alpha\, dt)^0 e^{-\alpha dt}}{0!} = e^{-\alpha dt}$$

and

$$p(1; dt) = \frac{\alpha\, dt\, e^{-\alpha dt}}{1!} = \alpha\, dt\, e^{-\alpha dt}$$

APPENDIX

Note that $e^{-\alpha dt}$ is defined as

$$e^{-\alpha dt} = \sum_{r=0}^{\infty} \frac{(-\alpha dt)^r}{r!} = 1 - \alpha dt + \frac{\alpha^2 dt^2}{2!} - \frac{\alpha^3 dt^3}{3!} + \cdots$$

Since $(dt)^r = 0$ for all $r > 1$, this reduces to $e^{-\alpha dt} = 1 - \alpha dt$
and $p(0; dt) = 1 - \alpha dt$

$p(1; dt) = (\alpha dt)(1 - \alpha dt) = \alpha dt$, and
therefore $p(0; dt) + p(1; dt) = 1 - \alpha dt + \alpha dt = 1$

That is, we have restricted ourselves to an interval of time sufficiently small so that only two events can occur—either no orders are placed at all, or one order is placed by a buyer.

We further assume that each buying firm is indifferent to which m selling firm fills the order and thus allocates its orders among the selling firms randomly. The probability that a particular selling firm receives an order generated by one of the buyers is just $\frac{1}{m}$. Further, since each of the buyers places his orders independently of the remaining buyers, the probability that a particular selling firm receives exactly g orders in the interval from t to $t + dt$ is (for $g > 0$):

$$p_m(g; dt) = \sum_{h=g}^{n} \binom{h}{g}\left(\frac{1}{m}\right)^g \left(\frac{m-1}{m}\right)^{h-g} \binom{n}{h}(\alpha dt)^h (1 - \alpha dt)^{n-h}$$

The expression can be thought of as being the sums, over all possible values of h, of the products of the probability that h orders are placed by the n buyers in the interval of length dt $\left[\binom{n}{h}(\alpha dt)^h(1 - \alpha dt)^{n-h}\right]$ and the probability that given that h orders have been placed by the n buyers, the particular selling firms will receive g of them—$\binom{h}{g}\left(\frac{1}{m}\right)^g\left(\frac{m-1}{m}\right)^{h-g}$. Since $(\alpha dt)^h = 0$ for all $h > 1$ over the small interval length dt, we need only consider two cases—where the firm receives an order and when it does not. Obviously

$$p_m(0; dt) = 1 - p_m(1; dt)$$

and from the previous expression

$$p_m(1; dt) = \left(\frac{1}{m}\right)n\alpha dt(1 - \alpha dt)^{n-1}$$

which reduces to

(since $(1 - \alpha dt)^{n-1} = 1 - (n-1)\alpha dt$ when $(\alpha dt)^r = 0$ for r > 1)

$$p_m(1; dt) = \frac{1}{m}n\alpha dt$$

and therefore:

$$p_m(0; dt) = 1 - \frac{1}{m}n\alpha dt.$$

Assume that the selling firms process orders one at a time in a first-come-first-served pattern. Assume further that service times (i.e., the times required to fill orders) are distributed in an exponential fashion. This is equivalent to saying that the *rate* of service is described by a Poisson distribution and if the average time that it takes to fill an order is $\dfrac{1}{v_m}$ then the rate of output is Poisson with mean v_m. Thus, given a sufficient backlog of unfilled orders, the probability that a selling firm fills k orders in an interval of length τ is:

$$S_m(k;\tau) = \frac{(v_m\tau)^k e^{-v_m\tau}}{k!}$$

Once again, if we restrict ourselves to an interval of length $\tau = dt$ where $(dt)^r = 0$ for $r > 1$ this probability reduces to:

$$S_m(k;dt) = (v_m dt)^k (1 - v_m dt) \text{ for } k = 0, 1 \text{ only.}$$

That is, dt is sufficiently small to allow the firm only to either complete the filling of an order or not complete the one it is working on. Then

$$S_m(0;dt) = 1 - v_m dt$$

and

$$S_m(1;dt) = v_m dt$$

Using these definitions it is possible to determine the probability that a given number of orders, say x, are either being worked on or are waiting for service in the *system* of a given selling firm. This is accomplished by noting that if at some time $t + dt$ the selling firm has x units in its system, it either had

(a) $x - 1$ units in its system at time t and had one new arrival and was unable to complete a service in the interval dt, or it had

(b) x units in its system at time t and either
  (i) had no new arrivals and was unable to complete a service during dt or,
  (ii) had one new arrival and was able to complete a service during dt, or finally it had

(c) $x + 1$ units in its system at time t and had no new arrivals and was able to complete a service during dt. This argument is summarized in the table below.

State of System at Time $t(x > 0)$		Number of Arrivals During Interval dt		Number of Services During Interval dt		Conditional Probability of Event
number	probability	number	probability	number	probability	
$x - 1$	$P_{x-1}(t)$	1	$P_m(1;dt)$	0	$S_m(0;dt)$	$P_{x-1}(t)\dfrac{n\alpha}{m} dt(1 - v_m dt)$
x	$P_x(t)$	1	$P_m(1;dt)$	1	$S_m(1;dt)$	$P_x(t)\dfrac{n\alpha}{m} dt v_m dt$
x	$P_x(t)$	0	$P_m(0;dt)$	0	$S_m(0;dt)$	$P_x(t)\left(1 - \dfrac{n\alpha}{m} dt\right)(1 - v_m dt)$
$x + 1$	$P_{x+1}(t)$	0	$P_m(0;dt)$	1	$S_m(1;dt)$	$P_{x+1}(t)\left(1 - \dfrac{n\alpha}{m} dt\right)v_m dt$

where

$P_x(t) =$ The probability that the selling firm has x units in its "system" at time t.

Then clearly the probability that the selling firm has x units in its system at time $t + dt$ is merely the sum of the conditional probabilities from the table, or;

$$P_x(t + dt) = P_{x-1}(t)\left[\frac{n\alpha}{m}dt - \frac{n\alpha}{m}v_m(dt)^2\right] + P_{x+1}(t)\left[v_m dt - \frac{n\alpha}{m}v_m(dt)^2\right]$$
$$+ P_x(t)\left[1 - \frac{n\alpha}{m}dt - v_m dt + \frac{n\alpha}{m}v_m(dt)^2\right]; x > 0$$

Noting that

$$\frac{P_x(t + dt) - P_x(t)}{dt} = \frac{dP_x(t)}{dt}$$

and dropping all terms of order $(dt)^2$ then

$$\frac{dP_x(t)}{dt} = -\left(\frac{n\alpha}{m} + v_m\right)P_x(t) + \frac{n\alpha}{m}P_{x-1}(t) + v_m P_{x+1}(t); x > 0$$

Restricting ourselves to the steady state or long run state of the system

$$\frac{dP_x(t)}{dt} = 0 = -\left(\frac{n\alpha}{m} + v_m\right)P_x(t) + \frac{n\alpha}{m}P_{x-1}(t) + v_m P_{x+1}(t); x > 0$$

Since the probability states of the system are independent of time this condition can be restated as:

(1) $$P_{x+1} = \frac{n\alpha}{mv_m}P_x + P_x - \frac{n\alpha}{mv_m}P_{x-1}; x > 0.$$

To determine $P_0(t + dt)$, note that only two cases are of concern: (a) the system has zero orders at time t and therefore services none during dt and, further, has no new arrivals during dt; or (b) the system has one order in service at time t, completes this item during the interval dt, and has no new arrivals during dt. In steady state these conditional probabilities are such that:

$$\frac{dP_0(t)}{dt} = v_m P_1(t) - \frac{n\alpha}{m}P_0(t) = 0$$

or

(2) $$P_1 = \frac{n\alpha}{mv_m}P_0.$$

Substituting (2) into expression (1) when $x = 1$ results in

(3) $$P_2 = \left(\frac{n\alpha}{mv_m}\right)^2 P_0 + \frac{n\alpha}{mv_m}P_0 - \frac{n\alpha}{mv_m}P_0 = \left(\frac{n\alpha}{mv_m}\right)^2 P_0.$$

Also expression (3) can be substituted into (1) for the case when $x = 2$.

Then

$$P_3 = \left(\frac{n\alpha}{mv_m}\right)^3 P_0 + \left(\frac{n\alpha}{mv_m}\right)^2 P_0 - \left(\frac{n\alpha}{mv_m}\right)^2 P_0 = \left(\frac{n\alpha}{mv_m}\right)^3 P_0.$$

Continuing in this fashion we can generalize:

$$P_x = \left(\frac{n\alpha}{mv_m}\right)^x P_0.$$

Note also that $\sum_{x=0}^{\infty} P_x = 1$ and therefore that:

$$P_0 \sum_{x=0}^{\infty} \left(\frac{n\alpha}{mv_m}\right)^x = 1$$

Then if $\frac{n\alpha}{m} < v_m$ (the condition for steady state)

$$\sum_{x=0}^{\infty} \frac{n\alpha}{mv_m} = \frac{1}{1 - \frac{n\alpha}{mv_m}} \quad \text{and therefore}$$

$$P_0 = 1 - \frac{n\alpha}{mv_m}.$$

Finally,

$$P_x = \left(\frac{n\alpha}{mv_m}\right)^x \left(1 - \frac{n\alpha}{mv_m}\right).$$

References

Morse, Philip M., *Queues, Inventories, and Maintenance,* (New York: John Wiley and Sons, Inc., 1958).

Saaty, T.L., *Elements of Queuing Theory,* (New York: McGraw-Hill Book Co., 1961).

INDEX

A

Absolute difference, in inventory
  levels, 63–64
Adaptation processes, 172
Adjustment, within structure, 223
Advanced analysis, 231–244
  points of departure, 232–236
  withdrawals, 231–232
Aggregate inventories, 58–60
Aggregate inventory costs, 84–89
  comparative, 68–72, 81–84
Aggregate inventory levels, 60–65
Agreements, of exchanging,
  106–107
Alderson, Wroe, 17, 18, 156, 180
Analysis, abstractions in,
  189–190
  advanced, 231–244
  dynamic, 241–242
  inventory, 51–52
  partial, 153–154
  See also Theoretical analysis
Assorting, 240
Attribute value, 171, 172

B

Bain, Joe S., 17
Balderston, Frederick, 18, 20, 21,
  25, 28, 34, 45
Baligh, Helmy H., 19, 156

B (continued)

Bargaining procedure, 40
Barger, Harold, 18
Behavior, vertical market
  structures, 12–13
Blending process, 172, 173, 176
Binomial order distribution
  pattern, 65–66
Boulding, Kenneth, E., 241, 242,
  243
Breyer, Ralph F., 14, 17, 18
Bucklin, Louis P., 156, 180
Buffer inventories, 121
Bund, Henry, 17
Buyers, indifference in suppliers,
  48
  waiting lines system, 105–106
Buying, 14
Buying market, segmenting, 101

C

Capacity, effective, 177
  expected process, 113–117
Capacity cost, and pre-order
  production, 176
Carroll, J.W., 17
Churchman, C.W., 126
Clark, Fred E., 17
Clewett, Richard M., 17
Collusion, and cooperation, 22
  and coordination, 188
Communication, 14

251

DATE DUE

1-12			
SEP 1 8 1975			
DE 6 '84			
GAYLORD			PRINTED IN U.S.A.